Iconography Of The West Front Of Wells Cathedral, With An Appendix On The Sculptures Of Other Medieval Churches In England

Charles Robert Cockerell

ICONOGRAPHY

OF THE

WEST FRONT

OF

WELLS CATHEDRAL,

WITH AN

APPENDIX

ON THE SCULPTURES

OF OTHER MEDIEVAL CHURCHES

IN ENGLAND;

BY

CHARLES ROBERT COCKERELL, R.A.,

PROFESSOR OF ARCHITECTURE IN THE ROYAL ACADEMY OF LONDON, D.C.L., HONORARY MEMBER
OF THE INSTITUTE OF FRANCE, OF THE ACADEMY OF ST. LUKE OF ROME, OF THOSE OF MUNICK
AND BERNE, AND OF OTHER SOCIETIES.

OXFORD AND LONDON,

JOHN HENRY PARKER.

M DCCC LI.

OXFORD:
PRINTED BY I. SHRIMPTON.

INDEX.

INDEX.

INTRODUCTION.

"AD QUÆ NOSCENDA ITER INGREDI, TRANSMITTERE MARE SOLEMUS, EA SUB OCULIS POSITA
NEGLIGIMUS: SEU QUIA ITA NATURA COMPARATUM, UT PROXIMORUM INCURIOSI, LONGINQUA
SECTEMUR: SEU QUOD OMNIUM RERUM CUPIDO LANGUESCIT, QUUM FACILIS OCCASIO EST: SEU
QUOD DIFFERIMUS, TANQUAM SÆPE VISURI, QUOD DATUR VIDERE, QUOTIES VELIS CERNERE. QUA-
CUNQUE DE CAUSA PERMULTA IN PROVINCIA NOSTRA, NON OCULIS MODO, SED NE AURIBUS
QUIDEM NOVIMUS; QUÆ SI TULISSET ACHAIA, EGYPTUS, ALIAVE QUÆLIBET MIRACULORUM PERAX
COMMENDATRIXQUE TERRA, AUDITA, PERLECTA LUSTRATAQUE HABEREMUS."

PLIN. EPIST. VIII. 20.

THE reproof which Pliny addressed to the Romans is entirely applicable
to ourselves; for if it could be shewn to the lovers of antiquity, that there
existed in any country of equal influence with England in the world's history, an
extensive but hitherto unedited commentary in living sculpture, of the thirteenth
century, upon its earliest dynasties, its Churchmen, and religious creed;
doubtless not a moment would be lost by the liberal and ingenious patrons of
such studies, in obtaining an accurate account of so precious a relic, however
distant the object and difficult the enterprise. And yet, such an one in the
bosom of our own country, and fulfilling these most interesting conditions,
has hitherto been disregarded, and may perhaps ere long elude altogether the
attention of which it is so worthy through the rapid decay and dilapidations
of time; because now, as in Pliny's days, "while we long for distant objects,
we are incurious about our own," and employ our funds and our energies in pro-
curing from Greece and Egypt the remains of their art, and of their dark
mythology, so foreign to our sympathies; while we neglect the deeply interesting relics of our own country and of our own religious antiquities,—
leaving them not only unillustrated, but unseen and scarcely heard of.

B

The sculptures of Wells Cathedral were designed to illustrate in the most ample and striking manner, the great and fundamental doctrines of the Christian Faith, its happy advent to this country, and its subsequent protection under the several dynasties to the date of their execution in 1214. For reasons hereafter to be explained, they relate also in a peculiar manner to the Anglo-Saxon originators of those laws and institutions which, under favouring Providence, have spread themselves together with our race over vast portions of the globe. They were conceived and executed by minds which enforced Magna Charta, and with Roger Bacon, Greathead, Scotus, and others, raised the intellectual character of our country to the highest grade of European civilization at that period. Fraught at once with the gravest and most important interests' of religion, history, and archæology, according to the learning and the taste of their day, they demand the best attention which can be bestowed upon them.

Professionally invited by the late Very Reverend Dean Goodenough, to advise on the application of the funds munificently raised by himself and the chapter for the repairs of the fabric of Wells Cathedral, I found myself irresistibly impelled, as much by a sincere admiration of these sculptures, as by a taste long ago imbibed in Greece and Italy, for reconciling the "disjecta membra" of ancient art, to unravel if possible a knot hitherto untied, and to penetrate through the quaintness of the style and the dilapidations of centuries, into their noble aim and purpose.

Having after much pleasurable labour satisfied myself fully of the admirable dignity and cogency of the design, and of the importance of these sculptures as historical and archæological evidence, I considered it my duty, in the absence of any previous explanation of a satisfactory, or even a rational kind, to lay before the Public such proofs and indications as my own unassisted drawings and engravings and notes on the subject could furnish, in order to invite those more careful and elaborate illustrations, which the funds of our learned societies alone are capable of affording in all their fulness, and of which the sculptures of Wells Cathedral are so entirely worthy.

I considered this monument as a yet undeciphered record of the religious, moral, and intellectual notions of their day, inscribed in stone, and preserved by a singular good fortune to our times, while others of a similar description have perished in religious or political revolutions; and I proposed by this Essay to do some measure of justice to this neglected work, and to the glory of our ancestors in an era no less remarkable for fine arts than for learning and chivalry, following the injunction of the ardent Bale. "As ye find a notable antiquyty, such as are the hystoryes of Gildas and Nennius amonge the Brytaynes, Stephanides and Asserius among the Englyshe Saxons, lete them anon be imprented, and so brynge them into a nombre of coppyes both to their and your owne perpetual fame[b]."

A strong professional motive (no less than of love of ancient art) has urged this undertaking, namely, the illustration, by this beautiful example, of the necessity and advantage to every work of magnificence, of a large admission of sculpture in carrying out architectural design; of the indispensable union of the sister arts, Sculpture (especially) and Painting, with Architecture, for the glory of art and of our holy religion.

The entire harmony of such an union with the canons and principles of the Anglican Church, has been triumphantly proved by the learned author of "The Ornaments of Churches considered[c];" in which the authorities of Luther, and Erasmus, together with the express opinions of the most illustrious reformers and doctors of the Anglican Church, are quoted at great length, and the whole subject treated with irresistible argument and eloquence.

I have to acknowledge the aid I have received in the prosecution of this study, from the late Very Rev. the Dean, whose ingenuity and learning were largely interested in it; from the Count Mortara, the Rev. J. Pollen, the Rev. J. W. Burgon of Oxford, and other obliging friends.

---

[b] Preface to Leland's New Year's Gift.   [c] See Appendix A.

PREFACE.

THE sculptures which adorn the western front of the venerable Cathedral of Wells, are beheld by no one without wonder and admiration. The most cursory observation of the learned eye recognises at once a grand design and order, which only the opportunity of leisure is wanting to explain; while the ignorant observer is conscious of that undefined veneration, which, for more than six hundred years, has imposed respect on the careless, and even on the spoiler, through the most evil times, and has preserved them with comparatively little injury to the present day.

Overwhelmed by the number, variety, and detail exhibited in these extended galleries of sculptures, and in the absence of any guide or key to their elucidation, the spectator receives but a confused impression, however striking. He acknowledges the questionable shape in which so many august and kingly personages, so many holy images of saints and martyrs, present themselves to his regard, and invite his meditations; but their due appreciation is obviously a work of patience and of spectacles, and even of the telescope, for many of their most precious details; and, to encounter the zephyrs at *Kill-Canon-corner*, (the name emphatically given to the best point of view,) he should be warmed, not only with enthusiasm, but in most seasons, with a good macintosh, provided with leisure, and recommended to that learned entertainment and hospitality of the Cathedral close, to which the ancient character given in Chaundler's Life of Bekington applies with equal force in the present day [a].

Doubtless in days of yore, when this magnificent work was still fresh in its

---

[a] In Chaundler's Life of Bekington, Ang. Sac., pars ii. p. 357, we have on this point, "Quid putas honoris, quid liberalitatis et cujusvis honestatis genus in nobili ac faceto Decano cæterisque Prælatis ipsis quos Canonicos vocant, reperies? moribus itaque religiosos, vita et honestate Clericos, hospitalitate illustres, gratos advenis atque affabiles, cunctis benevolos, primo discernes intuitu, ac deinde experientiâ docente id senties. Solent enim advenis et peregrinis tanto humanitatis officio obsequi; ut contendere videantur quis invitet, eum inhospitium que eum trahat," &c. &c.

glory, and the Benedictine brothers of the monastery were hourly ministering the holy offices of the cathedral service, some one of them would readily be found to expound the subject-matter of this "kalendar for unlearned men[b]," to the admiring folk assembled there on the holy day; or haply from the stone pulpit, immediately opposite the south-west corner, (the successor of one more ancient, erected by Bekington,) some eloquent preacher would expatiate on "the cloud of witnesses," on the facts so gloriously exhibited to their view, and enlarge upon the merits of those holy men and martyrs, those confessors, kings, and princesses, whose lives had been passed in the service of the Cross; that great cause which so intensely occupied our earliest Christian forefathers, more especially, either in the cloister or the camp.

But such explanations seem gradually to have been disused and forgotten, so that in 1450, scarcely two centuries later, William of Worcester was even at a loss as to the plain meaning of these sculptures. In his Itinerary he says[c]:

"Memorandum quod in occidentali et boreali parte ecclesiæ principalis Sancte Andreæ sunt tres magnæ boterasses cum tribus ordinibus magnorum ymaginum de veteri lege.

" Et in plana occidentali ecclesiæ sunt sex magnæ et altæ botterasses scitæ, ad latitudinem sex pedum et densitudinem circa trium virgarum cum tribus ordinibus magnarum ymaginum de nova lege sculptarum.

" Et in occidentali et boreali (2ª meridionali) parte dictæ ecclesiæ sunt duæ maximæ botterasses ad altitudinem circa LX. pedum cum tribus ordinibus sculptarum cum magnis ymaginibus de nova lege."

Had the topographer conceived the intention of these sculptures, or had they still been in his day the pride of Wells, as they certainly had been two hundred years before, it cannot be doubted that he would have expatiated more fully upon such works as could be equalled neither in this nor any other country; nor would he, under due observation and correct guidance, have confused the fourth and fifth tiers, which are purely historical and national, and are large statues, with the third tier, which are small ones, and relate to the Old and New Testament alone. His mention of the images is plainly *incidental* to his rude description of the architecture and general dimensions of the Cathedral, without the most distant

---

[b] See History of Benedictine Order, in Eustace's Classical Tour, vol. ii.   [c] Page 285.

notion of the comprehensive design of the sculptor in this magnificent work. And when we consider that the monastic establishment was, during the visit of the writer, (himself a Churchman,) in full discipline and order, the omission is remarkable; for it is hardly possible to suppose that the merit and the meaning of these works were already obscured.

Our worthy Fuller is the next author who adverts to the merits of Wells Cathedral; without particularly describing it, he yet displays his accustomed acumen and appreciation of these works. "The west front of Wells," says he, "is a masterpiece of art indeed, made of imagery in just proportion, so that we may call them 'vera et spirantia signa.' England affordeth not the like; for the west end of Exeter beginneth accordingly; it doth not like Wells persevere to the end thereof [4]."

In 1785 the zealous Carter, in his "Specimens of Ancient Sculpture and Painting," engraved five plates of these sculptures, preserving to us at least their number and state at that period, but the slightness of the performance sufficiently betrays his misapprehension, and the disregard in which he held them; and the short text added by Gough serves still further to diminish the interest they might otherwise have excited, and to involve his readers in the same darkness which obscured his own labours on the subject.

He quotes William of Worcester without remark, and proceeds to say that "if we should admit that some of them represent *kings and prophets of the Jews*, still there will be found intermixed *Christian kings, bishops, and warriors*, together with *several female* statues, without any distinguishing attributes except crowns." He supposes Bishop Harewell's statue (of a subsequent era, 1375) to be one of the series; he speaks of Ina as having founded the See, while he only founded the conventual church, with other errors which it would be a loss of time further to discuss. We must however always acknowledge our obligations to Carter, for having preserved and brought into notice in 1780 these and many other works of great interest.

Mr. Britton, in his "Cathedral Antiquities of England," has given us a precious work on the architecture of Wells Cathedral; and has engraved two plates, IV. and V., in elucidation of the sculpture. But he confines himself to the quotation of the

---

[4] Fuller's Worthies, iii. p. 89. See appendix B for a note on the west front of Exeter cathedral.

preceding authors, and adds nothing whatever to their interpretation.   He speaks of Carter's "slight etchings of the statues, too slight in drawing and too roughly executed, to inform the critical antiquary; and Mr. Gough's attempt to explain these statues, published in the same work, leaves them unexplained and undefined." "Any attempt," he adds, "to designate and describe all the statues and sculptured figures of this front, would require a long dissertation, and would *necessarily be occupied with much conjectural reasoning.*"

The illustrious Flaxman did not fail to seize at once the general scheme, and to describe its outline as presenting "the most useful and interesting subjects possible to be chosen, and testifying the piety and comprehension of the bishop's mind;" (see his Lectures on Sculpture;) but his remarks, in the highest degree valuable (as we shall proceed to shew) as the criticism of so signal a sculptor, do not attempt to develope the particulars of the scheme, or elucidate the historical or antiquarian matter with which it is enriched and magnified.

Collinson, in his History of Somersetshire, repeats the errors of his prede-cessors, adding "cardinals" to the list of worthies mentioned by others; Edgar Atheling with his *palmer's hat* (see catalogue) having no doubt suggested this to the topographer.

So late then as the year 1824, no satisfactory light has been thrown upon these precious relics of the learning and magnificence of our ancestors in the early part of the thirteenth century.   Not only have we been the idle possessors of so unexampled a specimen of sculpture of any country at that date, but the indolence of our antiquaries has left such an evidence unnoticed, while, at the same time, and in spite of them, they have suffered our countrymen to lie under the supercilious and absurd strictures of foreign writers, upon our incapacity in these elegant pursuits.   "The Abbé du Bos," says the indignant Barry, "the President Montesquieu, and the Abbé Winckelman, have followed one another in assigning limits to the genius of the English; they pretend to point out a certain character of heaviness and want of fancy, which they deduce from physical causes*." The learned Montfaucon, in the preface to his third volume, asserts that "the monuments of England are so few in the eleventh and twelfth, and even in the

* Spirit of Laws, c. ii. b. 14; c. xii. b. 14; b. xix. c. 27.   Abbé du Bos, part ii. c. 13; part ii. c. 14.   Histoire de l'Art, par abbé Winckelman, p. 48.   See works of James Barry, vol. ii. p. 177.

thirteenth century, that after the most *diligent search*, there are periods which do not furnish any." And yet we may challenge western Europe to produce an example of sculptural decoration, of any previous or subsequent era, which for magnitude and cogency of design, scriptural doctrine, and historical illustration, may compete with that of Wells.

The ' Imagines Majorum,' the worthy and the favourite subject of art with every illustrious race, from the early Greeks and Romans to our own times, have never been so largely and expensively treated in any recorded instance as by Bp. Trotman. For so extraordinary a display of zeal, devotion and outlay, we are to look for motives far more interesting and peculiar to the times than those of taste, as we shall proceed to shew in the following pages.

In considering the work itself, so truly expressed in the happy phrase of Asser, as applied to Alfred's horn-lantern, " concilioque artificiose atque sapienter invento,"—two important questions arise; first, who was its author, and what were the propitious circumstances which favoured its accomplishment in so complete and remarkable a manner? Secondly, whence the school in which so much skill in design and execution could be obtained?

These we find in perfect harmony with its merits, and singularly illustrative of that state of national politics and the personal circumstances of the bishop, which promoted the great work.

On the death of Savaricus, through Austrian influence bishop of Bath and Wells with Glastonbury, Jocelyn Trotman was elected by the joint chapters, as much on account of his amiable character[f], as for his theological and legal attainments, having been one of the chief justices of Common Pleas. He was consecrated at Reading under King John, in 1206, and sat in this See during thirty-six years, dying in 1242. He conferred many and conspicuous benefits on his native town and on the See; adding four manors and seven advowsons thereto; greatly increasing the number of prebends, and handsomely endowing them; and in conjunction with Hugh, bishop of Lincoln, founding the hospital of St. John in the town of Wells.

---

[f] Because, says the chapter, " in sinu Ecclesiæ nostræ, a primo lacte coaluit, et sine querela hactenus inter nos est conversatus." Anglia Sacra, pars i. p. 564.

But his architectural works are most remarkable; for he rebuilt the entire Cathedral from the presbytery westward[g], and the two episcopal chapels at Wells, still existing, and at Wokey, covering them with *vaulted ceilings*.

"Such a bishop," says the canon of Wells, "had not before been seen, nor has his equal since appeared[h]."

The patronymic Trotman sufficiently indicates his Anglo-Saxon origin, and, according to Godwin, he was a native of Wells, and received the principal part of his education there[i]. The elevation of an Anglo-Saxon to so important a See was a rare occurrence, and was naturally hailed by that people with the utmost satisfaction; for the words of Malmesbury, a century before, still applied,—that "England has become the residence of foreigners and the property of strangers at the present time, (1145), there is no Englishman either earl, bishop, or abbot. Strangers all, they prey upon the vitals of England; nor is there any hope of a termination to this misery."

The expectations so justly formed from the accomplished and practical spirit of Jocelyn Trotman, were retarded for a short time, in the dispute which arose between King John and Pope Innocent XIII. On the election of Langton to the See of Canterbury, Trotman had sided with the latter; and, together with the

---

[g] " Ecclesiam deinde ipsam Wellensem jamjam collapsuram (quamvis in ejus reparatione ingentes non ita pridem sumptus fecerat Robertus Episcopus) egregie refecit ac restituit, vel potius novam condidit. Nam partem multo maximam, quicquid nimirum presbyterio est ab occidente, demolitus est, et cum ampliorem tum pulchriorem redderet, structura excitata expolito lapide affabre insculpto, angustissima et spectatu, dedicavit Octobris vicesimo tertio, 1239."—*Godwin de Præsulibus*, p. 371. ed. 1743. See also infra, on the statue of Bishop Robert of Normandy.

[h] "Jocelinus fundavit multas Præbendas in Ecclesia Wellensi de novo, dotavit etiam omnes dignitates, personatus et officia dictæ Ecclesiæ in formâ adhuc durante: ipsamque Wellensem Ecclesiam vetustatis ruinis enormiter deformatam prostravit, et a pavimentis, erexit dedicavitque; assignans ei in dotem ad augmentum commune canonicorum manerium de Winescombe cum ecclesiâ; multosque alios redditus ad augmentum dictæ ecclesiæ perquisivit, unde ministri usque hodie sustentantur. Vicarios in Ecclesiâ singulis præbendariis ordinavit; tribus exceptis, quibus non provisit morte præventus. *Hic sibi similem anteriorem non habuit, nec huc usque visus est habere sequentem.* Tandem defunctus, in medio chori Welliæ honorificè sepelitur. Hic primo anno consecrationis suæ servitium 'B. Mariæ in ecclesiâ Wellensi fecit cotidie decantari. Capellas etiam *cum cameris* de Welles et Woky notabilitur construxit."—*Ang. Sac.*, pars i. p. 564.

[i] "Jocelinus (multis indiciis mihi videor comperisse) Welliæ natus est et magnâ ex parte educatus."—*Godwin de Præsulibus Anglia*, p. 371.

bishops of Worcester, Ely, and Hereford, had acted on the bold determination of publishing the pope's interdict on the kingdom; which so offended John, that he was banished in 1208, and passed five years in France, until the reconciliation of the king and the pope in 1214[k].

In the following year he received as a compensation for his sufferings, from the legate of the pope, (of whom, we shall see, he was a staunch partizan,) a portion of £27,000, which sum was raised for the purpose, and dispensed to the exiled bishops on that occasion.

He had also acquired, after much litigation with the monks of Glastonbury on the subjection of their monastery by the preceding bishop, four very productive estates, already mentioned; now given up on the condition of his resigning the title and jurisdiction assumed by his predecessor Savaric over the abbey of Glastonbury; confining his title for the future to Bath and Wells only, as formerly. The revenues of the See itself during the sequestration of King John amounted to £213. 14s. 6d., (about £5,000 of our present money,) and to this were to be added the contributions of the devout during twenty-five years.

Fortunately, the improvement of his taste in architecture kept pace with that of his funds. During his travels in France, the most magnificent works were in active progress, and could not have failed to engage his attention; he might have been present at the laying of the first stone at Rheims (1211) under the famous "*Lathomus*," Robert de Coucy[l]. At Rouen great works were in hand under Ingelramne: at Paris also, the church of Notre-Dame approached its glorious termination about that time; and the neighbouring buildings, especially the church of St. Stephen's, were removed, the better to display the wonders of its architecture. The activity of the English schools of art during that period, was not inferior to that of any other country; for Lincoln was at that time in earnest progress, and apparently Lichfield, Hereford, Salisbury and Worcester[m]. The works at Canterbury had been going on from 1175 to 1220, when Becket's

[k] "Paulo post hanc litem terminatam (with Glastonbury) in exilium profugere coactus est Jocelinus, ac in *Gallia* extorris quinque per annos degere."

[l] Architects accompanied the crusaders as engineers. Lewis the Ninth in the same century took out architects, whose names have reached us, expressly for the purpose of visiting the monuments of the East.

[m] See Appendix D.

Crown was accomplished to admiration, by William "The Englishman;" and great works were in progress at York also, and at St. Paul's Cathedral, London[n]. Thus, with funds so greatly improved, his experience so much enlarged, and his emulation so much excited, he was in a condition to vindicate the genius and the liberality of the Anglo-Saxon character, and shew to the usurping foreigners, who boasted that piety and learning were only to be found amongst themselves, what might be conceived and accomplished by the proscribed race: and how entirely he succeeded in this object cannot be questioned after a fair consideration of his unrivalled work. Unhappily the bishop does not appear to have left any explanation or commentary on his learned exposition of Christian doctrine, of national and local history. He has withheld from us his authorities, and all the immense interest which would have attached to such a document of his hand and time; for Godwin, who had access to the archives before they were burnt in 1643, would doubtless have quoted it, if existing in his day. He appears to have contented himself with a silent appeal to posterity,—however insensible hitherto to that appeal; and with the consciousness of having fulfilled his duty, to have said in the memorable words of his own immortal Alfred,

"I have desired to live worthily while I lived; and after my Life to leave to the men that should be after me, a remembrance in good works[o]."

This Anglo-Saxon party spirit, justified by hereditary affections and rights, had been the constant source of bitterness and animosity for nearly two centuries; bearing which in mind, we are struck with the fulness and dignity given to the Saxon dynasty on the west side, as compared with that of the Norman and Plantagenet on the north and east: and we recognise the animus and the boldness with which these national claims to the respect and veneration of posterity are asserted by our zealous and learned Anglo-Saxon bishop, in the face of the triumphant foreigners.

This undercurrent of internal politics, which has been more fully illustrated

[n] About this time letters hortatory were issued by the archbishops of Canterbury and York, and the bishops of Wells, Carlisle, Rochester, Coventry, and Norwich, to raise monies "for the provision of felling timber for the stalls in the quire of St. Paul's Cathedral," offering indulgences for a variety of terms; thus while Canterbury granted twenty days only, and York forty, Jocelin Trotman signalized his zeal and taste by granting thirty-eight days' indulgence.

[o] See S. Turner's Anglo-Sax., b. v. p. 36.

by Mons. Thierry [p] than by any other modern historian, had exhibited itself among the clergy no less than amongst the laity.

If the altar of Thomas à Becket had received in one year (1271) offerings to the amount of £600, (or £15,000 in modern money,) while that of our Saviour had received none, it was chiefly because Becket was an Anglo-Saxon; and now, in 1206, the pope had elected Stephen Langton *because he was an Englishman*, a title which he maintained shortly after in his defence of civil liberty, having been the chief instrument in obtaining the Magna Charta, and in requiring King John to *revive the laws of the good King Edward*, (in which act Trotman was also engaged [q],)

[p] " Between the refugees of the camp of Ely and the men of Sherwood—between Hereward and Robin Hood, there had been, especially in the north of England, a succession of partisan chiefs and outlaws, who, like them, were not without celebrity, but of whom too little is known for them to be considered as historical personages. The names of some of them—as Adam Bell, Clym of the Clough (or Clement of the valley), and William of Cloudesley, were long retained in popular memory. The adventures of these three men, who can no more be separated from one another than Robin Hood from Little John, are the subject of a long romance, composed in the fifteenth century, and divided into three cantos. There is not much faith to be attached to the particulars it contains; but we find in it many original traits, capable of communicating more forcibly to the reader the idea which the population of English race had formed of the moral character of those men, who, after the Conquest, chose rather to be banditti than slaves, and embraced the same way of life in England as the Klephtes in modern Greece."—*History of the Conquest of England*, vol. iii. p. 245.

The following is so characteristic of these passions in 1169, that its insertion may be excused. " William, an Englishman, of the municipal council of London, like his ancestors ever since the Conquest, had let his beard grow, from hatred and disdain of the Normans: he had made himself conspicuous by his zeal in defending his countrymen against oppression by every legal means. It appears that, in the municipal council held in the year 1196, the rich citizens of London who composed it, voted, according to custom, for such a distribution of the burden as should make only the smaller part of it fall on them. William Longbeard stood up against them; he charged them with injustice, and they answered by calling him a traitor to the king. ' The traitors to the king,' replied the Englishman, ' are those who defraud his Exchequer, by exempting themselves from paying what they owe him.' He actually passed the sea, went to King Richard's camp, and, kneeling before him, and lifting his right hand, asked of him peace and protection for the people. Richard promised to attend to it, which he never did. William became the head of a secret society, into which upwards of fifty thousand persons entered. After a public commotion he was seized by the Normans, one of whom, Geoffry, was instantly stabbed by William with the long knife, which, according to the fashion of the time, he wore in his girdle. He and his party took refuge in St. Mary de l'Arche, and defended the church for some time; at length wounded and taken, he was tied to the tail of a horse, dragged to the tower, and hung, together with his companions, all of English birth."— *History of the Conquest of England*, vol. iii. p. 284.

[q] At the coronation of Henry III. in 1217, the bishop, faithful to his political principles,

and especially in translating the bones of the English Becket with so much pomp and expense as to entail a heavy debt (long a burden to it) on the See of Canterbury.

The same spirit is exhibited also in the west front of the Cathedral of Lichfield, built towards the end of the same century; shewing plainly that it was rife throughout England at that period. Stavenby, Patteshulle, Wiseham, names of bishops of Lichfield, are sufficiently Anglo-Saxon to warrant the conclusion that a strong current of that interest then prevailed; the illustration of the Mercian dynasty was no less urgent at Lichfield, its ancient capital[x], than that of the kingdom of Wessex, its successful rival, was at Wells. Thus a laudable fashion prevailed at that period of constituting the ecclesiastical edifice a national monument at the same time.

But the circumstances of the times throughout the Christian world, were no less favourable to the development of art, than the national politics of Bishop Trotman in the present instance.

In 1204 Constantinople, the great capital of the middle ages, the seat and throne of all refinement in art, had been taken by the Franks. The Crusades had made the northern people familiar with the treasures of the Mediterranean; they beheld with admiration[s] the splendours of the Grecian chisel, and were inspired with the desire to reproduce their effects in illustration of their own religious fabrics: for the iconographic works of this age form the most remarkable feature of Christian art, and deteriorated successively, as they were further removed from their original models, down to the fifteenth and sixteenth centuries; in which, when the Holy Land ceased to be visited, and the remains of classical sculpture to be seen, statues were reduced in scale and dignity, until they assume the dimension of dolls, serving merely as subordinate decorations to architecture.

It must not either be forgotten, that during Bishop Trotman's era, " the Guilds, or incorporations of craftsmen, containing within them elements destined to alter

---

dictated (according to Matthew Paris) the terms of the oath taken by the young king, by which the great charter of English liberties was secured.

[x] See Appendix E for some account of the west front of Lichfield Cathedral.

[s] Though the mortified Greek, Nicetas Choniates, affects to say, " nil pulchrum amare norunt;" nor was the Helen ' amorum opus' sufficient " hos homines fereos mollire."

the whole condition of municipal society, were now rising simultaneously into importance throughout the commonwealth of Christendom; these bodies may be traced without difficulty to the colleges of workmen which subsisted in the Roman empire, and had, under that political dispensation, held an ambiguous place between servitude and freedom." To this, amongst other powerful causes, must be attributed the admirable progress of the building art in the early part of the thirteenth century.

And this leads to the second question which occurs for our consideration in the contemplation of this remarkable sculpture;—the school from which so much skill in design and execution might be supposed to emanate; a question which, to us, under the long and deplored severance of religion and the fine arts since the Reformation, and forgetfulness of the labours and the means of our early Churchmen, it seems difficult to solve; for though our antiquaries never for a moment doubt the capacity of our native architects, they are disposed invariably to refer the works of sculpture of those days to foreigners, and yet we may in the main attribute existing specimens in both arts equally to native genius without hesitation. We have been perfectly informed of the succession of types and illustrations of holy writ, imported periodically from Italy and Byzantium, from our earliest conversion; the *scriptorium* of every monastery reproduced these MSS., and practised limners copied and repeated these authoritative designs in all times; local schools of architects, and sculptors, and painters, exercised themselves in these arts indifferently and with equal merit, though academic specialities were not then established; and the body of masons, free or otherwise, who undertook a work, were able to carry out also its decorative and ornamental accompaniments in every detail.

Referring, as we commonly do, to Italy as the fountain of fine art, " It is very remarkable," says Flaxman, " that Wells Cathedral was finished in 1242, two years *after the birth of Cimabue*, the restorer of painting in Italy; and the work was going on *at the same time* that Nicolo Pisano, the Italian restorer of sculpture, exercised the art in his own country; and it was finished forty-eight years before the Cathedral of Orvieto was begun; and it seems to be *the earliest specimen* of such magnificent and varied sculpture united in a series of sacred history that is to be found in western Europe."

The first work of Nicolo Pisano (who was an architect as well as a sculptor) to which an authentic date can be affixed, is the sarcophagus of St. Dominico at Bologna, 1225 (eleven years after Trotman had begun his work); so that the learned d'Agincourt conjectures that he was born about 1200[t].   We are assured by the same authority that the Cathedral of Orvieto, in which it is pretended that the best works of Nicolo are to be seen, was founded in 1293, assigning to him the advanced age of 90; but with more probability, he adds, that these works may have been done in anticipation of the foundation, or may have been executed by his scholars from his designs.

But we must never forget that England was anterior, or at all events more advanced, already in the eighth century in Christian civilization than the other parts of western Europe, through the labours of the Venerable Bede, Aldhelm, Egbert, and Alcuin of York, the last of whom, in 782, invited by Charlemagne to take charge of the education of France, writes to the emperor "to permit him to send some of his young gentlemen into England, to procure such books as were wanted, and to transplant the flowers of Britain into France, that their fragrance may no longer be confined to York, but may also perfume the palaces of Tours."

England was the focus too, at this period, of missionary zeal;—sending Boniface, Wilifred, and others to the conversion of Germany, and being in constant communication with Rome: she was especially enriched, by the perseverance and learning of her Churchmen, with the literary and artistic treasures of that capital of Christian enlightenment.   In the latter end of the seventh century, "Benedict Biscop, the founder of the monastery of Weremouth, in Northumberland, made no fewer than five journeys to Rome to collect books and pictures."

"In his fourth voyage, 678," says the Venerable Bede, " he brought from Rome many pictures of the saints, for the ornament of the church of St. Peter which he had built: viz., a picture of the Virgin Mary, the mother of God, and the pictures of the twelve Apostles, which he hung up in the body of the church, on a partition of wood from the south to the north wall; pictures of the Gospel history, with which he decorated the south wall; and pictures of the visions of St. John in

---

[t] Two erroneous dates in this passage are corrected from the authority of d'Agincourt, who in the article of chronology ranks higher than our illustrious Flaxman.

the Apocalypse, with which he adorned the north wall; that all the people who entered this church, *though ignorant of letters*, might contemplate the amiable aspect of Christ and His saints in these pictures, wherever they turned their eyes." For his church of St. Paul at Yarrow, in his fifth journey, he brought " pictures of the concord of the Old and New Testaments, executed with wonderful art and wisdom; for example the picture of Isaac carrying the wood on which he was to be sacrificed, and Christ bearing the cross on which He was to be crucified, were placed next to each other; and in like manner the serpent lifted up by Moses in the wilderness, and the Son of Man lifted up on the cross [u]."

The encouragement thus given to learning, to the arts, and to religion, from the seventh century, notwithstanding the calamities of the country, by Alfred the Great and his successors, Edgar and others, had at least sustained them through the succeeding centuries; and we may question any great accession of light since their days through the boasted learning of foreigners, amongst whom the Normans more especially had but recently emerged from barbarism. A candid consideration of the piety and learning of England through the successive ages, and under the blessings of a firm government, from the Conquest down to the thirteenth century, will be sufficient to shew the high probability of a school of Art as illustrious in this country at that period, as in any other of western Europe, and that our accomplished and zealous bishop had no need whatever to look beyond its shores for all the assistance in art that he could want.

A material argument in favour of their native production is to be found in the fact that this sculpture is of stone from a well-known quarry in the neighbourhood, viz., Doulting, near Shepton-Mallet; and that if made elsewhere than at Wells, their size and number would have added very seriously, in that inland country, to the cost.

On the quality of the art employed in these works we can have no higher authority than that of Flaxman. " In speaking of the execution of such a work," says he, " due regard must be had to the circumstances under which it was produced, in comparison with those of our own times; there were neither prints nor printed books to assist the artist; the sculptor could not be instructed in anatomy, for there were no anatomists; some knowledge of optics and a

[u] Bed., Hist. Abbat. Weremouth, p. 295.

glimmering of perspective, were reserved for the researches of so sublime a genius as Roger Bacon some years afterwards."

"A small knowledge of geometry and mechanics was exclusively confined to two or three learned monks in the whole country; and the principles of those sciences, as applied to the figure and motion of man and inferior animals, were known to none; therefore this work is necessarily ill drawn, and deficient in principle, and much of the sculpture is rude and severe; yet in parts there is a beautiful simplicity, an irresistible sentiment, and sometimes a grace excelling more modern productions[v]." And the justice of these observations will be apparent to every unprejudiced observer.

The admiration claimed for these works must be understood in its due measure by the candid spectator; whoever distinguishes not between the mental qualities of conception and ideality, and the mechanical execution depending on imitation, anatomy, and academical practice, will scarcely excuse the defects, or enjoy the higher merits in which they abound. Regarded in the right spirit, we shall wonder at the inexhaustible resources of the artist in delineating the various and opposite characters of his multifarious composition,—in which no two are to be found alike, and in each of which we find the appropriate idea;—and the fulness of embodiment which sustains the "dramatis personæ" throughout, with an untiring energy of impersonation in costume, symbol, and action, which excites our warmest admiration.

We have the sanctity of the Monk, the meekness and abstraction of the supreme Pontiff; the Archbishop; the pious energy of the Bishop in the act of benediction; the prudent Abbot; the devoted Anchorite; the haughty and imposing King; the stark conqueror fiercely justifying his usurpation; the placid and impassible Confessor administering his good old laws; the lusty but hapless "Ironside;" the intrepid Harold encased in mail; the king, defender of the faith, treading upon the fallen pagan; the comely gallant prince and lover; the devout Nun; the majestic Queen benefactress,—who have retired from the pomps and vanities of the world: the lovely bride of Henry I., "the fair maid of Brabant," the theme of the troubadour; the inspired Evangelist, or the malignant sprite; each and all discovering a racy energy of conception, which the informed artist may

[v] Lecture 1.

envy. And though sometimes pushed almost to caricature, the better to explain the person, in keeping with the grossness of that day, these works contain beyond all doubt, lessons to the artists of our times, which ought not to be declined.

The sculptor, unaided by superscription, (which was not then in use, and was introduced only in subsequent styles,) was compelled to employ the most ingenious devices to make his characters understood; resources full of meaning, wit, and good taste, as we shall have occasion to see in the catalogue describing them.

We may apply to him the commendations bestowed by Mr. Sharpe on the style of the historian Malmesbury, whose records seem to have furnished our sculptor with his best materials. " He does not weary with a tedious detail, but in a moment some master-stroke is applied, some vivid flash of Promethean fire animates the canvass, and the perfect figure darts into life and expression ; hence we have the surly ferocious snarl of the Conqueror, and the brutal horse-laugh of Rufus. Malmesbury's history indeed may be called a kind of biographical drama, where by a skilful gradation of character, and a variety of personage, the story is presented entire, though the tediousness of continued narrative is avoided. Again by saying little on uninteresting topics, and dilating on such as are important, the mind, which perhaps recoils with indignation from the stupid indifference of an Ethelred, hangs with fond delight on the enterprising spirit and exertion of an Ironside *."

The poetic faculty, the fine sense of beauty, character, grace, and humour, are the gifts of nature ; technical and mechanical skill may be acquired by academy and happy circumstances. The union of these qualifications, which is requisite to perfection in a work of art, is indeed a rare felicity : their separate existence is a melancholy fact, exhibited by the history of schools ; in which for the most part mechanism and technicality usurp the higher attainment, and the wide distinction between the professional practitioner and the inborn artist is made apparent to us. But the end of all sound criticism should be to recognise these distinctions; to seize the poetical conception, however encumbered with a faulty execution, and

---

* Translator's Preface, p. xiv.

D 2

to appreciate in their true merit, the more exalted and the rarer qualities ; else the
poet descends to the grammarian, and the intellectual artist to a handicraftsman.

In contemplating the sculptures of Wells, these truths will be admitted ; and
we shall abundantly acknowledge those rarer qualities everywhere and throughout,
—lamenting only the absence of the inferior ones, by which they would have been
more effectually recommended to the understanding of all. The medieval artist
appealed sometimes to the imagination, and sometimes to the conscience ; and
thus gave a degree of sentiment to his works, which the moderns can scarcely
attempt,—much less attain. *Allegory* constitutes the intellectuality of the æsthetic
arts ; but it is wholly alien to the multitude in our own hard age, and we find the
greatest difficulty in adapting such conceptions to our customary criticism of the
fine Arts ; and yet, how desirable such noble motives in sculpture, painting, and
architecture,—calculated to appeal so much more universally, and readily, and
definitely, to the spectator, than any other in the circle of the fine arts ! Although
the symbols and the language of the graphic arts have long ceased to be vernacu-
lar amongst us, they are capable of being re-established ; and we may hope that
the reforming spirit of the present age may conduct us in that desirable path.

But it is the moral understanding of the artist which is most affected by
the contemplation of so vast an assemblage of Christian art, as contrasted with
the classical, contained in our museums or in ancient monuments. Habituated
to the Grecian model, in which the pride of life, the sensuality of beauty, a
superhuman energy, or an unreal Elysium are assumed, deluding with a beau-
ideal and disappointing to all human experience, he is brought here to the full
admission of the realities and the true conditions of human existence,—probation
by the sweat of the brow, and the grand achievement of eternal life. Art is here
employed to impress the great lessons of Truth, the warfare of the world, the
subjugation of the natural to the spiritual man, the honest employment of the
intellect in the great cause of religion. To classical eyes the Hercules becomes
the enduring warrior of the cross ; the demigod or the philosopher becomes the
saint or the holy martyr. Female gentleness and beauty in the veil, or clad in
sackcloth, minister to the infirmities, and assuage the afflictions of their fellow-
creatures, instead of its ruder passions ; no characters enter into this picture
which have not been signalized by some great good to society, or some great

triumph over all-absorbing self. Wisdom in its true sense, and varying energies of personal or intellectual strength, in a great cause, are the only passports to admission in these records.

The gentler sex, regarded in the heathen world as absolutely subordinate and subsidiary to human existence, according to Aristotle's idea of classing children and brutes in the same category,—here become the equals at least, and often the principal exemplars, of virtue and religion; " by weakness, strength is made perfect;" and the mothers of mankind are exhibited as the best helpmates to the happiness of the life that is to come, as well as of that which makes our present joy.

Such reflections, arising naturally in the course of this interesting department of history, yet become enforced especially upon the artist, with remarkable effect and strength by the cumulative view of the glorious company of saints and martyrs, " *oculis subjecta fidelibus,*" in this noble picture.

The expression which pervades the whole work is eminently Christian, and entirely formed upon the poetical figures of the Old and New Testament; the imagery of which, as contrasted with classical art, is every where remarkable. The Virgin 'tramples on the dragon;' 'the seed of the woman bruises the serpent's head;' the Kings 'tread down their enemies;' and 'ye shall tread down the wicked;' and God shall 'tread down Satan under your feet;' 'the humble and meek are exalted;' the 'angels stand about the throne:' Angels minister in every part of the picture, and the agency of evil spirits is equally apparent every where[y].

We are impressed too with the soundness of authority and the purity with which all doctrinal subjects are illustrated, and the absence of that apocryphal and legendary matter, and often disgusting machinery of miracles, devils, and pitchforks, and the impertinence of pun and rebus, which disfigure cotemporary and subsequent works both of literature and art. We may conceive it not improbable that the bishop had read the edifying letter upon this subject, written by St. Bernard to the abbot of St. Thierry in 1125. " For," says he, " what purpose can be answered by those monsters in painting and sculpture which are found in our cloisters or on our walls, in the sight of those who lament their sins ; where is the advantage

[y] See also Psalm xviii. 37, 38; xlvii.; lviii.

of this fine deformity, or this beauty deformed, of these hideous monkeys, furious lions, or monstrous centaurs [a]?"

From these, the sculptures and the taste generally displayed in the works at Wells, are quite free ; and this consideration furnishes a strong argument in favour of the enlightening influence of the unadulterated Word, upon the Churchmen of that period, in favour no less of fine art than of every other intellectual work.

It will be remembered that the great corruptions of the Church began immediately after the age of Trotman. The victories achieved by the pope over the English crown during the reigns of Henry II., Richard, and John, and the enormous abuses which thence grew up in this country, paved the way for that false learning which followed, and for the discontinuance of the study of the word of God, from whence alone true light can be derived. The yet unprinted letter of Roger Bacon to the pope on this subject, confirms this fact in a remarkable manner. The following passage is furnished by a friend at Oxford[a], as a striking though neglected evidence of the state of biblical learning in that day.

" Quartum peccatum est," says Bacon, " quod præfertur una sententia Magistralis textui facultatis Theologicæ, scil. liber sententiarum. Nam ibi est tota gloria Theologorum. Et ibi quilibet facit onus unius equi. Et postquam illum legerit quis, jam præsumit se de magisteri Theologiæ, quamvis non audiant tricesimam partem sui textus. Et bacularius qui legit textum, succumbit lectori sententiarum parum [?]. Et ubique et in omnibus honoratur et præfertur. Nam parum ille qui legit sententias habet principalem [?] horam legendi secundum suam voluntatem, habet et socium et cameram apud Religiosos. Sed qui legit Bibliam, caret his, et mendicat horam legendi, secundum quod placet lectori sententiarum. Alibi qui legit Sententias disputat, et pro Magistro habetur. Reliquus qui textum legit, non potest disputare, sicut fuit hoc anno Bononiæ, et in multis aliis locis, quod est absurdum. Manifestum est igitur quod textus illius facultatis subjicitur uni sententiæ Magistrali[b]."

[a] Apud Mabilionem inter opera Sancti Bernardi, cap. xii.

[a] Mr. John W. Burgon, of Oriel College, Oxford.

[b] From the copy of a MS. letter of Roger Bacon, to Pope Clement, preserved in the Bodleian Library, (Cod. MSS. Bodl. Digb. 218,) quoted by Hody, in his work *De Bibliorum textibus originalibus*. Fol. Oxford, 1705, p. 419. The original MS. abounds in contractions, and is hard to read.

The letter treats of the necessity to the theologian of a study of the original language, and of the corruptions of the Vulgate. In the course of the letter occurs the preceding curious testimony of a contemporary, to the preference then given to the works of the Schoolmen ; and the comparative neglect into which the word of God had fallen.

DESCRIPTION OF THE SCULPTURES.

GREAT historical and diocesan interest was involved in the See of Wells which was one of those three created, with Crediton and St. Petræ, out of the Sees of Sherborne and Winchester, by Edward the Elder, A.D. 905.

Wells was in the heart of that kingdom of Wessex, which conquered the other kingdoms of the so-called heptarchy, and finally established the race of Cerdic on the throne of these realms for nearly three centuries; such a boast was more gratifying to the men of Wessex, than we are now able to appreciate, civilization sweeping away, as it does, those provincialisms and nationalities which formerly influenced our countrymen so much more strongly than at present. In illustration of this fact, so glorious to the west of England, very naturally deemed paramount by the learned and patriotic Bishop Trotman, upwards of six hundred figures, in statues, or very high relief, varying from about two feet to eight feet high, in great part historical, adorned the western front, and the two returns north and south, of the Cathedral[a].

That so vast and extended a series might be duly disposed with ample and convenient space for their collocation, a peculiar arrangement of the architecture and an unusual dimension were required[b]; the two towers, in the old Norman fashion, placed at the extremities of the western front and incorporated into the design, thus afforded the space necessary for its exhibition.

[a] The Parthenon comprised about the same number of figures in the pediments, metopes, and frieze round the cella. To compare the works of Phidias with those of the untutored and unrecorded sculptor of Wells, may be startling, but the fact is remarkable as exhibiting the vastness of the work.

[b] The front of Wells is 147 ft., while that of Notre Dame at Paris is only 136 ft., and at Amiens 116 ft.; that of Rouen is 188 ft., but the two towers at Rouen cannot be said to form part of the design of the front.

The front of Wells, according to Cæsarcanus, would be called Hexastyle, as having six buttresses, those of France are generally Tetrastyles, having four buttresses only.

E

The doorways also are remarkably limited in their width and elevation, that the series of sculpture might be as little interrupted by these necessary features as possible[e].

The architecture was thus regarded but as the frame in which was to be displayed " a kalendar for unlearned men," a picture illustrating the chief doctrines of the faith, its sacred history, its happy advent into this country, and its protection through successive spiritual Guides and temporal Princes.

The front is divided horizontally into *Nine tiers or zones* of sculpture extending throughout the whole surface ; it is so divided, perpendicularly, that all that refers to the spiritual characters, and treats " *de vetere lege*," is placed to the south of the western door ; and all that refers to the temporal characters, and " *de nová lege*," is placed to the north.

Again we are to remark that the statues on the six buttresses to the west, and three to the north and east, are much larger in the fourth and fifth, the historical Tiers, and (with only one exception) invariably sitting, while the others stand ; the former refer to the most illustrious characters of history, either the great kings of the Saxon, Norman, and Plantagenet dynasties, the special protectors of the Church, or to the bishops of Wells promoted to the See of Canterbury up to the year 1244 ; the latter refer to the kings in regular succession, princes, Churchmen, and worthies of both sexes.

Proceeding to the explanation of these nine tiers or zones of sculpture, we find, *in the first Tier*, upon the basement, sixty-two niches once containing the messengers of the Gospel from the earliest to the latest time. Thus according to St. Paul[d], the Church is " built upon the foundation of the Apostles and the Prophets." Unfortunately the far greater part of their contents have been destroyed by the iconoclasts of the sixteenth and seventeenth centuries ; especially

---

[e] Durandus, c. i. 26, says the door of the Church is Christ; according to that saying in the Gospel, " I am the door, by Me if any man enter he shall be saved," (John x. 9.) The Apostles are also called doors. The smallness of the extreme doors, north and south, alludes to Matt. vii. 13, " Enter ye in at the strait gate." Other reasons also contributed to this characteristic peculiarity in the architecture of that period ; the door, offering the scale to the entire design, is kept small to give effect of magnitude to the architectural elevation both externally and internally, and again, the smallness of the door, according to Durandus, had a symbolical meaning.

[d] Eph. ii. 20.

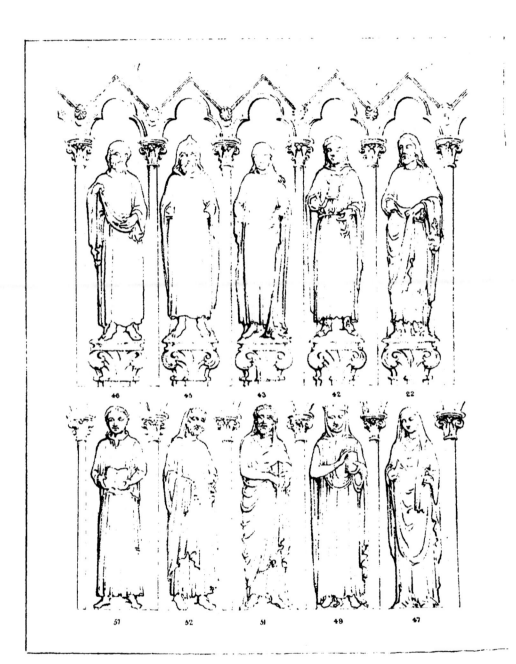

in the Somersetshire riots in 1685, when the archives also of the Cathedral were miserably burnt; a few only of the characters intended by the 62 statues are distinctly recognisable, and we are left to conjecture the rest.

To the south of the western entrance (invariably esteemed the most holy, side) are twenty-two niches in this tier, two of which only still possess their statues*. These are not sufficiently characterized to enable us to pronounce upon the personages intended : but judging from their position under the series of the Old Testament, and from the practice in France and elsewhere, (which was to place the most venerable and sacred characters to the south,) these figures may possibly have represented the four major, and the twelve minor Prophets; and also Moses, Aaron, Melchisedec, Noah, &c.

The twenty-two niches north of the western door, doubtless illustrated the first mission of the apostles in England. Here we may conclude were SS. Peter, Paul, James, and Andrew, (whose preaching in this country was traditionally asserted in those days,) together with Joseph of Arimathea, said to have been the founder of Glastonbury, Claudia Rufina, Græcina, King Lucius, Faganus, Duvanus, St. Albanus the proto-martyr, &c. &c. Two only of these (42[f] 43) remain ; on the breast of one is an object held up in both hands, which is not distinguishable, but had doubtless its important signification. On the north side of the north tower, the figures of this tier are better preserved, and some of them may be clearly identified. They undoubtedly refer to the second mission to this country under St. Augustine, whose figure (46) holding the pallium, the symbol of his occupation of the first archiepiscopal chair in England, is quite unquestionable. No. 45 may be Luidhard, his predecessor. Then follow four of the gentler sex, habited in matronal, and one in a queenly vestment, and crowned. These may be the blessed help-

---

* See specimen, fig. 22, a very dignified figure, having a mantle thrown over the left arm, terminating as it appears in a lion's mask, and fig. 21; neither of them having any discernible characteristic. The plate of the geometrical elevation represents these statues as restored, the better to convey the original design. The lithograph perspective represents the actual state of the western and northern fronts.

[f] "In Exodus (xxviii. 22) it is commanded by the divine law, that on the breast of Aaron the breastplate of judgment should be bound with strings, because fleeting thoughts should not occupy the mind of a priest, which should be girt by reason only." "To bear the fathers thus imprinted on the breast is to meditate on the lives of ancient saints without intermission."—Dur., p. 65.

mates to these apostles, Bertha [s], and Eadburgha, and others, by whose influence
their labours were crowned with a happy result.

No. 51 may well be St. Birinus, the special apostle of the west of England,
who, thirty-nine years later, (635,) arrived at the court of Kinegils, king of
Wessex ; he holds in his hands the "corporalia," as the credentials of his
mission, and sufficient evidence to us of his identity. "Proceeding from Genoa
through France," says Milner, "our apostle came to the sea-port on the channel,
from which he was to embark for our island. Here having performed the sacred
mysteries, he left behind him what is called 'corporal,' containing the blessed
Sacrament, which he did not recollect until the vessel in which he sailed was some
way out at sea. It was in vain to argue the case with the pagan sailors who
steered the ship, and it was impossible for him to leave his treasure behind him.
In this extremity, supported by a strong faith, he stepped out of the ship upon the
waters, which became firm under his feet, and walked, in this manner, to the land ;
having secured what he was anxious about, he returned in the same manner on
board the vessel, which had remained stationary in the place where he left it.
The ship's crew were of the nation to which he was sent, and being struck with
the miracle they had witnessed, lent a docile ear to his instructions. Thus our
apostle began the conversion of the West Saxons, before he landed upon their
territory. This prodigy," adds Milner, "is so well attested by the most judicious
historians, *that those who have had the greatest interest to deny it, have not
dared openly to do so* [h]."

The five following figures, 52—56, are not so favourable to interpretation, though holding books and symbols of various descriptions. 57, a priest
holding a pictured tablet to his heart, may represent the active and zealous

[s] "Ethelbert, king of Kent, had married a Christian lady, Bertha, the daughter of Caribert,
king of Paris, who had a French bishop (Luidhard) for her chaplain, and a church in Canterbury for
the practice of her religion, where St. Augustine and his companions on their arrival were permitted to
sing, pray, say mass, preach, and baptize, without molestation."—Bede, Ecc. Hist., lib. i. c. 26. A
similar circumstance, paved the way for Paulinus to preach to the Northumbrians. "Edwin their king
sent an embassy to Ethelbert in order to demand his daughter, Eadburga, in marriage, who, as well
as her father, was a zealous Christian. The offer was accepted, but upon condition that she might be
at liberty to practise her religion. This furnished an opportunity for St. Paulinus, who accompanied
her, to introduce Christianity into the north."—Milner's History.

[h] Milner's Hist. and Survey of Winchester, c. vi p. 68.

Benedict Biscop, who made five journeys to Rome, from 678 to 685, for the purpose of collecting pictures and missals, &c. for his monastery at Weremouth, as already related.

58, 59, and 60, have indications of the same kind, which may serve to identify them to those whose industry and skill may be more fortunate than my own.

In the second Tier, in thirty-two quatrefoils, are angels issuing from clouds, having two wings, a nimbus on the head, with scarfs elegantly and variously disposed, and holding in their hands, mitres, crowns, and scrolls, the emblems of the temporal and eternal rewards to the faithful listeners to these predications, and proclaiming the glad tidings of Salvation.

In the third Tier (in which the illustration of the Old and New Testament is proposed [i]) to the south of the western door are seventeen subjects from the Old Testament,—to the north seventeen from the New, and fourteen others in the north and east, making forty-eight in all : many of them remaining, and all remarkable for the scriptural correctness, simplicity of expression, and absence of apocryphal matter ; the particulars of these are given in the catalogue.

The birth of the Saviour, typified in the Old Testament, and so largely illustrated in the New, and the blessed Virgin, are appropriately represented in this series in two groups ; first, in the spandrel of the arches of entrance and within the porch, are the Virgin and Child. She is grandly dressed, and seated on a throne, and treading on the serpent, according to Gen. iii. 15, "The seed of the woman shall bruise the serpent's head [j]." An acolyte elegantly disposed on either side administer incense. The ground was originally painted in ultramarine, the mouldings gold and red. The figures appear to have been partly gilt, and a nimbus, crown, or other ornament, was attached by bolts or nails to the back ; in the south portal, at Amiens, three angels sustain the nimbus over the head of the " Vierge dorée [k]."

The second representation alludes to the coronation of the Virgin, and is

---

[i] Some idea of these is given in the accompanying lithograph.

[j] Psalm xci. 13 ; Rev. xx. 2.

[k] Most of the ornaments and figures of the porches of Amiens Cathedral, as well as those of the transepts, have still the remains of different colours, and of gilding upon them, according to the oriental system of decoration imported to Italy by the Greeks. In the East indeed mosaic had been invented and much used by the early Christians in their pictorial decorations, thus intending to realize in the most striking manner the idea of the new Jerusalem built of precious stones.—See Rev. xxi., and Appendix E.

placed above the point of the porch. The heads have been destroyed by the zealous reformers ; who, (to their credit be it remembered,) while they respected all that was scriptural, everywhere defaced the apocryphal.

The adoration of the Virgin more especially was an abuse which commenced in this century ; and the canon of Wells expressly records the fact, that Trotman was a great promoter of it : " hic primo anno consecrationis suæ servitium B. Mariæ in ecclesia Wellensi fecit cotidie decantari."

We must not omit to mention that in the soffit of the great western doorway, are ten small female figures with canopies, and pedestals of very elegant sculpture, which probably refer to the ten commandments, but no symbols or details help us to any further explanation. They are not perceived until we are within the porch, and form no part of the external decoration : they are therefore rather connected with a moral idea than an artistic feature. The placing of the ten commandments over and around the heads of the comers to the temple, is not only appropriate as the symbol of the old and new Law illustrated on either side, but singularly characteristic of the Founder in his legal capacity, as one of the king's chief justices of Common Pleas. Bishop Trotman seems to have felt that the Divine law and the law of the land should be identical ;—that he who would write those laws in his heart, would have no need of human legislation. He entirely coincided with the opinion of his own immortal Alfred, whose great endeavour it was to impart the spirit of the law of God to the temporal legislation of his kingdom. Alfred's statutes are prefaced by the Decalogue ; to which he has added also a selection from the Mosaic precepts, and the canons of the first apostolic council. " Do these," he continues, " and if these commands be obeyed, no other doom-book will be required."

The fourth and fifth Tiers display in 126 niches the effigies of those lords, spiritual and temporal, under whom, as God's vicegerents upon earth, the blessings of religion, learning, and good government, have been cherished and defended in this country. Amongst these are introduced the progenitors, illustrious Alliances, and worthies of the Anglo-Saxon history more especially, and also of the Norman and Plantagenet dynasties. All these, with the exception of ten or twelve, are so distinctly recognisable, either by symbols, costume, significant action or locality, as by the help of history, to leave no reasonable doubt as to their identity,—as the catalogue will explain.

In the sixth Tier we have the Resurrection in ninety-two subjects, containing about 150 statues in high relief, about 4 ft. high,—rising from the tomb at the sound of the trump in the last day. In these groups, all the expression of hope and joy, repentance, fear, and despair, are displayed in the most awful, and at the same time natural manner. They awaken by degrees from their long sleep, heave up their tomb-stones, and draw themselves slowly from the earth with difficulty, as scarcely awake; hail with emotion the joyful summons; or tear their hair, and call upon the rocks to cover them; some have upon their heads the symbols of their office in this world; kings and queens, though naked, are recognised by their crowns; bishops by their mitres; while their bodies, like the rest of mankind, are denuded of all their earthly pomp and paraphernalia.

The third in the lithograph plate (in which specimens are selected and placed here in illustration of their design and character), is found immediately over the Conqueror; no doubt alluding to the account which he especially and his queen Matilda, have to render of all their wrongs inflicted upon the Anglo-Saxon race.

A bishop naked, but recognised by his mitre, and hiding his face with his hands, is placed over the series of bishops on the south side. The expression of all, especially of the women, is admirably natural, and may challenge the works on the same subject by the Pisani at Orvieto, given in d'Agincourt's third vol., plate xxxiii., in which a puerile grimace and action, and machinery of shapeless devils and serpents, betray a conception of the subject assuredly inferior to that at Wells.

In the seventh Tier are at present 15 niches, in which the hierarchy of heaven is represented by the angels. Six appear to sound the last trump, but nine of these, immediately under the Apostles, are remarkable as representing the nine orders of angels especially invoked on the pious benefaction of ecclesiastical establishments [1].

---

[1] Wharton, Anglia Sacra, vol. ii. p. 10. Ethelred, king of the Mercians, A.D. 681, gives a certain property to Malmesbury, when he uses these terms: "Quod si quis tyrannicâ potestate fretus demere sategerit; sciat coram Christi *novemque angelorum ordinibus* rationem redditurum," and the same imprecation is used in other similar instances. King Ina conveys a property to Malmesbury much in the same terms, p. 11, Ang. Sac. "in ultimo examine coram Christo et angelis ejus rationem reddere."

It is important to bear in mind that the angels, according to the canons of our own Church, stand on the same authority as in Bishop Trotman's time, in the following order:

1. Cherubim.
2. Seraphim.
3. Thrones.
4. Powers.
5. Dominions.
6. Authorities.
7. Angels.
8. Archangels.
9. Principalities [m].

It will be observed that the division of the nine niches has no correspondence with that of those above, which are twelve in number; and are therefore designed with special signification of these nine ministers of grace. It may be presumptuous in a layman to attempt their definition, but as their several symbols are in some instances distinctly recognisable, the following remarks are hazarded. Four have the appearance of archangels, each clothed by four wings; the first of these appears to be Michael: the second may be Raphael, Medicina Dei; he holds a basin of incense in his hands, the vapours of which wave as they ascend; the third, Gabriel, seems in act of annunciation with upraised hands: the fourth may be Uriel, having in his hand the wooden shovel or flabellum with which the grain is sifted from the chaff when thrown into the air [n].

We may remark on the angels having two wings only, that the second in the series appears like the angel of prayer; the fourth bearing a sword may represent the angels "that excel in strength;" the fifth in the centre clothed in a vesture of the utmost dignity and beauty, may be the angel of grace; the sixth in warlike guise and fully armed may be the "destroying angel;" the ninth holding a book may be the angel of the Revelations.

These remarks are offered to the learned in this mysterious subject as aids to their interpretation merely. It may be mentioned that the east window of the Lady's chapel contains also the nine angels [o].

In the eighth Tier the twelve apostles in statues of about 8 ft. high, stand

---

[m] See Dionysius Areopageta, and Bollandi Acta Sanctorum.

[n] In King Canute's charter to Glastonbury he says, " and should any one endeavour, on any occasion, to break in upon, or make void the enactment of this grant, let him be driven from the communion of the righteous by the FAN of the last judgment."—Malmesbury, c. xi.

[o] See Appendix on Worcester Cathedral.

in majestical order and very fine design, with their several distinctive symbols and costume, worthy of the most careful observation and comparison with other authorities.

The first is undoubtedly St. Peter, as evinced by the globe in his hand, and the crown on his head[p]; Bishop Trotman's adhesion to the papistic party, is here asserted in a signal manner. The second may be Matthew, holding his gospel; the third may be Thomas; the fourth Simon the Canaanite holding a sword, his constant symbol; the fifth may be James the son of Zebedee, standing next to his brother the sixth, St. John, holding a chalice in his hand; the seventh is Andrew, designated by his cross, to whom the church of Wells was dedicated; the eighth may be Philip; the ninth, by the instrument of his martyrdom which he holds in his hand, the flaying knife and his own skin, can be no other than Bartholomew; the tenth is James, the son of Alpheus, recognised by the club with which as bishop of Jerusalem he suffered martyrdom; the eleventh may be Thaddeus; and the twelfth is Matthias.

In the ninth Tier are three niches from which the statues (except the feet of the Saviour in the centre) have been removed by the iconoclasts. These doubtless contained the Christ sitting in judgment; the Virgin and John the Baptist, on either side, the types of the old and the new law, and the intercessors on the last solemn day.

Thus have we in this magnificent series of sculpture, adorning the front of Wells Cathedral, the most glorious picture of prayer and praise that can be presented to the Christian spectator; a sort of homily, rude indeed, but in earnestness and propriety not surpassed by any other example we are acquainted with. In contemplating its comprehensive design, the mind that animates every part of it, the sumptuousness of its execution and fulness of illustration, we are reminded of the noble hymn of St. Ambrose, which, as the Pæan which inspired and guided every operation of peace or war in those days, it may not be

[p] It is to be observed that the first of these statues, St. Peter, is crowned, which is an unusual, if not a singular instance of such a representation of that Apostle; the sculptor might quote Durandus as his authority for this addition; who (without at all meaning to be jocose) justifies these liberties in the artist, on the ground, that ' pictoribus atque poetis quodlibet *addendi* semper fuit equa Potestas.' The note of his candid editors, Messrs. Neale and Webb, upon this is, "a false reading of course : yet not without its appropriate sense, the power of adding any ornamental circumstance !"

a conceit, unsuited to the period, to suggest as the meaning which it was
proposed to embody in this work [q].

Resuming the order of *these nine Tiers*, we trace each successively in the
verses of the " Te Deum."   In the *first* we read :—

" The glorious company of the Apostles praise Thee.   The goodly fellow-
ship of the prophets praise Thee."   •

" The noble army of martyrs praise Thee."

In the *second* :—" To Thee all angels cry aloud, the heavens and all the
powers therein."   And over the central door in the same Tier

" Thou art the King of Glory, O Christ ; when Thou tookest upon Thee
to deliver man, Thou didst not abhor the Virgin's womb."

In the third, fourth, and *fifth* :—" The holy Church throughout all the world
doth acknowledge Thee."

In the sixth, seventh, and *eighth* :— " When Thou hadst overcome the sharp-
ness of death ; Thou didst open the kingdom of heaven to all believers."

" We therefore pray Thee help Thy servants, whom Thou hast redeemed with
Thy precious blood."

" Make them to be numbered with Thy saints, in glory everlasting."

" O Lord, save Thy people and bless Thy heritage."

In the ninth :—" We believe that Thou shalt come to be our judge."   The
whole work proclaims

" Day by day we magnify Thee, and we worship Thy name ever world
without end."

---

[q] When in the sixth crusade the army had crossed the Nile, and assaulted Damietta, they took
possession of the enemy's camp, singing the hymn " Te Deum Laudamus." When the deputies sent
by King John to the pope, to entreat the confirmation of the bishop of Norwich, as primate of Canterbury, were required by the pope to prefer the Cardinal Stephen de Langton, " they concurred in so
doing (with the exception of the chief deputy); and singing the ' Te Deum,' while they murmured in
their hearts, led the cardinal to the altar."

Dante writing in this century, and describing the sound of the doors of purgatory, as they were
opened to him, says,

> " Io mi rivolsi attento al primo tuono
> E, *Te Deum Laudamus*, mi parea
> Udire in voce mista all' dolce suono."

DETAILED ACCOUNT OF THE SCULPTURES;
SOUTH, OR SPIRITUAL SIDE.

HAVING thus offered a general view of the religious and historical intention of these sculptures, I proceed to describe the latter more particularly, as less obvious and as highly illustrative of the historical and artistic purpose of these effigies, and of the record of these characters.

An important division in the west front, established by ancient superstition, was that which attributed greater sanctity to the southern end than the northern [a]. In the first tier this distinction is exhibited in the more apostolical costume of the two remaining figures, 21 and 22, already remarked upon, as probably referring to the Prophets; in the third tier, in the adaptation of the Old Testament; and in the fourth and fifth tiers, in the occupation by the lords spiritual (almost exclusively) of the southern side. While the preachers of the first and second missions; the New Testament; and the temporal lords, occupy the northern half of the west front, as also its continuation in the north and east sides of the north tower. These cardinal divisions of the picture are pointed out in the accompanying index.

We are also to remark the pre-eminence given to the buttresses. In these the most illustrious characters are of larger dimensions and enthroned, (see their names printed in large characters in the index;) while the others are standing. Thus in the three southern buttresses we have Edward the Elder, and the five archbishops translated from Sherborne, or Wells, previous to 1214. So in the northern half of the west front, we have on the three buttresses, Alfred, S. Dunstan, Athelstan, Edred, Edward, and Edgar. We proceed with the description of the former.

In an illiterate age the history of the Bishops is the history of civilization : the Clergy were then the depository and the guardians of all knowledge, and all law human and divine; the confidential advisers of the crown, and the intercessors for the people; and the only cultivators of the arts, the utilities and the refinements of life. The altar was the corner-stone of the fabric of monarchy, constantly directing and

---

[a] For reasons of the sanctity of the south side, see Bingham Origines Ecclesiasticæ, or the Antiquities of the Christian Church; also Staveley in his History of Churches, Martene, Lyndewoode and others.

It is however remarkable that at Orvieto this order is reversed. The subjects of the Old Testament being to the north.

sometimes absorbing all its powers.   The Anglo-Saxon period especially com-
prises some of the most interesting and touching events of Christian history ; it
was then that the good seed was sown for the second time in this country, and
not only grew rapidly over our land, but by the burning zeal of its missionaries
soon extended its branches beyond the seas. The blood of martyrs shed by pagan
or by ruthless hands marked each step of its holy warfare during four centuries,
in which its labours and its triumphs approach the miraculous, and it was then that
was stamped that form of Church government which we enjoy at this day.

An order thus paramount has always therefore formed one of the most interesting subjects of history, and accordingly with the Venerable Bede, Alfred, Malmesbury, and Godwin, the Gesta Pontificum have always had their parallel record
with the Gesta Regum ; and as relates to personal character and civilization in
peaceful progress, the former has an incalculably higher interest ; for while Kings
are illustrious by hereditary right, Bishops are more emphatically so by the far
higher rights of natural gifts and acquired virtues.

In these venerable effigies then, we behold the conservative power of Christendom, the human authors of every good institution ; and in their characteristic
attitudes of benediction, the blessings and the benefactors of mankind.   The
uniformity of their office and costume imparts to these effigies a regimental mono-
tony, and we are unable to recognise with certainty the individuals intended ;
this is the more to be regretted since, as the chief actors in the multifarious scenes
of life, the sculptor might have designated them with no less variety of symbol
than on the temporal side, had he been permitted ; sometimes armed against the
pagan with sword and hauberk, like the intrepid and unfortunate Werstan, at
Brenanburg ; as counsellors and clerks in the most valorous, and the most solemn
acts of kings ; in missionary perils, then indeed most dangerous ; or in holy
exhortation amongst a barbarous people ; now constructing an organ, now limn-
ing a saint, designing a church, inditing a chronicle, compounding a learned
medicament, or transplanting from a foreign land some effectual relic, or some
precious fruit tree, or exotic herb of mickle grace to the gardens of England ;
sometimes too, the victims of evil passions, like other men, especially after the
Conquest, when for a long period, foreign oppression made injustice triumphant.

We count thirty-six bishops and holy characters on the spiritual side, but the bishops of Wells preceding Trotman, were twenty only in number[c]; to whom then are we to attribute the others?

It will be remembered that Wells, as a conventual church, was included

[c] Bishops of Sherborne.

Aldhelmus	705	
Forthere	737	
Herewald	——	
Ethelnod	——	
Denefrith	——	
Wilbert	812	
Ealhstan	823	
Edmond	867	
Ethelrage	871	
Alfsius	——	
Asser	910	
Sighelm	889	
Ethelwold	898	

Bishops of Wells.

Athelmus	909	Archbishop of Canterbury.
Wolfelmus	924	Do. Do.
Elphege	927	
Wolfelmus	938	
Brithelmus	959	Do. Do.
Kyneward	973	
Segar	997	
Adelwynus	1000	
Burwold	——	Martyr.
Leovingus	1001	Archbishop of Canterbury.
Eathelwynus	1023	Ejected.
Brethwinus	1026	
Merewint	1034	
Dudoc	1060	
Giso	1088	
John de Villula	1123	Physician.
Godfrey	1135	
Robert	1166	
Reginald Fitz-Jocelyne	1191	Archbishop of Canterbury.
Savaric	1205	
Trotman	1206	

during 200 years in the diocese of Sherborne: both these were founded by Ina; it is highly probable therefore that those bishops of Sherborne who preceded the institution of the See of Wells, by Edward the Elder, figured here.

We shall proceed then to suggest the intention of the figures according to this view,—" If perchance," as Malmesbury says with reference to the history of the bishops, " I may be able to win any thing worth notice out of the mintage of antiquity."—c. viii.

We should gladly have distinguished the individuals on this side of whom history has preserved any records, as we have been enabled to do on the temporal side; but, as already observed, the uniformity of their attitude and dress precludes the possibility of our doing so; the materials indeed for such a history are incidental only, and meagre, from the destruction of their records; and Wharton's Anglia Sacra has preserved little more than their names.

We should gladly have distinguished Kynewarde, the sixth bishop, who was most active in Edgar's time in expelling the married clergy. Ethelwyne, the eleventh, who was ejected from the See, we know not why. Dudoc, the fourteenth, was a Saxon, why preferred to a native we do not learn. Giso, the fifteenth, appointed by the Conqueror, was active in building a cloister, dormitory, and refectory for the monks[d]. The simoniacal John de Villula, the sixteenth, enriched by medical practice at Bath, purchased of Rufus (as we are told) the entire city of Bath, remunerating himself in some sort by taking down Giso's works, and appropriating the property of the monks. Robert the Norman, the seventeenth, is said to have repaired the Cathedral Church of Wells, and to have rebuilt that of Bath entirely. The nineteenth, Reginald 'the Englishman,' the

---

[d] Much scandal has attached to the fame of this prelate; Rodburne accuses him of " bribery to the king," and Matthew Paris, alluding to his medical profession, asserts that he obtained his episcopal seat from the willing king " albo unguento manibus ejus delibates." It is very interesting to trace at the east end of the actual church the remains of the church begun by this bishop through " the mammon of unrighteousness," and probably completed by Bishop Robert. And it is again pleasing to trace almost to our times his last remains, in the passage of our earliest antiquary Leland: " This John," says he, " pulled down the old Chirch of St. Peter at Bath, and erected a new, much fairer, and was buried in the middle of the Presbyteri thereof, whos image I saw lying there 9 yere sine, at which tyme all the Church that he made lay to wast, and was onrofed, and wedes grew about this John of Tours sepulchre."—Itin., vol. ii. f. 39.

friend of Henry II., and envoy to the pope on his reconciliation after the murder of Thomas à Becket : Reginald purging himself by oath, as particeps in any sort by word or deed or writing before the pope consecrated him to this See.

In his life we have an interesting evidence of the state of the town of Wells previous to his episcopacy in the fact recorded,—" that he made Wells a free borough, relieving it from all servile duties to the See."

The memory of Savaric, the twentieth bishop, was especially odious ; he was related to the infamous duke of Austria, Leopold, and affected great regard for Richard I. in his captivity, with a view, however, to an ample reward by the bishopric of Wells, and the entire jurisdiction of Glastonbury also. The consent of Richard to these exorbitant demands, and of the monks of Glastonbury, were made the conditions of the king's release. The abbot went over to Germany to plead their exemption, but in vain.

Great difficulty will be found in assigning names to the rest of the episcopal and venerable characters figured in this series, and the attempt to do so must be somewhat arbitrary.

We find bishops of Wells translated to Canterbury before 1204	5
Remaining bishops of Wells	16
The archbishops on the south pier, perhaps Ethelgar, and the martyr Elphige	2
Bishops of Sherborne	13
	—
	36

Proceeding to the description of the statues on the south* of the western door, the spiritual side of the Cathedral, we observe No. 1, a spirited statue standing upon a pedestal and about 5 ft. high, on the south pier of the central window.

Judging from his conspicuous position, the crown he wears, and the model of a church held in his left hand, to which he points with his right, this can be no

---

* For reasons of sanctity of the south side see Bingham, Origines Ecclesiasticæ, or the Antiquities of the Christian Church ; also Staveley in his History of Churches ; Martene de Antiquis Ecclesiæ ritibus ; Lyndewoode in his Provinciale ; Martene de ritibus monachorium.

It is recorded by Bentham (Hist. of Ely) that Dunstan presiding at the dedication of this Cathedral, dedicated " the east end to St. Peter, the south side of it to the blessed Virgin," p. 74.

other than the venerable Ina, who, with Offa and Ethelbert, founded the Anglo-Saxon "Doom-book," and signalized a long reign of thirty-seven years by remarkable merits.   He first collected and established the seventy-six laws which formed the nucleus and earliest foundation of Anglo-Saxon legislature.   His valour and prudence gave that preponderance to Wessex which ultimately enabled his descendant Egbert to become the Bretwalda of the other kingdoms of the so-called heptarchy, and to maintain the pre-eminence of the house of Cerdic for 265 years. He improved the ecclesiastical administration by founding the See of Shireburn, (A.D. 703,) and in the same year the conventual Church of Wells, which he dedicated to St. Andrew, (704); and rebuilding and enlarging Glastonbury, and other monasteries.

'King Ina sent for Greek masters from Athens; Aldhelm was versed in Hebrew.'   He bestowed his patronage with discriminating sagacity, as evinced in the promotion of Aldhelm, subsequently the refounder of Malmesbury, and Winfrith who ultimately became the apostle of Germany, under the assumed name of St. Boniface.   At length, accompanied by his Queen Æthelburgh, he went a pilgrim to Rome, where rejecting every vestige of earthly pomp and clad in homely garb, but declining (according to Lappenberg') to cut off his long hair, the mark of dignity amongst the Saxons as well as amongst the Franks, he passed the remainder of his days with his constant wife in privacy and devotion.

Ina was the founder of the Saxon school or college at Rome, of which mention is constantly made in subsequent history as the retreat of our pilgrims, and the school of English youth.

It was rebuilt by Ethelwolfe, enriched and adorned by Ethelbald of Mercia.

William of Malmesbury relates a characteristic anecdote of their retirement from the world by the contrivance of the queen.

No. 41, standing upon a pedestal against the north pier of the central window, is the Queen Æthelburgh, a graceful statue, towards which the sculptor has directed the king's regard with characteristic attention.

To her girdle is suspended the "aulmoniere," the symbol of her charity, in her right she probably held the model of the convent at Barking to which she

' See Thorpe's Translation, vol. i. p. 267.

ultimately retired, and in her left is apparently a roll signifying perhaps the charters and endowments she obtained in favour of monastic institutions[e].

No. 2. is the statue of a bishop, who, from his contiguity to the king, Ina, very probably represents Aldhelmus, the first bishop of Sherborne (705) appointed by Ina. He was nephew to the king, abbot of Malmesbury, and spoken of (by Bede and Malmesbury) in exalted terms, as "wonderful for ecclesiastical and liberal erudition," "a mind clear, and almost divinely inspired." His poetry was the delight and consolation of Alfred, and his work on the eight principal vices, his Enigmas, and his "Praise of Virginity," made him celebrated; an ancient MS. copy of this latter work, with a portrait of Aldhelmus himself, exists in the library of the archbishop's palace at Lambeth. Strutt has given us an engraving of it in plate xvi. "For his extensive knowledge of the Greek and Latin tongues," says Lappenberg, "he was indebted to the school of Canterbury, more especially to Hadrian, abbot of St. Augustine's in that city, who did not come to England till Aldhelm was near thirty years old; though his earlier instruction, particularly in dialectics, he owed to the abbey of Maildalfesburh, (the modern Malmesbury,) founded by a Scot." We have it from Alfred, that Aldhelm found no surer way of interesting his countrymen than by singing sacred and other poems to them on the bridge at Malmesbury, as they came into the market.

No. 3. may be Forthere, the second bishop of Sherborne, who accompanied the Queen Frithogtha in her pilgrimage to Rome (737), where he died. The scrip or reliquary suspended to his girdle is the distinctive mark of pilgrimage. Montfaucon has given us an engraving of the consecrated scrip for relics, which, with the oreflamme, accompanied Philip Augustus from St. Denis in the fifth expedition to the Holy Land.

---

[e] "Amongst others of our West-Saxon kings," says Milner, "who relinquished their crowns about this time in order to embrace a monastic life, were Sigebert, king of the East Angles; Ethelred, and Kenred his successor, kings of Mercia; Sebba and Offa, kings of the East-Saxons, and Ceolwulph and Egbirght, kings of the Northumbers." .. "Above thirty kings and queens made this sacrifice within the two first centuries after the conversion of our ancestors." .. "Those who condemn this abdication," adds Milner shrewdly, "as superstitious when performed for the sake of religion, would extol it as an act of heroism, if it were grounded on a philosophic contempt of wealth and state; or on a preference of the calm pleasures of a domestic life, or of studious retirement."—Milner, History of Winchester, ch. vi. p. 79.

The nine immediate successors of Forthere in the See of Sherborne, were Herewald, Ethelnod, Denefrith, Wilbert, Ealhstan, Edmond, Etheleage, Alfsy, Asser, Sighelm, Ethelweard, and are, I think, represented by the Nos. 4, 6, 7, 8, 9, 11, 13, 14, 12, 15, and 16, which will be described in the following pages.

The presiding figure, enthroned on the first buttress, No. 25, is undoubtedly Edward the Elder, the founder of the episcopal church of Wells in 905, and very properly placed on the south side.

No. 5, under Edward the Elder, is Athelelmus, first bishop of Wells, translated to Canterbury A.D. 924, and who crowned Athelstan at Kingston on Thames, A.D. 926.

No. 10, Wolfelmus, translated from Wells to Canterbury 927. Both these are in the act of benediction.

No. 30, Brithelmus, translated to Canterbury 959.

No. 37, Leovingus, translated to Canterbury A.D. 1013, after the murder of Archbishop Elphege by the Danes, he himself having been imprisoned by them for seven months, and exiled for a time. The mitre of this figure is conical and peculiar, the position is also uneasy and constrained, as if to express the affliction and persecution under which the archbishop had laboured.

No. 17 is Reginald Fitz-Jocelyn, the last translated from Wells to Canterbury (A.D. 1191) to the episcopacy of Trotman.

No. 27, Elphegus, and 28, Wulfelmus, the third and fourth bishops of Wells, have no celebrity, that I am aware of, attached to their names, though living in the active and illustrious reigns of Athelstan, Edmond, Edred, and Edwig. Brethelmus, No. 30, the fifth bishop, translated to Canterbury in 959, appears to have remained there but one year, and to have returned to Wells, holding his episcopal office there thirteen years longer. We can have no better key to the series, or more conclusive evidence of the personage intended by the sculptor, than his significant posture and the pallium held in his outstretched hands.

Bishops Kyneward, Segar, and Adelwynus, (29, 31, 32,) have no distinction in history, save as they were contemporaries with the sufferers in the Danish persecutions, from 981 to the final conquest by those barbarous invaders.

Bishop Burwold the martyr, the ninth bishop, should be distinguished by some special symbol, which however I have not been so fortunate as to discover : his episcopate appears to have been as short as it was fatal.

Leovingus, the tenth bishop of Wells, appears to have sat some years in this See previous to his translation to Canterbury, where his loyalty to Edmund Ironside and the Saxon party subjected him to especial persecution, as expressed by his effigy enthroned on the third buttress, and already remarked upon. The Saxon Chronicle characterizes Leovingus as "a very upright man before God and the world."

The eleventh bishop, Eathelwynus, No. 34, had but a short episcopate, terminating unhappily by his ejection from the See; on what occasion is not (that I am aware of) recorded in history, though the event and reasons might well be expected to appear in his effigy; another interesting recognition in this series reserved for more happy and attentive investigation. The twelfth bishop, Brithwynus, is distinguished by the record of his superintendance of the removal of the relics of St. Elphege from London to Canterbury in 1023; at which ceremony King Canute and his Saxon queen Emma assisted. Whether the full canonicals, in which the effigy, No. 35, appears, and a book, recording perhaps the holy commission in his hand, while his predecessors were without them, may be considered significant of his identity or not, remains for the consideration of the more careful observer.

No. 36, in full canonicals, may be Merewint, the thirteenth bishop, who had been abbot of Glastonbury. No. 38, Dudoc, the fourteenth bishop of Wells, was sent with others by Edward the Confessor to the great synod held at Rheims, "to the intent that they should report to the king what was determined there concerning Christendom." No. 39, Bishop Giso, the fifteenth bishop, consecrated at Rome 1060, whither he had been sent by the same pious monarch, together with Walter, bishop of Hereford, for the purpose of having certain doubts on the subject of religion resolved by the holy See; "being men, not only learned, but of good conversation, and not guilty of simoniacal practices." "When Giso entered upon his See," says the Canon of Wells, "he found but ten canons; according to others only five; who were reduced to beggary in consequence of the spoliations of Harold, earl of Kent, by whom this Church had been deprived both of its ornaments and possessions." "Complaining unto the king of this outrageous havoc," says Godwin, " he found cold comfort at his hands ; for whether it were for fear of Harold's power, or his wife's displeasure, he caused no restitution to be made ; only the queen was content to give of her own manors those of Mark and Modesley unto the Church."

No. 40 may be John de Villula, the sixteenth bishop, a French physician, already mentioned.

No. 18, now empty, may have contained the effigy of Bishop Godfrey, the seventeenth bishop, a foreigner as usual, a native of Belgium, who had been chaplain to Adelecia, the second queen of Henry I., whose effigy we may see in the north front of the church. To the king was owing the gift of Dogmersfield, long after the episcopal residence of the bishops of Bath and Wells.

No. 19, the eighteenth bishop of Wells, Robert of Normandy, another foreigner, appointed by the interest of the bishop of Winchester with his brother Stephen. Robert enjoyed a long episcopate, which he honorably employed in the repair of the Cathedral church of Wells, during the disastrous times between the usurpation of Stephen and the murder of Becket. Warton tells us of this prelate, (Ang. Sac. pars 1, p. 561,) " Complevit fabricam Ecclesiæ Bathonensis per Johannem Turonensem inchoatum, dedicavit ecclesiam Wellensem. Multas ruinas ejusdem ecclesiæ destructionem ejus in locis pluribus comminantes egregie reparavit." As the bishop died in 1166, previous to the introduction of the pointed style in this country, it is in the highest degree improbable that the actual Cathedral could have been executed by him.

No. 17, the nineteenth bishop, Reginald Fitz-Jocelyne.

No. 20, Savaric, the twentieth bishop.

Thus have we completed the catalogue of these holy men, leaving much for further discovery by scaffolding and other means of closer investigation, and we can have few more curious subjects of enquiry than the symbolism by which these interesting characters are designated, and the lights which may thereby be thrown upon their acts, and the estimation in which they were held in the thirteenth century.

Ninth Tier.

NORTH TOWER.

Eighth Tier.

St. Peter.
St. Matthew.
St. Thomas.
St. Simon.
St. James.

The nine Angels.

Seventh Tier.

Sixth Tier.   The   Re su rrect io n.

Fifth Tier.

99	98	97	96	95	94	93		92	91	90	89	88	87		86	85	84	83	82	81		80
	Johannes Scottus.	Turketul.	ST. DUNSTAN.	St. Elphege.	Grimbald.	Ethelward.		Ethelfleda.	St. Neot.	Earl of Mercia.	ALFRED.	Gothrum.			Otho.	Charles the Simple.	ATHELSTAN.	Edgiva.	Elgiva.	Hugh.	Echflæda.

Fourth Tier.

60	59	58	57	56	55	54		53	52	51	50	49	48		47	46	45	44	43	42		41
Harold.	Edmund Ironside.	Edgitha.	EDRED.	Hardicanute.	Harold I.	Emma.		Osburga.	Canute.	Ethelred.	EDMUND.	Edward, Martyr.	Edwy.		Ethered.	Ethelbert.	EDGAR.	Ethelbald.	Ethelwolf.	Egbert.	Ethelburga.

Third Tier.

18	17	16	15	14		13		12	11		10	9		8	7	6		5	4		3		2	1
Transfiguration.	The Anointing.	Christ preaching.	Christ in the wilderness.			Mission of the Apostles.		John in the wilderness.	Christ among the Doctors.										Nativity.					St. John.

Second Tier.   The   Angels.

First Tier.

THE   TEMPORAL   SIDE.

North Door.

(Pp. 45, 46.)

SOUTH TOWER.

St. Philip. | St. Bartholomew. | St. James the Less. | St. Thaddeus. | St. Matthias.

e nine Angels.

The Resurrection.

		Aldthelmus.	Edgitha.		EDWARD THE ELDER.	Edfleda.	Elphege.	Wulfhelm.	Kyneward.	BRITHELMUS.	Sigar.	Alwyn.	Burwold.	Ethelwynius.	Brithwyn.	Merewint.	LEOVINGUS.	Dudoc.	Giso.	Villula.
Edgiva.	O		Edgitha.			Edfleda.	Elphege.	Wulfhelm.	Kyneward.		Sigar.	Alwyn.	Burwold.	Ethelwynius.	Brithwyn.	Merewint.		Dudoc.	Giso.	Villula.
21	22	23	24	25	26	27	28	29	30	31	32	33	34	35	36	37	38	39	40

	Aldthelmus.	Forthere.	Herewald.	ATHELELMUS.	Ethelnod.	Denefrith.	Wilbert.	Ealstan.	WOLFELMUS.	Headmund.	Asser.	Etheleage.	Alfsy.	Sighelm.	Ethelweard.	Bao FITZ-JOYCELYN.		Robert.	Savaric.
1	2	3	4	5	6	7	8	9	10	11	12	13	14	15	16	17	18	19	20

	Creation of man.	Creation of woman.	Eden.	Temptation.	The Almighty in the garden.	Adam and Eve labour.	Cain's sacrifice.		Sentence.	Noah building.	The Ark.	Sacrifice on Ararat.	Isaac and Rebecca.	Isaac's blessing.	Death of Jacob.	
2	3	4	5	6	7	8	9	10	11	12	13	14	15	16	17	18

The Angels.

21 22

THE SPIRITUAL SIDE.

South Door.

DETAILED ACCOUNT OF THE SCULPTURES

ON

THE NORTH, OR TEMPORAL SIDE OF THE WEST FRONT.

THE history of the Anglo-Saxon kings is the history of chieftains whose mental and physical powers gave them a personal pre-eminence amongst men, and although hereditary rights were fully acknowledged, they yielded readily to those rights which nature had disposed for the more energetic acts of war or government. Amongst a refractory and half-civilized people, and bordering nations of the so-called Heptarchy, the sword was the only effectual sceptre in this island during 600 years, 250 of which were passed in struggles, rendered still more deadly and perpetual by the desolating and atrocious inundations of the Northmen, whose unexpected descent, like flights of locusts, with every east wind, on the whole circuit of our coasts, threatened annihilation to the inhabitants, and to every germ of civilization. Alfred fought nine pitched battles in one year, and Edmund Ironside five, three of them under the walls of London. The deep and ineffaceable scars of these encounters in the dykes which traverse our island, or the innumerable tumuli which occur in all parts of it, attest the pertinacity with which every inch of English ground has been contended through the length and breadth of the land. During those long centuries every man, not a " nidering," bore his sword ever on his person; and might count upon his using it in deadly contest once at least in each year of his pilgrimage; his house and family ever subject to the fire and sword of the ruthless enemy; and his cities defended by stockades and timbered walls only, awaited combat, perhaps destruction, at every moment.

In such a state of things the wonder is that sound religion and good laws should have been planted, and could have survived, and that institutions of piety and learning could have been originated or have found the means of existence; and yet in those disastrous times were firmly laid those deep and solid foundations on which the whole fabric of our national existence now stands and flourishes. The same energy which those rude and hardy Anglo-Saxons put in such continual exercise, appears in the powerful and masterly outlines drawn out by them, of every thing great and good in our present constitutional system; as if the same dire necessity which war enforced, elicited also in religious and peaceful institutions efforts equally original, energetic, and meritorious.

To the institutes of Ina, Ethelbald, and Alfred, our present laws are to be traced. To the religious foundations of the same law-givers, with Alfred, Edward the Elder, and Edgar the Peaceable, we trace the present form, and even number, of our episcopal governments, though our population is forty-fold. The latter found the means of establishing during his reign an average of three monasteries for religion and learning per annum. These considerations force upon us the conviction of wisdom and virtues in those ancestors of ours, which entitle their history to the fondest study and admiration; from which neither their supercilious treatment from our early historians, even from Milton and Burke in some instances, nor the still earlier absurdities and superstitions of the monkish writers, should deter us.

Far different is the interest of records of kings and people, thus written amidst sufferings and struggles and aspirations towards better things, from those of Europe in more recent periods, when the established power, the luxuries and the corruptions of courts, have enervated and debased the human character; and the contrast of their simplicity, their earnestness, and their virtues, with the very reverse of these pure qualities exhibited in the latter, imparts a freshness and a delight in the study and contemplation of them not easily found in other pages.

It does not appear that any of the children of Japheth have been more powerful instruments in the progressive scheme of improvement in our species designed by providence than the Anglo-Saxon. And our boast is that we still bear upon our persons and in our language the undisputed impress of their lineage, their institutions and genius. We acknowledge that their virtues and sufferings have brought about (as gold tried and refined in the furnace) that political and moral existence under which we flourish in this our day, nor can we ever forget that the glories of our more modern history are but the fruits of that noble tree which they planted; the majestic strength of which in its matured growth now overshadows, protects, and distinguishes our empire and its dependencies.

Amongst a people devoted to freedom, the Anglo-Saxon native history has always therefore occupied the brightest talents, from the immortal Shakespeare [a] and Milton, to Burke and Macintosh. In more recent days it is to the admirable Sharon Turner, Sir F. Palgrave, Dr. Lappenberg, the Conybeares, and others, that we owe its more correct and detailed appreciation, through their elaborate investigations.

In the thirteenth century we shall proceed to shew how warmly these truths were felt, and how learnedly and how splendidly they were exhibited by Bishop Trotman and his Anglo-Saxon coadjutors, in Wells Cathedral.

To the north of the west door, it was proposed in the fourth tier to illustrate in succession the temporal princes under whom the Church had flourished, from Egbert, king of Wessex, whose preponderating (800) influence had first united the kingdoms of the so-called Heptarchy [b], and had established him as the bretwalda of the several states, down to Henry III., the reigning prince during Bishop Trotman's episcopacy.

The successive princes of the throne established by Cerdic were,

	A.D.		A.D.
Egbert .	800	Edwig .	955
Æthelwulf .	837	Edgar .	959
Æthelbald .	857	Edward the Martyr	975
Æthelbert .	860	Æthelred II.	978
Æthelred I. .	866	Edmund Ironside .	1016
Alfred .	871	Canute .	1017
Edward the Elder .	901	Harold .	1035
Athelstan	925	Hardicanute .	1039
Edmund	941	Edward the Confessor	1044
Edred .	948	Harold .	1066

[a] Shakespeare has well displayed its dramatic interest in his Lear, Cymbeline, and Macbeth; and the Anglo-Saxon annals are still rich in historical and political pathos. In no histories can be traced more awfully the hand of the avenging Nemesis, than in those of the perfidious and ambitious Offa and his Mercian dynasty; or the adulterous Edgar, and the retribution of his crime on the ill-fated successors of the house of Cerdic.

[b] The modern historians abjure the term ' Heptarchy,' as altogether unauthentic and inaccurate.

We have seen that on the south, or spiritual side, two only temporal princes, as founders of the conventual and episcopal churches, Ina and Edward the Elder, were admitted, but on this, the temporal side, Churchmen are exhibited in all instances, (except those of Alfred and Athelstan,) as the tutelary and presiding influences on whom all the beneficial acts of kings depended[*].

In the principal front, the west, it was intended not only to magnify the Saxon dynasty altogether, but to gratify the western people of Wessex more especially, as having conquered the rest of England after a rivalry of more than three hundred years, and established the race of Cerdic as supreme in the realms of England, and this consideration will account for the importance and the expense attached to the church of Wells by Bishop Trotman. Of this illustrious race Alfred was justly considered the great luminary, he is therefore placed conspicuously on the top of the central buttress, surrounded by his family and the worthies of his reign.

The scheme of the sculptor required that the regular succession should be interrupted by placing on these prominent buttresses in larger and sitting images (while the others are standing) the most distinguished kings and personages of the period. Thus these six places are occupied by Alfred "the Great," as we have seen, No. 89 ; his grandson Athelstan, the "Lord of the West Saxons," the "Giver of Bracelets," No. 84 ; his grandson, Edmund "the Magnificent," No. 50 ; his great grandson, Edgar the Peaceable, No. 45 ; and Edred, successor to the "fourfold empire of the Anglo-Saxons and Northumbrians, pagans and Britons," No. 57 ; lastly, on the top of the northern buttress sits the master-spirit of the tenth century, St. Dunstan, (No. 96,) round whom all the leading events of nearly fifty years are centered. The index, No. 1, will shew the succession of kings and worthies, to the description of whose characters we refer the reader in the subsequent pages, 74, &c.

[*] This influence is admirably described as applied to Ina ; " has animi regalis dotes animabat stimulis monitionem pater Aldhelmus ; cujus ille præcepta audiebat humiliter, suspiciebat granditer, adimplebat efficaciter."

THE FIRST TIER OF SCULPTURES

OF THE ENTIRE WEST FRONT.

A MUCH more detailed notice of this tier, in addition to what has already been given is not in our power. It may however be noted that the sixty-two statues of the same stand upon lias marble pedestals of great elegance and expense. Also that the 0 in the key, as in other niches, signifies the empty niche; and that the engraver has filled these niches in the plate of the west elevation in order to express the original effect of this tier. The variety of character and costume in those which still remain is sufficient to arrive at the important conclusion, that the second mission of St. Augustine is certainly represented in the north front, and therefore the previous thirty-three were occupied by the first mission, and possibly the hagiology of England, or the prophets. Their loss is the more to be deplored as they would have given us clearer notions of the martyrology of the English Church according to Trotman, and we recur for consolation to the happy sentence of the worthy and eloquent Fuller. "It was indeed pity to have erected a monument in memorial of these unknown martyrs, whose names are lost. The best is, God's calendar is more complete than man's best martyrologies; and their names are written in the book of life, who on earth are wholly forgotten."

In this series we have the light of truth and Gospel knowledge introduced into this country traditionally by the Apostles, continued through the second mission of Augustine down to the days of Bishop Trotman in regular succession, through the bishops of Sherborne and Wells; a very noble design, dignifying and completing the history of the Church in this country.

From the ecclesiastical the transition to the doctrinal may be deemed sufficient reason for proceeding to the consideration of the second and third tiers in the following pages.

THE SECOND TIER OF SCULPTURES

Consists of angels issuing from quatrefoils, deeply sunk in the spandrels of the arches of the first tier. They seem to " cry aloud;" and to " proclaim the glad tidings of salvation," brought by the holy messengers below. They issue from clouds in the dress of acolytes, having a nimbus on the head, and a scarf variously and elegantly cast over their shoulders. In their hands are held the rewards spiritual and temporal, which bless the hearers of the word, the mitre or the crown, and sometimes a book. They are thirty-three in number, and all differ in their form and composition.

The coronation of the Virgin in a niche surmounting the central arch may be considered as included in this tier. The figures are headless, but are composed with much dignity and grace, and on the back of the niche may still be traced the remains of painting and gilding, with which it was originally adorned. Specimens of these are thrown together in a lithographic plate.

THE THIRD TIER OF SCULPTURE

Is illustrative of the dispensations of the Almighty as recorded in the Old and New Testaments in forty-eight subjects, occupying large quatrefoils and in very high relief.

To the south are eighteen, comprising the history of the Creation down to the twelve patriarchs.

To the north are eighteen, and twelve others in the same tier, on the north and east sides of the north tower, comprising the history from the Nativity to the Gift of the Holy Ghost, so that the entire subject of Revelation and the three Persons of the Trinity, are completely displayed, a design as complete as it is admirable. The expressions which Will. of Worcester employs, " de vetere lege," and " de novâ lege," (extended too largely by him to the statues,) apply properly to the third tier of sculpture only.

Proceeding from the central west door southward, we have

No. 1, empty.

No. 2 and 3, the creation of man and of woman; subjects treated with so much dignity and expression, as to have deserved the especial notice of Flaxman, who has given them in his lectures on sculpture.

No. 4, the planting our first parents in the garden of Eden.

No. 5, the temptation, Adam and Eve embraced, listen to the serpent, his body curled upon the tree, and his head between them.

No. 6, two figures in conversation with a third, may be the discovery in the garden after the fall.

No. 7, empty.

No. 8, Adam delves and Eve spins.

No. 9, the sacrifices of Cain and Abel, the smoke of the irrespective altars descending and ascending.

No. 10, empty.

No. 11, God's wrath provoked, and the destruction determined on, is admirably expressed. The Almighty, in great majesty, approaches a man who sits pensive (his head reclining on his hand) on the side of a hill, upon which trees and herbs are growing; from behind the pensive head starts forth a young and arch demon, who stretches forward his hand, with prodigious energy and life, and laughing, puts out his tongue in derision. The conception and the execution are equally illustrative and admirable.

No. 12, Noah in workman's garb, with a cap on his head, tied under his chin and covering his ears. He is inclined towards a bench, with his tools under it, the back-ground is entirely occupied by the frame of the Ark.

No. 13, the Ark very remarkably and significantly described. It is raised pyramidally in four tiers, each having open arcades, in which the beasts and birds are seen; the door is in the side, and the flood below.

No. 14. The Ark rests on Ararat, and Noah sacrifices. Much mutilated, as also the following,

No. 15, apparently the meeting of Isaac and Rebecca.

No. 16, Isaac on his bed, and reclining his head on his hand, blesses Jacob, who stands over him. Flaxman also describes this subject.

No. 17, Jacob blesses the patriarchs, " and gathers up his feet into the bed."

No. 18, empty.

Returning to the centre door, and proceeding northward, we have thirty subjects of the New Testament.

No. 1, an angel with wings, in an attitude of inspiration, and finely composed, having a book before him, supported on the back of an eagle. Described also by Flaxman.

This figure resembles that commonly given to the Evangelist St. John, whose Gospel, and especially the Revelations, was the favourite study of the monks, " the difficulty of which," says Malmesbury, " exercises the talents of its readers even in the present day [a]."

No. 2 and 3 are unfortunately lost.

---

[a] Book i. ch. 3.

No. 4, much mutilated, yet plainly displays the Nativity..

The six following are also wanting, a circumstance much to be regretted, as they would have offered comparisons with the apocryphal subjects admitted into this series of the New Testament at Notre Dame and Amiens.

No. 11, Christ amongst the doctors, of whom four are seated, in attitudes of attention; one is in a cowl, one presides in a rostrum, while the young Christ is raised on a small pedestal. Joseph and Mary are in the background, the latter holding a kerchief in her hand, as having " sought Him sorrowing."

No. 12, John the Baptist clothed in camel's hair, quaintly expressed in abundant locks, and sitting in the wilderness.

No. 13, a preacher addresses nine persons; and may represent the Sermon on the Mount.

No. 14, empty.

No. 15, a single figure, may be Christ in the wilderness.

No. 16, a preacher addresses eight persons, possibly the mission of the Apostles.

No. 17, five persons sit at a table, possibly the feast of Matthew.

No. 18, a small figure on a mount, surrounded by many figures, possibly the feeding of the five thousand.

No. 19, six figures sitting, may be the feeding of the four thousand.

No. 20, a tree under which a person is crouching with three figures surrounding. This may be the call of Nathaniel, or the cursing of the barren fig-tree.

No. 21, Christ on a colt, riding into Jerusalem, two persons by His side. The gate is pointed, under it are two holding palm branches, others look from the towers and battlements.

No. 22, three figures majestically dressed and disposed, the centre being crowned, the train or cloak of the one to the right is officiously held up by a small devil having wings. On the other side is a small devil adjusting the lid of a money-box. This can be no other than Judas betraying the Saviour to the chief-priests for the thirty pieces of silver.

No. 23, the Last Supper; John reposes in the bosom of the Saviour; in front is a page kneeling on one knee, as constantly seen in the festive scenes of the middle ages. Under the table are bottles and a small basket.

No. 24, empty.

No. 25, a figure raised on a pedestal: on the die of which is a small devil; two approach on the left, and seven others are above and around; this can only be Christ before Pilate.

No. 26, the Saviour bears the cross, four or five figures much defaced around Him.

No. 27, much defaced, but the attitudes proclaim the raising of the cross.

No. 28, three small figures and a large one, much defaced; may have represented the declaration of the Ascension to Salome and the two Marys.

No. 29, empty.

No. 30, Christ rises from the tomb, an angel with extended wings on either side, three armed guards are below in astonishment. This is a very grand composition, but much defaced.

No. 31, six figures majestically dressed, but much defaced. This can be no other than the day of Pentecost.

Thus terminating this interesting series of man's redemption through the Father and Son, with the declaration of the third Person in the Trinity; and giving as full and correct exposition of sacred history as can be found or desired in this or any other age, and one which contrasts most advantageously with those which we gather from the most remarkable of the French cathedrals, executed about the same period. See note.

NOTE.

At Amiens, (begun 1220,) Mons. Gilbert's " Description de la Cathedrale d'Amiens," describes six subjects of the Old, and fourteen of the New Testament. Of the former, No. 1, the creation of Adam: No. 2, the creation of Eve: No. 3, their occupation of Paradise: No. 4, their fall: No. 5, their expulsion: No. 6, they eat bread in the sweat of their brow. Of the New Testament, No. 1, a person points out to the Magi the star in the east: No. 2, Herod gives orders to seek the Messiah: No. 3, the

Magi embark in a boat, the head and shoulders of the boatmen concealed by a large hat. On this subject Mons. Gilbert remarks with abounding faith, p. 52 :—" le voyage des mages dans une barque á voiles, offre, ainsi que deux autres traits dont nous parlerons plus bas, des circonstances qui etoient ignorèes dans cet honorable mission; n'ayant pas eté consignèes dans l'ecriture sainte, elles supposent que l'on possedait, á l'epoque de l'execution de ces bas reliefs, plusieurs traditions qui ne sont pas parvénue's jusquá nous."

No. 4, the Magi asleep are advised by an angel in a dream not to return to Herod but to return by another route.

No. 5, Herod gives an order to two servants to burn the boat which transported the Magi to Bethlehem. One of them is armed with a torch.

No. 6, they break up the vessel and throw the fragments into the fire.

No. 7, Herod on his throne: No. 8, the massacre of the Innocents: No. 9, "by one of those rude transitions," says Mons. Gilbert, "which we often meet, this bas relief presents Jesus recognised by the pilgrims at Emmaus, in the breaking of bread."

To the right of the spectator, No 10, the Virgin giving birth to the Saviour: No. 11, a notary registering the birth : No. 12, the flight into Egypt : No. 13, the young Christ amongst the doctors : No. 14, the Virgin and Joseph discover and take Him home.

In Notre Dame of Paris, Mons. Gilbert cites no subjects of the Old Testament, but in the portail of St. Anna, in the south, he enumerates twelve bas-reliefs of the New, with episodes highly characteristic of a country renowned then, no less than now, for its gallantry.

No. 1, " Saint Joseph veut se separer de Marie, qui le supplie les mains jointes de ne pas l'abandonner; il s'en va sans vouloir l'entendre."

No. 2, "Joseph est ramené par un ange; il demande pardon á genoux; la vierge le reléve et lui pardonne." This last scene is represented in the twentieth subject of the stalls at Amiens, executed in the year 1508, and conveying to us in a remarkable manner the same spirit nearly three hundred years subsequently. In the elegant work by Messrs. Jourdain and Duval, " Sur les Stalles de la Cathedrale d'Amiens," we read, "20°, S^t. Joseph revient de son doute—S^t. Joseph, à genoux devant sa divine Epouse et presenté par deux anges, s'excuse de la pensée quil a eu de s'en separer, en meme tems quil adore dans son sein virginale le verb de Dieu fait chaire. Marie lui tend avec bonté la main, sans quitter le livre des saintes ecritures quelle feuillète de l'autre main. Le baton, la besace et le sac ficele posés à terre, font encore souvenir du projet de fuite clandestine qu'avait conçu le Patriarche. Tout ce tableau est un livre, poetique et pieuse traduction du texte sacré."

No. 3. " Joseph conduit la vierge chez lui."

He farther observes upon the costume of Joseph,

" La coiffure de tête, que portent Saint Joseph, et plusieurs patriarches, representèe au dessus des portes de Notre Dame, consiste en un espère de chapeau rond, dont les aisees sont tres petites, et que est surmonté d'un Bouton."

No. 4, the high-priest Zacharias on his knees before an altar, in which is a lamp, receives the revelation by the angel Gabriel. The altar is at the top of the stairs.

No. 5, the Annunciation: No. 6, the Visitation of the holy Virgin to her cousin Elizabeth: No. 7, the Nativity of Christ, over the bed of the Virgin the cradle in which the child lies is warmed by the cattle.

No. 8, behind Joseph is the annunciation to the shepherds. No. 9, Herod holds a council with the Magi on the birth of the young King.

No. 10, the Magi having quitted Herod, go to Bethlehem with their horses. No. 11, the Magi address Joseph, who presents them to Jesus, already grown to boyhood. No. 12, the presentation at the Temple, the doves carried by Joseph, and the young Christ by the Virgin.

In the cotemporary work at Rheims, we have eighteen subjects of the Old Testament of nobler conception than the preceding.

No. 1, creation of the world figured by the Almighty, holding a cup in one hand, symbol of the waters, and a fruit in the other, of the earth. No. 2, creation of angels, figured by one adoring and rendering thanks for his existence. No. 3, Adam created and Eve issuing from his side. No. 4, the union of Adam and Eve, the type of marriage. No. 5, the Almighty dictates the first laws from a book, to our first parents in the garden of Eden. No. 6, Eve disobedient gathers the forbidden fruit, and gives it to her husband. No. 7, the expulsion. No. 8, Adam condemned to labour. No. 9, Eve spins. No. 10, Cain represented as a smith labouring at the anvil. Attached to this a sculptor and a carpenter are at work to typify the labours of the fine arts.

No. 11, Cain cuts timber in the forest.

No. 12, the Almighty appears to Abel from the heavens.

No. 13, the acceptance of Abel's sacrifice represented by a person holding fruits in his right and in his left conducting a lamb.

No. 14, Cain, jealous of his brother, kills him with the jaw-bone of an ass.

No. 15, an angel presents a small figure to the Almighty, a symbol of the soul of the just Abel. No. 16, prophecy of the birth of Christ, figured by a sage opening a scroll. No. 17, the Saviour appears holding a terrestrial globe in His hand. No. 18, a group of various figures, much broken, which may be the twelve Apostles, the earliest missionaries of the Gospel.

At Strasbourg, in the principal gateway, are thirty-four subjects of the Old and twelve of the New Testament.

1. Creation of the world: 2, the spirit of God upon the face of the waters: 3, creation of the sun and moon: 4, separation of the waters from the earth: 5, creation of the firmament: 6, of trees and plants: 7, of birds and fishes: 8, of quadrupeds: 9, of man and woman: 10, injunction to abstain from the forbidden fruit: 11, Eve deceived seduces Adam: 12, God calls Adam: 13, Adam and Eve driven from paradise: 14, the

birth of Cain and Abel: 15, Adam delves and Eve spins: 16, sacrifices of Cain and Abel: 17, fratricide of Cain: 18, flight of Cain.

In another tier,

19, Abraham on his knees before the angels imploring the salvation of Lot and of Sodom: 20, sacrifice of Abraham: 21, ark of Noah: 22, insult of Cham: 23, the dream of Jacob: 24, Moses and the burning bush: 25, the brazen serpent: 26, Moses striking the rock: 27, the successors of Moses, Joshua, and Judah: 28, Othniel, first of the judges: 29, Elias drops his mantle on Elijah: 30, Jonas thrown on shore from the whale's mouth: 31, Samson contends with the lion: 32, the king Hezekiah prays for health: 33, Joshua sets up a stone under the oak at Shechem: 34, conversion of the king Manasseh.

The subjects of the New Testament are, 1, entry into Jerusalem: 2, the last supper: 3, before Caiaphas: 4, the flagellation: 5, the crown of thorns: 6, the crucifixion: 7, the entombment: 8, the resurrection: 9, His apparition to the disciples: 10, St. Thomas touching the wound with his fingers: 11, the ascension: 12, Judas hangs himself.

These four examples, taken from renowned contemporaneous works, are sufficient to shew a fair comparison of Bishop Trotman's treatment of theological illustration with the generality of authors in that day.

The elegant works of Messrs. Jourdain and Duval upon the Cathedral of Amiens, now in part only published, will set this comparison in a still clearer light, as also the careful investigations on the Cathedrals of France now in progress throughout all the departments.

THE FOURTH AND FIFTH TIERS.

HISTORICAL SERIES OF THE WEST FRONT.

THE SPIRITUAL SIDE.

In the fourth and fifth tiers of sculpture, Bishop Trotman proposed to illustrate the celebrities of England during 526 years: to enumerate, embody, and identify to the beholder, all those distinguished characters who had shed the light of religion, civilization, and renown upon their age; and by whose agency the progress and the interest of its history is to be estimated.

This extended and magnificent picture justly referred to the race of Cerdic, and the country of Wessex especially; as that stock and kingdom of the octarchy, from whence, under Providence, all these blessings had flowed with so fertilizing a stream; he shewed that the civil and military glory of this portion of our island, was coincident with the establishment of Christianity at Glastonbury, and proportioned duly to the superior enlightenment, which might be expected to flow, by natural consequence, from that "nursing-mother of saints," which, by every evidence and tradition, was the earliest and the most fruitful of all the religious institutions of western Europe.

This front, and its sculptured illustrations, thus constituted a national monument, at once illustrative of the triumph of Christianity in England, and of the acts and the prosperity of those who were best guided by its blessed influences. It was a tribute, at the same time that it was an incentive to the patriotism of the west country, to assert by such a monument as this, in the face of England and of Europe, the claims to respect which this ancient province had possessed preeminently; but which now, in Trotman's time, under a new race of kings, and a transferred seat of government, were well-nigh forgotten.

The scheme of this historical picture is worthy of our best attention. We

shall admire the exact adaptation of the one hundred and twenty historical characters to the architectural symmetry, number, and position of the niches; the
appropriate adjustment of the pre-eminent characters in the front of the buttresses,
seated on thrones, while the rest are standing. The historical justice with which
that pre-eminence is determined, without the omission of a single renown during
the five hundred and twenty-six years which it illustrates, and, at the same time,
without a single idle figure in the whole composition.

The west front is entirely occupied by the Saxon dynasty, while the smaller
portion (the north and east fronts) is devoted to the Norman and Plantagenet
dynasties; thus meting, with perfect justice, (though not like a good courtier of his
day, for Plantagenet Henry was then reigning), the regard due towards the former,
which had made the glory of this country during five hundred and seventy-one
years, as compared with the latter, which had scarcely accomplished one hundred and
seventy years; dynasties having had no part in the original institutions of the
country, and having scarcely done more than to uphold and fortify them;
while they had introduced many internal evils of foreign wars and connections,
which absorbed and wasted its best blood and treasure for many years.

The central door and window of the west front divide the picture into two
series, the southern (always esteemed the most sacred side) being devoted to the
spiritual princes and guides, the northern to the temporal princes, alliances,
and worthies, with some exceptions, which we shall find most entirely justified by
the spirit of the times, as well as by strict historical justice.

Proceeding then to the catalogue of these figures of the fourth and fifth tiers,
and beginning at the central door, to describe those (forty-two in number) occupying
the south side of the west front, which we term the spiritual side, we have first to
remark, that the six figures enthroned on the three piers, are Edward the Elder, the
founder of the episcopal church of Wells, and the five Archbishops promoted to
the See of Canterbury from that of Wells, from the foundation of the See in 909,
to the time of Bishop Trotman in 1209.

Ina, the founder of the conventual church, is well entitled to a niche on the
spiritual side, though not pre-eminently in front of a buttress; and five of the family
of Edward the Elder have been equally honoured with niches on this side, reducing
the bishops, or lords spiritual, to thirty-three of the whole number.

Great indeed is the interest attached to the history, however scanty, of these
venerable Prelates, Lords as they are, not by inheritance, or the right of kings, as
those on the temporal side ; but by that more divine right of original and improved
gifts, and virtues, by which as messengers of the Word, they controlled and guided
the unruly wills of a savage People, and introduced by degrees all those blessings
of law, and order, and civilization, which gradually made the happiness and
prosperity of the country.   In early history especially, these spiritual Lords appear
as the arbiters of peace and war, conspicuous as the most active agents of good,
and enforcing their superior knowledge and influence in a manner, and by acts,
equally important with the highest temporal powers.   In fact, the gesta Pontificum,
and the gesta Regum, were held in equal estimation by every writer, from Bede or
Malmesbury to Godwin, occupying their pens with no less fulness, as God's messengers on earth, and with much deeper interest, than the temporal Lords themselves.   But we have to regret, that their memoirs are scanty and insufficient,
giving us but meagre accounts of their beneficent agency in all the most material
events of those times.

In the fourth tier, and over the central door, we have two small statues
raised on pedestals ; Ina and Ethelberga.

No. 1, wearing a crown, and in regal attire, having a church in his left, to
which he points with his right, while he looks earnestly towards his queen.
No. 41, is King Ina, the first figure on the spiritual side, and very properly
placed here as the founder of the conventual church at Wells, and the restorer of
Glastonbury abbey ; which he almost rebuilt and largely endowed.   Ina enjoyed a
long reign of thirty-seven years, which he illustrated by conquests, by a code of
seventy-six laws, (the earliest known to us amongst the Anglo-Saxons, those of
the Kentish kings excepted,) by his ecclesiastical foundations, already named, and
especially by the institution of the See of Sherborne.

A significant notice of Ina's liberality and discrimination is evinced in his
patronage of Aldhelmus, the famous abbot of Malmesbury, afterwards appointed by him as the first bishop of Sherborne ; and again, in his employment
of Winifrith in some important political negociations, the missionary, known afterwards as Boniface, the apostle of Germany.

Finally, according to the pious aspirations of that day, he made a pilgrimage to Rome, accompanied by his queen, Ethelberga, and died there in the Saxon college. This part of his history, as given by Malmesbury, is so characteristic of the spirit of the times, as to warrant its insertion here.

Ina's queen was Ethelburgha, a woman of royal race and disposition, who perpetually urging the necessity of bidding adieu to earthly things, at least in the close of life, and the king as constantly deferring the execution of her advice, at last endeavoured to overcome him by stratagem. For on a certain occasion when they had been revelling at a country seat with more than usual riot and luxury, the next day after their departure, an attendant, with the privity of the queen, defiled the palace in every possible manner with excrement of cattle and heaps of filth; and lastly, he put a sow which had recently farrowed, in the very bed where they had lain. They had hardly proceeded a mile, ere she attacked her husband with the fondest conjugal endearments, entreating that they might immediately return thither whence they had departed, saying that his denial would be attended with dangerous consequences. Her petition being readily granted, the king was astonished at seeing a place which yesterday might have vied with Assyrian luxury, now filthily disgusting and desolate; and silently pondering on the sight, his eyes at length turned upon the queen. Seizing the opportunity and pleasantly smiling, "where, my noble spouse," said she, "are the revellings of yesterday? where the tapestries dipped in Sidonian dyes? where the ceaseless impertinence of parasites? where the sculptured vessels overwhelming the very tables with their weight of gold? where are the delicacies so anxiously sought throughout sea and land to pamper the appetite? Are not all these things smoke and vapour? have they not all passed away? Woe be to those who attach themselves to such, for they in like manner shall consume away. Are not all these like a rapid river hastening to the sea? Reflect, I entreat you, how wretchedly will these bodies decay, which we pamper with such unbounded luxury; must not we who gorge so constantly, become more disgustingly putrid? The mighty must undergo mightier torments, and a severer trial awaits the strong." Without saying more, by this striking example she gained over her husband to those sentiments which she had in vain attempted for years by persuasion. Thus after his triumphal spoils in war, after many successive degrees in virtue, he aspired to the highest perfection and went to Rome. There not to make the glory of his conversion public, but that he might be acceptable in the sight of God alone, he was shorn in secret, and clad in homely garb grew old in privacy. Nor did his queen, the author of this noble deed, desert him, but as she had before incited him to undertake it, so afterwards she made it her constant care to soothe his sorrows by her conversation, to stimulate him when wavering by her example; in short, to omit nothing that could be conducive to his salvation. Thus united in mutual affection in due time they trod the common path of all mankind. This was attended as we have heard with singular miracles, such as God often deigns to bestow on the virtues of happy couples.

No. 41, a graceful female statue, having a roll or charter in her left, her right broken off; the "aulmoniere," the emblem of her charity, suspended to her side. Belonging strictly to the temporal side, this must be the faithful Ethelburga, who cannot be separated from her King, even in the order of our catalogue.

We count thirty-three venerable images of bishops and holy men, in the fourth and fifth tiers of this, the spiritual side, of the western front; but the predecessors of Bishop Trotman in the See of Wells, were only twenty: to whom then are we to attribute the thirteen remaining? The answer to this difficulty on the threshold of our enquiry, is suggested by the consideration that the conventual church of Ina had been governed during more than two hundred years by the bishops of Sherborne, until the See of Wells was instituted; and that the thirteen in excess correspond exactly with the number of the bishops of Sherborne whom history has recorded in that interval.

No. 2, a bishop in the act of benediction, with full pontificals, may safely be pronounced as Aldhelm, the first bishop appointed by Ina to the See of Sherborne (in 703), which See was created by Ina, and was a subdivision of the See of Winchester, after the death of Hedda. Aldhelm was celebrated as an Anglo-Saxon poet and writer, of equal merit (according to Dr. Lappenberg) with his cotemporary the venerable Bede. "Whereby," says the caustic doctor, "a greater lustre is conferred upon his name than that which his rank-adoring countrymen attribute to him in the record that he was himself of royal descent." "In enumerating and characterizing the works of Aldhelm," continues he, "no observation is more descriptive both of him and his nation, even in our days, than that which distinguishes pomp as a leading quality[a]."

No. 3, a bishop having a remarkable bag suspended by a string to his neck, apparently intended for a reliquary, which he also holds in his right, while his left (now broken) seems to have held a pastoral staff. Such distinctives may well suit Forthere, the second bishop of Sherborne, who accompanied the Queen Fredigotha to Rome, where the best treasures which he could collect in the estimation of those times, would be the relics of the saints.

Nos. 4, 6, 7, and 8, bishops in the attitude of benediction, without any peculiar

---

[a] England under the Anglo-Saxon Kings, vol. i. p. 265. See Life of Aldhelm, Anglia Sacra, pars i. p. 2.

distinctions, may be the successors to the See, Herewald, Ethelmod, Denefrith, Wilbert, whose acts are not recorded.

No. 9, though no more distinguished than the others, and in the same attitude, has figured in history in a manner that should entitle him to the sculptor's peculiar notice. This figure occupies the place of the warlike Ealhstan, the seventh bishop of Sherborne, who passed more than fifty years in office, and in the achievment of many remarkable acts; in 823 he carried war into Kent, and drove Baldred from his throne, and subsequently, assisted by the Alderman Osric, he gained several victories over the Danes in the west. In 825 he encouraged the Prince Ethelbald in his pretensions, and dictated the division of the kingdom with his father Ethelwulf. He died in the midst of the Danish troubles in 867, during the reign of Ethelred I.

No. 11 should be Headmund, the eighth bishop, who was slain at Meredun, in one of the nine pitched battles fought against the Danes in the year 871, which cut off kings as well as people, and placed the immortal Alfred on the throne, after the death of his three brothers.

The next figure, No. 12, in the corner of the middle buttress, and Nos. 15 and 16, in that of the end buttress, are bishops in full pontificals, and in the act of benediction, having books in their hands; while Nos. 13 and 14, conspicuously placed in front of the tower, are deprived of all the honours of their order, and habited as monks, with cowls and long beards; the latter having his two hands listlessly tucked in his girdle.

These five figures complete the number of thirteen bishops of Sherborne, corresponding with the recorded names of Etheleage, Alfsy, and the illustrious Asser, Sighelm, and Ethelwold; but Asser has the precedence of Etheleage and Alfsy, by a licence often taken in favour of the better illustration of the subject in these sculptures. As these (Etheleage and Alfsy) were the bishops of Sherborne at a disastrous period for the Church, through the desolations of the Danes, and during the extreme degradation and ignorance into which the Clergy had fallen, the demonstrative Sculptor may have adopted this significant manner of expressing the lamentable decline of learning and piety which Alfred deplores in his own writings. "So clean was learning fallen out of England, that very few were they," says the royal author, "on this side the Humber, who could understand their daily prayers in

K

English, or translate any letter from the Latin.   I think there were not many
beyond the Humber; they were so few, that I indeed cannot recollect *one single
instance* on the south of the Thames, when I took the kingdom."—"When I
recollect all this, I also remember how I saw, before that every thing was
ravaged and burnt, that the churches through all the English nation stood full of
vessels and books, and also of a great many of the servants of God," &c. &c.—
" thanks be to Almighty God, that we have now some teachers in our stalls [b]."

Thus in place of the chronological order of succession, Etheleage, Alfsy, Asser,
Sighelm, Ethelwold; I have presumed, for the reasons already stated, on the more
illustrative order of Asser, Etheleage, Alfsy, Sighelm, Ethelwold.

Asser's celebrity arises from his invaluable biography of "the most perfect
king recorded by history," and from his connection with Alfred as his tutor,
invited from St. David's to pass half his time in his court to teach Latin to his
royal pupil.   "When I remembered," says Alfred, "how the learning of the
Latin tongue before this was fallen through the English nation, and yet many
could read English, then began I, among much other manifold business of this
kingdom, to turn into English the book named Pastoralis, or the Herdsman's-book,
sometimes word for word, sometimes sense for sense, so as I had learned it from
Plegmund, my archbishop; and Asser, my bishop; of Grimbald, my mass priest;
and of John, my mass priest; and as I understood, and could most intellectually
express it, I have turned it into English."   Such were the fruits of Asser's tuition.

Sighelm's celebrity is not less deserved, but through a course distinct from
Asser's.   By the enlightened liberality of Alfred, this bishop was sent to the
Christians of St. Thomas in India, apparently to contribute to their necessities, to
promote commercial enterprise, and to procure relics.   " I wish," says Dr. Vincent,
in his voyage of Nearchus, "that more authority for this remarkable mission
existed, than is to be found in the tradition of Sherborne; for Alfred deserves
any honour that can be added to his name."

"Ever intent on alms-giving," says Malmesbury, "he confirmed the privileges
of the Churches, as appointed by his father, and sent many presents over sea to
Rome, and to St. Thomas in India. Sigelm, bishop of Shireborne, sent ambassador
for this purpose, prosperously penetrated into India; a matter of astonishment

[b] Alfred's Preface, p. 82; Wese's Asser.

even in the present time. Returning thence, he brought back many brilliant exotic gems, and aromatic juices, in which that country abounds, and a present more precious than the finest gold, part of our Saviour's cross sent by Pope Marinus to the king."

The last of the bishops (the thirteenth) of Sherborne, who had episcopal jurisdiction over Wells, is Ethelweard, the youngest son of Alfred, who died twenty-one years after his father, a learned prince, educated at Oxford.

Having thus arrived at the period in which Edward the Elder founded the episcopal church of Wells, in 909, we naturally expect to find this zealous king distinguished with the same honours bestowed already on Ina, the founder of the conventual church; accordingly we discover him enthroned on the first buttress, south, No. 25, in royal apparel, at the head of his bishops and archbishops; the only temporal prince, except Ina, admitted in this, the spiritual side; a position equally deserved by the piety and utility of his foundation.

"Greatly inferior to his father Alfred in literature, but greatly excelling him in extent of power," Edward reigned 23 years, deriving all the fruits of that system of piety and virtue, which his illustrious father had so sedulously planted, and blessed with a family of fifteen children, six "on the spear side," and nine "on the spindle side," and educated under all that discipline which might be expected from the son of Alfred: "for Edward," says Malmesbury, "had brought up his daughters in such wise, that in childhood they gave their whole attention to literature, and afterwards employed themselves in the labours of the distaff and the needle, that thus they might chastely pass their virgin age. His sons were so educated as first to have the completest benefit of learning, that afterwards they might succeed to govern the state not like rustics but philosophers[e]."

A more complete success could not possibly have attended the principles which Alfred had instilled, and the edifying habits of his royal son; for his grandsons became the greatest princes of the Saxon line, and his grand-daughters contracted European alliances of the most splendid rank, as we shall proceed to shew in the proud memorials with which this remarkable monument is adorned.

Before we proceed to note the Prelates of the See of Wells, we must advert to those princesses, who stand on either side of the patriarchal monarch, and who,

[e] Book i. chap. 5.

K 2

illustrious by their piety, were deemed worthy of niches in the spiritual side, no less than the bishops themselves.

The first, No. 23, an elegant statue, her head veiled, her right in her necklace, and her left holding her garment, may have been Ethelhilda, his fourth daughter, a lay sister.

No. 24 is empty ; but may be conjectured to have contained the statue of his second daughter Eadflæd, who became a nun.

"Eadflæd and Ethelhilda, vowing celibacy to God, renounced the pleasure of earthly nuptials, the first in a religious, the second in a lay habit. They both lie buried near their mother at Winchester [d]."

No. 26, in the habit of a nun, may well have been Eadburgh, of whom Malmesbury relates [e], that "Edward the Elder, of whom I have before spoken at large, had by his wife Elfgiva, several daughters. Amongst these was Eadburga, who, when scarcely three years old, gave a singular indication of her future sanctity. Her father was inclined to try whether the little girl would lean to God or to the world, and had placed in a chamber the symbols of different professions, on one side a chalice and the gospels, on the other, bracelets and necklaces. Hither the child was brought in the arms of her indulgent attendant, and, sitting on her father's knee, was desired to choose which she pleased. Rejecting the earthly ornaments with stern regard, she instantly fell prostrate before the chalice and the gospels, and worshipped them with infant adoration. The company present exclaimed aloud, and fondly hailed the prospect of the child's future sanctity ; her father embraced the infant in a manner still more endearing. "Go," said he, "whither the Divinity calls thee ; follow with prosperous pace the Spouse whom thou hast chosen, and truly blessed shall my wife and myself be, if we are surpassed in holiness by our daughter." When clothed in the garb of a nun, she gained the affection of all her female companions in the city of Winchester, by the marked attention she paid them, nor did the greatness of her birth elevate her, as she esteemed it noble to stoop to the service of Christ. Her sanctity increased with her years, her humility kept pace with her growth, so that she used secretly to steal away the socks of the several nuns at night, and carefully washing and

[d] Malmesbury, book i. chap. 5.
[e] Book i. chap. 5.

anointing them, lay them again upon their beds. Wherefore, though God signalized her while living by many miracles, yet I more particularly bring forward this
circumstance, to shew that charity began all her works, and humility completed
them ; and finally many miracles in her life-time, and after her death, confirm the
devotion of her heart, and the incorruptness of her body, which the attendants at
her churches at Winchester and Pershore relate to such as are unacquainted with
them."

Immediately under King Edward, and enthroned upon the same buttress, is
the venerable figure of an archbishop, No. 5, the head and hands much defaced.
This can be no other than Athelmus, the first bishop of Wells, who on the death
of holy Plegmund, was advanced to the archbishopric of Canterbury, in the year
923, one year before the death of his royal master.

No. 10, also an archbishop, his left raised to his breast as a confessor, his
right in benediction, is Wulfhelm, the second bishop of Wells, a man of great
sanctity and erudition, subsequently, like his predecessor, advanced to the primacy,
where he presided over several synods, appointed by King Athelstan, on ecclesiastical affairs.

No. 27, a bishop in benediction, is Elphege, the third bishop of Wells.

No. 28 is Wulfhelm, the fourth bishop of Wells.

No. 30 is an archbishop enthroned on the second pier, and in a remarkable
attitude, holding in extended arms a drapery, and looking towards the kings to
the north. This is Brithelm, the fifth bishop, a monk of Glastonbury, appointed
to the See in 956, and in the following year raised to the primacy ; which in 959
he renounced at the instance of King Edgar, in favour of St. Dunstan. " A good
and prudent man," says Godwin, " but of too mild a nature to exercise those
stripes upon the rebellious monks, which were necessary for good discipline,
whereupon King Edgar, having commanded him to retire from the primacy, he
went back to this See of Wells."

To express this remarkable fact in the history of the See of Wells, the sculptor
has presented the archbishop as holding his robe of office, the pallium, in his hands,
and offering it to Edgar, who sits below him on the north. A more happy expe-
dient for the recognition of this amiable personage, could not possibly have been
divined. The spectator is at once struck with the singularity of the action, and

finds one of the most effectual keys to the explanation of the whole subject of these sculptures.

The dignity of Brithelmus required that licence, of which we have already spoken, of transposing the chronological order. Thus the following bishop, No. 29, is made to precede the archbishop. This " good prelate of manners mild," died in 975, ten days after King Edgar.

No. 31 is Sigar, abbot of Glastonbury, and seventh bishop of Wells, in full pontificals, and in the act of benediction.

No. 32, in the dress of an abbot, holding a book in his hand. This should be Alwyn, the eighth bishop ; but history has not recorded any sufficient occasion for the remarkable eccentricities of this costume, amongst the bishops of Wells.

No. 33 and 34 are habited like monks, with cowls, long beards, and scrips to their girdles, and stand immediately over those similar figures, already described, of the See of Sherborne ; and may be supposed to illustrate the second Danish persecution, and the lamentable degradation of the clergy in the beginning of the eleventh century. They stand in the places of Burwold, the ninth bishop, and martyr in 1000 ; and the eleventh bishop, Ethelwyn, in 1013.

The tenth bishop, Leovingus, having been promoted to the primacy after the cruel martyrdom of Archbishop Elphege by the Danes in 1013, is placed on the summit of the third buttress, No. 37, in full pontificals, but even here the sculptor has not failed to demonstrate those lamentable times by the diminished size and dignity of the mitre which he wears. The Saxon chronicle characterises Leovingus as " a very upright man before God and the world." He crowned the brave but unfortunate Edward Ironside in 1016.

No. 35 is the twelfth bishop, Brithwyn, distinguished in history as having presided on the removal of the relics of the martyr Elphege, 1023, from London to Canterbury, at which ceremony the King Canute, and his Queen Emma, attended.

The bishop is accordingly restored to the full episcopal canonicals of which his immediate predecessors are deprived, and he holds in his left a book which may possibly signify the record of the horrors done to the martyr Elphege, and the restoration of the church to its pristine consequence.

No. 36, a bishop in full canonicals, is the thirteenth in the See of Wells, Mereardit, abbot of Glastonbury, and promoted in 1027.

No. 38 is Dudoc, the fourteenth bishop, who was sent by Edward the Confessor to the great synod held at Rheims, with two others, " to the intent that they should report to the king what was determined there concerning Christendom."

No. 39, Bishop Giso in full canonicals, consecrated at Rome 1060, whither he had been sent by Edward the Confessor, together with Walter, bishop of Hereford, for the purpose of having certain doubts on the subject of religion resolved by the Holy See, " being men not only learned but of good conversation, and not guilty of simoniacal practices."

" When Giso entered upon his See," says the canon of Wells, " he found but ten canons, according to others only five, who were reduced to beggary in consequence of the spoliations of Harold, earl of Kent, by whom this church had been deprived both of its ornaments and possessions."   " Complaining unto the king of this outrageous havocke," says Godwin, " he found cold comfort at his hands ; for whether it were for fear of Harold's power, or his wife's displeasure, he caused no restitution to be made ; onely the queen was content to give of her own manors those of Mark and Modesley unto the church.

" After the death of King Edward, Giso was fain to flee the land, till such time as Harold, the sacrilegious usurper, being vanquished and slaine, William the Conqueror was a meane to restore, not only him to his place and country, but his church also to all the other had violently taken from it, except what had been given to St. Peter's at Gloucester."

Bishop Giso built a cloister, dormitory, and refectory, for the monks of Wells, and died in the twenty-second year of the Conquest.

No. 40 is John de Villula, a French physician, who having amassed wealth by medical practice at Bath, purchased the See of Wells of Rufus, 1088, pulled down Giso's works at Wells, and built a palace in its place, and transferred the See to Bath, the abbey of which he obtained of the king " by anointing his hand *with white salve*," says Matthew Paris.   He rebuilt the church in that city. Leland says, " this John pullid doun the old church of St. Peter at Bath, and erected a new, much fairer ; and was buried in the middle of the presbyteri thereof, whos image I saw lying there 9 years sins, at which tyme all the church that he made lay to wast, and was onrofid and wedes grew about this John of Tours sepulchre."

No. 18, now empty, doubtless contained the statue of Bishop Godfrey, the seventeenth in this See, a foreigner as usual, a native of Belgium, and chaplain to the fair queen Adelicia, the second wife of Henry I., who gave him the manor of Dogmersfield, in Hampshire, long the summer residence of the bishops of Bath and Wells.

No. 19, Robert of Normandy, another foreigner, appointed by the interest of the bishop of Winchester, with his brother King Stephen; a long-lived prelate, having been thirty years in his See, which he repaired through disastrous times and disputes which afflicted the country from the usurpation of Stephen to the murder of Becket: he died in 1166. So that his repairs of Wells Cathedral from ruin and destruction were probably completed between 1150, and that period when the Pointed style, in which it now appears, under the hand of Bishop Trotman, was certainly not practised in this country.

"Complevit fabricam Ecclesiæ Bathonensis per Johannem Turonensim inchoatam. Dedicavit Ecclesiam Wellensem—*multas ruinas ejusdem Ecclesiæ destructionem ejus in locis pluribus comminantes egregie reparavit*[1]." These expressions will hardly warrant the attribution of any part of the present Cathedral to Robert.

No. 17, Reginald Fitz-Jocelyne, of foreign family, though born in England, was appointed by Henry II. in 1174; a man of business, ambassador to the pope from the king to remove all imputation of the murder of Becket from his royal master. A sportsman also, having obtained lands from Richard I. to sustain those diversions; and liberal to the burgesses of Wells, whom he relieved from all *servile offices*, constituting the town of Wells a free borough.

"In consequence of some services rendered to the monks of Canterbury, they were induced to elect him as their archbishop in 1194, and, being present, they seated him by violence in the archiepiscopal throne. At first he strenuously, and with tears, refused to accept the proffered dignity; but on the following day being asked whether he assented to the election, he answered, that 'so far from being ambitious of that place, that it was a great grief to him to be chosen, and that he would be very glad they would take some other in his room; howbeit,' quoth he,

[1] Ang. Sac., pars i. p. 561.

'if they will needs stand to their election, though with grief and heart's sorrow, I must and will accept the same.'" In the December following, being taken suddenly ill, he put on a monk's cowl and died.

The archbishop appears here in full canonicals, though death had scarcely given him time to put them on.

No. 20, Savaric, though born in England, was of foreign extraction, (like all his predecessors from the Conquest,) as having been related to Henry VI., emperor of Germany, by whose influence he added Glastonbury to the See, the emperor making this addition a condition of the liberation of Richard the First from imprisonment by Leopold of Austria. He was appointed 1194, and died in 1205, making room for the illustrious Joceline Trotman.

In the extreme buttress, and looking south, are two archiepiscopal figures, enthroned in the fourth and fifth tiers. Their names must be matter of mere conjecture, and there are no distinctive characteristics whatever by which they may be known; I have therefore ventured to suggest that they may have been intended for Archbishop Plegmund, who originally consecrated the See with Edward the Elder, and Stephen Langton, the reigning primate, cotemporary and intimately connected with our illustrious Bishop Trotman in political affairs.

THE FOURTH AND FIFTH TIERS.

HISTORICAL SERIES OF THE WEST FRONT.

THE TEMPORAL SIDE.

HAVING described the prelates of Sherborne and of Wells from the eighth to
the thirteenth centuries, those lords spiritual and "messengers of the Word"
who had guided the princes of Wessex and the interests of its Church during that
period of history, we now proceed to those temporal lords under whom, as God's
vicegerents upon earth, the Church and State had been equally directed.

The northern portion of the west front is devoted wholly to that illustrious
Saxon dynasty, which shed such peculiar interest and glory on the history of this
country during more than 500 years. "Quæ quidam historia," says Archbishop
Parker, "non mediocrem mente tua voluptatem infundet, neque minorem adferet
cum voluptate utilitatem, si in præclarissimarum rerum contemplatione defixus, te
ad earum imitationem, et quasi imaginem totum effinxeris. Etenim quæ delectatio
major quam clarorum virorum studia, res gestas, mores, vitas denique, ortus,
obitus, (tanquam tabulas bene pictas) quotidie intueri * ?"

Here, as in the southern portion of this front, the three prominent buttresses
are employed to illustrate, by larger dimension, and by enthroned and sitting
figures, those more distinguished princes, whose acts and influences have been the
most signal. And though such a collocation somewhat deranges the regularity of
their succession, they serve eminently to assist the spectator in identifying the
series, and to explain their relative merits in the estimation of Bishop Trotman
and the historians of that day.

* Preface to Asser's Life of Alfred.

Thus we have Alfred in the summit of the central buttress, as the chief luminary of that constellation of merits which made the success and glory of the dynasty of Cerdic during 200 years. To his left is Athelstan, to his right the prodigy of his age, and second only to Alfred himself in energy and influence, St. Dunstan; and below are his great grandchildren Edred, Edmond of the second, and Edgar of the third generation.

The minor stars of this galaxy appear in the fourth tier from Egbert to Harold, and the princes' ministers, and alliances, who contributed so much to their glory, are in the fifth tier.

The first figure on the temporal side, in the fourth tier, and over the western door, is Ethelburga, the zealous queen of Ina, already described.

The second, No. 42, a dignified figure, crowned, clad in a long mantle, having had a sword in one hand and a sceptre in the other, (now broken,) and trampling upon an enemy clad in a hauberk, grasping a sword, with spurs on his feet, is undoubtedly the victorious and accomplished Egbert; who versed in men and manners, and especially in the art of war, during his sojourn in the court of Charlemagne, obtained the glorious title of Bretwalda of all England, uniting for the first time the octarchy of Saxon kingdoms, which had torn the vitals of the country for so many years. He died in 837. See annexed plate.

No. 43, his son Ethelwulf, who reigned twenty-one years in constant warfare with the Danes, and is also accompanied with the appropriate symbol, a vanquished enemy under his feet. He was the progenitor of the four succeeding monarchs. He made his pilgrimage to Rome in 855, and on his return through France, he married Judith, the daughter of the French king, and died the year following, 857. As the founder of tithes in this country, he was entitled to special honours from the Church at all times.

No. 44, a kingly figure crowned, but having neither sword nor sceptre, nor the vanquished under his feet. This is doubtless Ethelbald, the eldest surviving son of Ethelwulf, who scandalized the Church by marrying his father's widow Judith. He had also, during the absence of his father at Rome, severed the kingdom ·by his intrigues, and the assistance of Ealstan, the warlike bishop of Sherborne, and died three years after (860) with an inglorious reputation; which the sculptor has thus visited upon his image, by depriving it of the usual symbols of royalty.

No. 46, a graceful crowned king, trampling on the foe, his right having a sword, and his left in his necklace, is Ethelbert, who reigned six years in constant warfare with the Danes. This king and his predecessor were buried at Sherborne, a circumstance to be remarked, as shewing the importance of that See, and illustrating the record of its bishops given in the spiritual side.

No. 47 is a crowned king holding a sword in his right, and a candlestick in his left, to signify his devotion; but as an unfortunate, though a brave prince, he has no foe under his feet. This is Ethelred I., brother of the late king, and third son of Ethelwulph, who during a reign of five years was in continual warfare with the Danes, who utterly destroyed the monasteries of Bardeney, Croyland, Peterborough, and Ely, and the cities of Thetford, Nottingham, and Reading. Malmesbury's recital of the last battle at Eschendun is so characteristic of the prince and of the times, that it is subjoined[b].

"One battle memorable beyond all the rest was that which took place at Eschendun. The Danes having collected an army at this place, divided it into two bodies; their two kings commanding one, all their earls the other. Ethelred drew near with his brother Alfred. It fell to the lot of Ethelred to oppose the kings, while Alfred was to attack the earls. Both armies eagerly prepared for battle, but night approaching deferred the conflict till the ensuing day. Scarcely had morning dawned, ere Alfred was ready at his post, but his brother, intent on his devotions, had remained in his tent, and when urged on by a message that the pagans were rushing forward with unbounded fury, he declared he should not move a step till his religious services were ended. This piety of the king was of infinite advantage to his brother, too impetuous from the thoughtlessness of youth, and already far advanced. The battalions of the Angles were now giving way, and even bordering on flight, in consequence of their adversaries pressing upon them from higher ground; for the Christians were fighting in an unfavourable situation; when the king himself, signed with the cross of God, unexpectedly hastened forward, dispersing the enemy and rallying his subjects; the Danes, terrified equally by his courage and the Divine manifestation, consulted their safety by flight. Here fell Osey their king, five earls, and an innumerable multitude of common people."

No. 89. On the summit of the middle buttresses is enthroned the next king

---

[b] Book ii. c. iii.

in succession, the glorious Alfred, "the shepherd of his people," "the wisest of men," "the darling of the English," "the truth-teller," and by all times proclaimed "the Great," the only king of England to whom history has awarded this title.

It is rather by position and the surrounding figures, than by any peculiar attribute, that the identity of Alfred is to be traced; the sculptor seems to have been abashed by the greatness of the original, and time has made too much havoc even on the remains, to encourage a delineation of their actual state, though it might be said, with the enthusiastic Spelman, that "the pieces we have being mangled, and wanting the joints and edges wherewith they should agree among themselves, they seem rather the rubbish of a broken statue, than the whole parts of a perfect image. But, Sir, he was of that merit, that even the dust of his feet was not unworthy of collecting, nor did the most venerable of all the Romans' ashes deserve a more sacred urn."

Of a character which has attracted the homage of every historian, from Asser to Voltaire, and whose life, so often written, has never failed deeply to affect every reader, gentle, humble, or royal, it is difficult to speak with becoming reverence or effect. His prowess as a commander, his faculties as a statesman, his enthusiasm for virtue, his irrepressible and ardent love of literature, of song, and of the fine arts; his deep piety, his bodily constant infirmities, his romantic misfortunes and adversity, his simplicity and gaiety of heart, his devotion to his family and his people, his tenderness towards his mother and his wife, even the failings of his early life, (proving at least that he was human,) and his immense public services, all cast a halo of glory and of interest round the person of Alfred, which all ages will delight to contemplate as one of the fairest and most consolatory of mortal characters.

We can only notice this imperfect image in Wells cathedral as another (hitherto unrecognised) testimony of a learned period to the merit and the lustre of this mirror of kings; thus appropriately exhibited as the glory of his times and dynasty, and the pride and comfort of every succeeding generation of his countrymen.

And though every literary age has delighted to dwell on the life of this "monarch of the erudite and the religious," and that the brightest talents (of whom Sharon Turner is the last) have made him the theme of their happiest efforts, yet will the solid virtues and the romantic adventures of Alfred, present to all the varied feelings and talents of our race the most interesting and affecting, and at the same time, ever fresh pictures which biography can furnish.

The painter and the poet find their most touching subjects in his varied life; as an outlaw in the herdsman's cottage, as the harper in the Danish camp, rallying his persecuted and dispirited countrymen to battle and to victory; or in the bosom of his family, seated on his rush floor, earnestly listening to the reading (by the light of his newly-invented horn lantern) of Orisini the herdsman, or sacred writ, by Plegmund, or Asser, or Grimbald; his shield and hauberk at his side; in the midst of daily and nightly alarms from the incessant northmen, or as diligently translating into mother tongue in his well-regulated hours, for the love, instruction, and delight of his countrymen, those stores which he had obtained himself with so much joy, and toil, surrounded with the duties and cares of a troubled court.

Proceeding with our catalogue, the next in succession is Edward the Elder, his son, and worthy successor to the crown of his renovated country, who, with his numerous family, and their illustrious alliances, his renowned successors, seemed to justify for a time the application to his image of the prophecy of Isaiah, by the ardent Spelman in his life of Alfred: "Thou shalt raise up the foundations of many generations, and thou shalt be called the repairer of the breach, the restorer of paths to dwell in."

As the founder of the See of Wells, Edward the Elder was enthroned on the first buttress of the spiritual side, and has been already described.

It was to this prince that the touching and celebrated exhortations of his dying father were addressed.

No. 84, the next monarch in succession, is Athelstan, the eldest son of Edward the Elder, a prince entirely worthy of his progenitors in military prowess, no less than his pious habits and foundations. Athelstan, in Saxon phrase, "the lord of the west Saxons, the giver of bracelets." Malmesbury relates that "Europe resounded with his praises, and extolled his valour to the skies; foreign princes with justice esteemed themselves happy if they could purchase his friendship either by affinity or presents; Harold, king of Norway, sent him a ship with a golden beak, and a purple sail, furnished within with a compacted fence of gilded shields," &c. &c.

"He levelled with the ground the castle which the Danes had formerly fortified in York, (after the great battle of Brananburg,) that there might be no place for disloyalty to shelter in, and the booty which he found there, and which was very considerable, he divided man by man to the whole army. For he had prescribed himself this rule of conduct, never to hoard up riches, but liberally to spend all his acquisitions either on monasteries or on his faithful followers. On these during the whole of his life he expended his paternal treasures, as well as the produce of his victories. To the Clergy he was humble and affable, to the laity mild and pleasant, to the nobility rather reserved, from respect to his dignity; to the lower classes, laying aside the stateliness of power, kindly condescending. He was as we have heard of proper stature, thin in person, his hair flaxen, as I have seen by his reliques, and beautifully wreathed in golden threads. Extremely beloved by his subjects from admiration of his fortitude and humility, he was absolutely terrific to those who rebelled against him by his invincible courage."

Amongst the praises of Athelstan we must not forget his promotion of that liberty which has ever been characteristic of England.

"Athelstan," says Palgrave, "made many good laws, and the traditional recollections of his government seem to shew that he desired the welfare and freedom of his people. It was currently believed that he bestowed great privileges and franchises upon the town of Beverley, saying

> As free,
> Make I thee,
> As heart may think, or eye can see.

When the good folks of the borough began to regard it as conducive to their welfare and importance that they should be able to send members to the House of Commons, Athelstan's charter was pleaded more than once, as the foundation of their parliamentary right; and throughout the west of England there was scarcely a town in which the statue of Althelstan was not erected[e]."

In this statue, Athelstan (literally the "gem" or the "precious stone") is distinguished by a large brooch on the breast, a symbol which the sculptor did not fail to place conspicuously for the purpose of identification. His crown, too, which is historically stated to have exceeded the ordinary elevation, is also remarkable.

[e] Palgrave's Anglo-Saxon Period, c. x. p. 217.

He has his hands imposingly advanced on his knees, his right leg raised on a pedestal.

Athelstan was crowned at Kingston-upon-Thames, in which till recently (1735,) according to Palgrave[d], stood an ancient chapel, ornamented with the statues of the Anglo-Saxon kings, who took possession of their kingdom by standing upon a great stone, or fragment of a rock, which at no very distant period was still preserved in the churchyard.

No. 50 is Edmond, "the magnificent," but the ill-fated; who perished by the hands of the assassin Leof the outlaw, on the anniversary of St. Augustine, (946,) after a reign of six years, at Pucklechurch, in Gloucestershire. He was the fourth son of Edward the Elder.

The unfortunate king is enthroned under his grandfather Alfred, a comely statue, his right elevated, probably holding a sceptre, now broken, his left imposingly advanced on his knee.

"St. Dunstan," says Malmesbury, "at that time abbot of Glastonbury, had foreseen his ignoble end: being fully persuaded of it from the gesticulations and insolent mockery of a devil dancing before him. Wherefore, hastening to court at full speed, he received intelligence of the transaction on the road. By common consent then, it was determined that his body should be brought to Glastonbury, and there magnificently buried in the northern part of the tower. That such had been his intention, through his singular regard for the abbot, was evident from particular circumstances. The village also where he was murdered, was made an offering for the dead, that the spot which had witnessed his fall might ever after minister aid to his soul."

The succeeding monarch was Edred, fifth son of Edward the Elder, a sickly prince, placed on the throne on account of the extreme youth of his nephews, the heirs of Edmund; who, however, by the energy of his advisers, Turketul, his uncle, the chancellor, and Dunstan, still abbot of Glastonbury, vanquished the rebellious Northumbrians, and pacified his kingdom. "In the meantime," says Malmesbury, "the king prostrate at the feet of the saints, devoted his life to God and St. Dunstan, by whose admonition he endured with patience his frequent bodily pains, prolonged his prayers, and made his palace altogether the school of virtue. He

[d] c. x. p. 201.

died accompanied with the utmost grief of men, but joy of angels; for Dunstan learning by a messenger that he was sick, while urging his horse in order to see him, heard a voice thundering over his head, 'Now King Edred sleeps in the Lord.' He was buried in Winchester cathedral*."

The statue of this king is enthroned on the third buttress, under the statue of the all-directing Dunstan. The head of this statue has been injudiciously restored by a very incompetent hand. His left was raised to his breast in the attitude of a confessor. His feet are bare, as ever prostrate before the saints.

No. 48, a comely and crowned statue, the left raised to his necklace, in the conventional grace assumed by the sculptors of the thirteenth, his right is broken; at his feet is a figure which from its drapery, though much defaced, may be taken for an ecclesiastic. These symbols well correspond with Edwy, the ill-fated son of Edmond, who fell a sacrifice to the disputes of the married and the monastic orders both in reputation and in life, (958,) after three years' reign only. The romantic and melancholy story of the beautiful Elgiva, and the cruelty of the archbishops Odo and St. Dunstan towards the royal pair, give a sad interest to the history of this prince, and the times in which he lived, and indeed obscurity no less, from the partial records of the monks.

The succeeding monarch, Edgar "the peaceable," "the honour and delight of the English," the second son of Edmond, reaped all the advantages which the virtues and the prowess of his ancestors had produced, enjoying a reign of seventeen years of unparalleled prosperity, receiving homage from all the neighbouring princes as 'Bretwalda,' 'Emperor,' 'Basileus of all England.' His political position was enforced by a fleet composed it is said of 5000 vessels, which continually circumnavigated the coasts. The favourite of the monastic orders, and the founder of forty monasteries, Edgar's merits are exalted, and his vices mitigated by the monkish writers.

Edgar's effigy, enthroned in the first buttress, is remarkably significant of his history; his head, unlike those of other kings, is without a crown, his right is raised to his breast as a confessor, and in his left he appears to have held a monastery, his feet are bare. The sculptor had well calculated on the evidence

* B. ii. c. vii.

M

which this singularity among the royal and crowned statues would afford, and the spectator is at once attracted by so unusual an omission. The crimes of Edgar were chiefly against the fair sex. Malmesbury[1] relates those licentious acts by which, says he, "some persons endeavour to dim his exceeding glory." When the most hideous of these adulteries reached the ears of St. Dunstan, "the king was vehemently reproved by him, and underwent a seven years' penance, though a king: submitting to fast, and to forego the *wearing of his crown* for that period." —"However these things may be, this is certain, that from the sixteenth year of his age when he was appointed king, till the thirtieth, he reigned *without the insignia of royalty;* for at that time the princes and men of every order assembling, he was crowned with great pomp at Bath (Ake-mannes-Cæastre, literally the city of aching men or invalids,) survived only a few years, and was buried at Glastonbury."

No. 51. The blessing of the just had descended from Alfred to the fourth generation, and we now arrive at that melancholy period of Saxon history, which seems to exhibit a terrible retribution for the crime of Edgar. His eldest son, Edward the Martyr, was cruelly murdered by the adulterous mother of the second son, Ethelred; with whom came into the dynasty of Cerdic that imbecility, or the sword, which never again departed from their house; and the history of David and Uriah was enacted in this country with additional delinquency, and more awful visitations.

Malmesbury relates: "Meanwhile King Edward conducted himself with becoming affection to his infant brother and his stepmother; retained only the name of king, and gave them the power; followed the footsteps of his father's piety, and gave both his attention and heart to good counsel. The woman, however, with that hatred which a stepmother only can entertain, began to meditate a subtle stratagem, in order that not even the title of king might be wanting to her child, and to lay a treacherous snare for her son-in-law, which she accomplished in the following manner. He was returning home, tired with the chase, and gasping with thirst from the exercise, while his companions were following the dogs in different directions as it happened; when hearing that they dwelt in a neighbouring mansion, the youth proceeded thither at full speed, unattended and unsuspecting.

[1] B. ii. c. viii.

as he judged of others by his own feelings. On his arrival, alluring him to her with female blandishment, she made him lean forward, and after saluting him, while he was eagerly drinking from the cup which had been presented, the dagger of an attendant pierced him through. Dreadfully wounded, with all his remaining strength he clapped spurs to his horse in order to join his companions; when one foot slipping, he was dragged by the other through the trackless paths and recesses of the woods, while the streaming blood gave evidence of his death to his followers. Moreover, they then commanded him to be ingloriously interred at Werham; envying him even holy ground when dead, as they had envied him his royal dignity when living."

The young king is represented as holding a sceptre in his right, and the cup or chalice in his left, significant of his martyrdom, and he tramples on a figure which is much defaced, but according to the demonstrative system of the sculptor, may well have represented his detestable stepmother.

The succeeding monarch, the base-born Ethelred the Second, seemed to have brought the curse of his parents upon his unhappy country, which by his acts was afflicted in a variety of ways, leading to the ultimate destruction of the Saxon dynasty, and ruin of the country. He bought off the Danes by three enormous subsidies, whom on another occasion he caused to be assassinated throughout the land in one day, wasting the wealth, revenues, and spirit of the country during thirty-eight long years, and bringing it into the entire subjugation of the Danes. Finally abandoning a crown he could no longer maintain, and retiring into Normandy, he died in 1016.

Dunstan died in the tenth year of this reign, and from the comparative prosperity of those in which his energy and judgment had full exercise, we may judge of the greatness of his powers and abilities, and find an irresistible argument in favour of his disputed merits. It is certain that had Dunstan lived, the melancholy fate of this country subsequently might have been averted. The merits of Edmond, the vigour of the decrepid Edred, the powers by land and sea, and the peace which blessed the reign of Edgar, are thus all attributable to the counsels of Dunstan.

The statue, No. 51, which represents this wretched king, Ethelred II., is crowned, holding apparently in his right a sceptre, and his garment in his left.

Under his feet is a remarkable figure, reposing in perfect ease, *and leaning upon his elbow*, and quite unlike the figures so placed, which are usually in attitudes of crushed and vanquished foes.

This singular position may well have been designed to caricature the imbecile king himself, and the demonstrative sculptor gladly availed himself of Malmesbury's description of his indolent character, to identify, amongst so many, the peculiarity by which he was known.   Malmesbury says[e], " In the meantime, the king, admirably calculated for sleeping, disregarding these important transactions, would only yawn, and if ever he recovered his senses enough to *raise himself upon his elbow*, he quickly relapsed into his original wretchedness, either from the oppression of indolence, or the adverseness of fortune.   His brother's ghost also, demanding dire expiation, tormented him.   Who can tell how often he collected his army? how often he ordered ships to be built? how frequently he called out commanders from all quarters? and yet nothing was ever effected.   For the army, destitute of a leader, and ignorant of military discipline, either retreated before it came into action, or else was easily overcome."

" History contains few reigns," says Dr. Lappenburg with his accustomed point, " so long and so disastrous as that of this unhappy prince; but merited as his misery was, the Catholic Church has, nevertheless, enrolled him among her martyrs."

In this statue, at all events, we find historical justice fully vindicated by the Catholic Bishop Trotman, and Ethelred's character ignominiously exposed, although two hundred years had elapsed since these sad events.   The sculptor of this figure, and his patron Trotman, have participated and expressed the discouragement of the country, for we have no crowned head until we arrive at Edward the Confessor on the north buttress, and even that crown is depressed and insignificant, as if diminished in glory, compared to those of the other Saxon monarchs.

The next in succession, is the gallant and interesting Edmund Ironside, crowned by Archbishop Leovingus in 1016.   Recommended to the spectator with all the honours due to him, as a valiant prince at least, however unfortunate, and fully competent to vindicate the ancient renown of his race, had Heaven and the

e B. ii. c. x.

treacherous Streon permitted it. His statue, No. 59, is one of the best composed and most striking in the whole series, and is inadequately shewn in the annexed plate. He is clad in a hauberk, which covers his head and chin and feet, he holds the sheath in his left, and draws the sword with characteristic expression; the tragical and atrocious manner of his death is related by Malmesbury, b. ii. c. x.

The placing this statue out of the regular series, together with that of Harold also irregularly, I consider to have been intended by the sculptor simply as a more palpable demonstration of these chivalrous characters, and to interest the spectator with the becoming images of two valiant Englishmen, worthy of their name and country, however unfortunate. Had they been placed with rigorous exactness in the series, the admired Edmund would have been placed in the corner of the buttress, comparatively obscure, and Harold would have been placed east of the Confessor, almost equally obscure. Such a dislocation, and for such objects, was quite consistent with the scheme laid down by the sculptor and the architect, and of which we have already remarked so many instances.

No. 52. The kingly figure next to Ethelred II., crowned and holding his sceptre in his left, and trampling on the foe, *who is still struggling*, is Canute the Danish conqueror and usurper of the English throne.

His wise and glorious reign during nineteen years, and his benefactions to the Church, entitled him to the honours here bestowed on his image, in contra-distinction to those of the succeeding Danish monarchs, as we shall proceed to shew.

The following female and royal statues, Nos. 53 and 54, are of Queens, elegantly composed, and most conspicuously placed. The first holds a book in her left, and her position immediately under Ethelflæda and Alfred, might incline us to attribute the revered name of Osburga, the mother of Alfred, to this statue. The pretensions however of Gunhilda, daughter of Canute by the English dowager queen, Emma, and wife of Henry III., emperor of Germany, might contest this honour. For the display of so illustrious an alliance is quite in character with the spirit of these sculptures throughout. See her remarkable history in Malmesbury, b. iii. c. xii.

But Osburga, the mother of four kings, the affectionate companion of Alfred in all his good and evil fortune, to whose maternal culture we owe the birth of that literary spirit which dignified Alfred, and his country through him, in so glorious a manner, should rather have the preference, more especially on account of the significant symbol, the book, which she carries in her hand.

"It chanced," says Palgrave, "one day that Alfred's mother, Osburga, (and not as some suppose the Frenchwoman Judith,) shewed to him and his brothers a volume of Anglo-Saxon poetry, which she possessed. 'He who first can read the book, shall have it,' said she. Alfred's attention was attracted by the bright gilding and colouring of one of the illuminated capital letters. He was delighted with the *gay*, and enquired of his mother, 'Would she really keep her word?' She confirmed the promise, and put the book into his hands; and he applied so steadily to his task, that the book became his own [h]."

There can be little doubt of the identity of the figure 54, as of the dowager queen of Ethelred II., Emma, daughter of Richard, duke of Normandy, whom the politic Canute married; thus conciliating his new English subjects to the usurpation of the Saxon crown. The issue of this marriage in Hardicanute, who succeeded to the throne, and Gunhilda, who became empress of Germany, fully justified this act of policy.

But a prior title to the distinction of a statue, was, that Emma by her first husband was the mother of Edward the Confessor, the last scion of the beloved Saxon stock.

No. 55. The following mean and unkingly statue, with a crown so depressed, as hardly to be recognisable, and trampling upon a foe, is Harold Harefoot, the successor of Canute in 1035.

No. 56. The following king, in still meaner attire, *without a crown*, but trampling on the foe, is Hardicanute. The impious treatment of his brother's remains, his insults to the Church, and the oppression of his subjects, were thus visited on his image by Trotman's carver. The undignified character of both these statues of the Danish princes, and the absence of the crown on the latter, may signify their disputed succession, and their division of the kingdom, which ought to have been united, as well as of the worthless princes whom they represent.

No. 58, a remarkably graceful queen, holding a book in her right, and

[h] Anglo-Saxon Period, p. 162.

pointing with her left to her brother Harold, and her husband, Edward the Confessor, is undoubtedly Edgitha, the virgin wife of the last of the Saxon kings. Besides her personal and literary merits, she had peculiar claims to be recorded in Wells, as having endowed the See with several valuable estates.

"Shortly after the king (Edward the Confessor) took Edgitha, the daughter of Godwin, to wife; a woman whose bosom was the school of every liberal art, though little skilled in earthly matters: on seeing her, if you were amazed at her erudition, you must absolutely languish for the purity of her mind, and the beauty of her person. Both in her husband's lifetime, and afterwards, she was not entirely free from suspicion of dishonour; but when dying, in the time of King William, she voluntarily satisfied the bystanders of her unimpaired chastity, by an oath. When she became his wife, the king so artfully managed, that he neither removed her from his bed, nor knew her after the manner of men. I have not been able to discover whether he acted thus from dislike to her family, which he prudently dissembled from the exigency of the times, or out of pure regard to chastity: yet it is most notoriously affirmed, that he never violated his purity by a connexion with any woman. But since I have gotten thus far, I wish to admonish my reader, that the track of my history is here but dubious, because the truth of the facts hangs in suspense."

Ingulf knew the Queen Edgitha, and describes her as beautiful, meek, modest, faithful, virtuous, and the enemy of no one. She had none of the barbarism of her father and brothers, (Godwin, and Harold, and Tosh,) she was even *literis apprime erudita*, a lady of learning. He adds, "I have often seen her, when only a boy, I visited my father in the royal court. Often as I came from school, she questioned me on letters and on my verse; and willingly passing from grammar to logic, she caught me in the subtleness of argument. I had always three or four pieces of money counted by her maiden, and was sent to the royal larder for refreshment."

No. 61, the next in succession, is Edward the Confessor. But the admission of his statue to this, the western front, was not compatible with the scheme of this sculpturesque illustration. He could hardly be said to belong to the happiest memory of the Cerdic dynasty, and, however virtuous and amiable, he would not be considered as one of that galaxy of Saxon princes, which it was proposed to exhibit there in all its splendour. At the same time a conspicuous position was due to him, at least of a secondary quality, and he is accordingly enthroned in the first buttress of the northern front.

The sculptor could not possibly have expressed in a more significant manner the mild and impassible character of the holy king. His head crowned with a *low* crown, and in his left the sceptre. His right leg crossed over the knee of his left in the attitude of counsel; he appears as the affable and peaceful king, the idol of his subjects. The contrast of his image with that of the fierce and imposing conqueror in the next buttress of that front, is a masterpiece of the sculptor.

In it we identify the description of Malmesbury[1], "In these exercises, of hunting with hounds, and pouncing of birds, after hearing divine service in the morning, he employed himself whole days. In other respects he was a man by choice devoted to God, and lived the life of an angel in the administration of his kingdom. To the poor and the stranger, more especially foreigners, and of the religious order, he was kind in invitation, munificent in his presents, and constantly exciting the monks of his own country to imitate their holiness. He was of just stature; his beard and hair milk white, his countenance florid, fair throughout his whole person; and his form of admirable proportion.

"Thus full of years and of glory, he surrendered his pure spirit to heaven, and was buried on the day of the Epiphany, in the said church, (Westminster,) which he, first in England, had erected after that kind of style, which now, almost all attempt to rival at enormous expense. The race of the West Saxons, which had reigned in Britain five hundred and seventy-one years, from the time of Cerdic, and two hundred and sixty-one from Egbert, in him had ceased to rule."

We have now to return to the west front, and to observe the last figure in the series of kings, preceding, and standing next to Edward, though chronologically posterior to him. An awful warlike figure, clad in full armour, cap-à-pied, with the kite-shaped shield, spurred, and striding in all the energy of the usurper Harold, with admirable expression. It was a consolation to the Saxon spectator to contemplate this daring leader, whose success in a long career of arms, down to the battle of Standford Bridge, had given him undue confidence in himself and his followers. Nineteen days after that tremendous battle, with a difficult and tedious march of his harassed troops from the north, and with inferior numbers, he in-

[1] B. iii. c. xiii.

cautiously gave battle to the wary Norman, prepared with his fresh troops, after a repose of fifteen days on the shores of Sussex. At least, he died a glorious death, and accomplished all that valour and devotion could effect; and the sculptor has done his best to recommend his subject to the favourable regard of his country-men, by the intense character with which he has invested his image.

Having thus displayed the succession of kings from Egbert to Harold, figured in the fourth tier, we have now to point out those of the fifth tier, the minor and subsidiary celebrities, princes, princesses, holy men, and foreign alliances, who made up the glory of the Saxon period, and who are scarcely less interesting and illustrative of the spirit of the times in which they flourished, than the kings and bishops themselves.

Beginning then, as before, from the centre of the west front, and proceeding northward, we have No. 82, a most graceful queen, with an ornamented diadem and scarf, a veil gracefully thrown over her head and shoulders, her left in her necklace, and her right having apparently held a sceptre, may well be Ethilda. "The fourth daughter of Edward the Elder," says Malmesbury, "in whom the whole essence of beauty had centred, which the others only possessed in part; was demanded from her brother by Hugh, king of the Franks. The chief of this embassy was Adulph, son of Baldwin, earl of Flanders, by Ethelswitha, daughter of King Edward. When he had declared the request of the suitor in an as-sembly of the nobility at Abendon, he produced such liberal presents as might gratify the most boundless avarice; perfumes such as had never been seen in England before; jewels; but more especially emeralds; the greenness of which, reflected by the sun, illumined the countenances of the by-standers with agreeable light; many fleet horses with their trappings, and, as Virgil says,

"champing their golden bits;"

an alabaster vase so exquisitely chased that the cornfields really seemed to wave, the vines to bud, the figures of men actually to move, and so clear and polished that it reflected the features like a mirror; the sword of Constantine the Great, on which the name of its original possessor was read in golden letters; on the pommel on thick plates of gold, might be seen fixed an iron spike; one of the four which the Jewish faction prepared for the crucifixion of our Lord; the spear of Charles

N

the Great, which whenever that invincible emperor hurled in his expeditions against the Saracens, he always came off conqueror; it was reported to be the same which, driven into the side of our Saviour by the hand of the centurion, opened, by that precious wound, the joys of paradise to wretched mortals; the banner of the most blessed martyr Maurice, chief of the Theban legion, with which the king in the Spanish war used to break through the battalions of the enemy, however fierce and wedged together, and put them to flight; a diadem, precious from its quantity of gold, but more so for its jewels, the splendour of which threw the sparks of light so strongly on the beholders, that the more stedfastly any person endeavoured to gaze, so much the more was he compelled to avert his eyes; part of the holy and adorable cross enclosed in crystal, where the eye pierced through the substance of the stone, might discern the colour and size of the wood; a small portion of the crown of thorns, enclosed in a similar manner, which, in derision of His government, the madness of the soldiers placed on Christ's sacred head. The king (Athelstan) delighted with such great and exqui- site presents, made an equal return of good offices; and gratified the soul of the longing suitor by a union with his sister. With some of these presents he enriched succeeding kings; but to Malmsbury he gave part of the cross and crown; by the support of which, I believe, that place even now flourishes, though it has suffered so many shipwrecks of its liberty, so many attacks of its enemies. In this place, he ordered Edwin and Ethelwin, the sons of his uncle Ethelward, whom he had lost in the battle against Analaf, to be honourably buried, expressing his design of resting here himself."

No. 81 is undoubtedly the suitor himself, Hugh the Great, not as Malmes- bury calls him " king of the Franks," but the father of Hugh Capet, who obtained the royal dignity in 987. The crownless head of this statue bears a remarkable testimony to the accuracy of Trotman's history, for it is habited as a prince and not as a king, with a cap (and not a crown), gracefully placed sideways on his head; and suspended to his side, is the formidable sword of Constantine, above described.

"Hugh the Great," says Palgrave, "by whose influence Raoul had been raised to the royal dignity, possessed so much power, that he was often called ' Rex Francorum,' or King of the French, though he had no real claim to such a

title, and as the means of securing his authority, he anxiously sought the friendship and alliance of our Athelstan. He visited London, offering rich gifts : the
sword of Constantine the Great, and the lance of Charlemagne ; by which, as
it was believed, victory had always been ensured to the fabled emperor of
chivalry. Hugh's main object was to obtain one of the sisters of Athelstan in
marriage ; Hugh probably feared that Athelstan would incline to support the
pretensions of his nephew, Louis d'Outremer ; but if he, the Rex Francorum, could
have another sister of Athelstan, sitting by his side as his consort, the Anglo-
Saxon king might be inclined to overlook the claims of the son of his sister
Edgiva, by Charles the Simple [k]."

Nos. 82 and 83, two very elegant female figures, clad in simpler guise, but
full of dignity, may be Edgiva, married to Charles the Simple, king of France, and
Elgiva, to Otho, son of Henry the Fowler, emperor of Germany, whose statues,
85 and 86, represent crowned kings of great dignity ; the former, having the foe
under his feet, stands to the right of King Athelstan.

"The sisters of Athelstan shared in the estimation acquired by their brother's
conduct and success. Otho, the son of Henry, the emperor of Germany, sought
the hand of one of these noble ladies, and another became the consort of Louis,
duke of Aquitaine. These continental Princes might have matched themselves
much nearer home, so that some strong and special inducement must have led to
their union with the daughters of England."

It was Turketul, their cousin, the chancellor, who conducted these royal
damsels to Cologne, on their way to the dominions of Otho.

"Charles the Simple, the lineal representative, and heir of Charlemagne, had
taken refuge in England to avoid the storms of the revolution. Here he was
hospitably received, and having espoused the fair Edgiva, daughter of Edward,
and sister of Athelstan, he continued a dependent upon the kindness or bounty of
the Anglo-Saxon nation. Eudo had not reigned very long, when great discon-
tent against him prevailed. A deputation was therefore sent to England, for the
purpose of recalling Charles the Simple, who with his English wife quitted this
country, and was crowned at Rheims, 898. Charles being defeated subsequently,
922, by Hugh the Great, was expelled again by that fickle people, and died in

[k] Palgrave's Anglo-Saxons, p. 215.

captivity. His son by Edgiva, born in England, became king of France, under the title of Louis d'Outremer.

Such was the desire of the continental princes to ally themselves to the Saxon kings at that time, and justly are these memorials presented to the spectator, in this glorious picture of that illustrious dynasty.

No. 87 is empty. To the left of Alfred, some character attached to his time and history probably stood here.

No. 88, a figure to the left of Alfred, clad in a hauberk, discovering his face, with armour of a singular form, upon his legs a sword and belt, and apparently a kite-formed shield, now broken, is probably Gudrum the Dane, the symbol of Alfred's noblest exploit in war.

Not long after the vision of Cuthbert, announcing success to Alfred's arms, " Alfred venturing from his concealment in Ethelingai," says Malmesbury, " hazarded an experiment of consummate art. Accompanied only by one of his most faithful adherents, he entered the tent of the King Gudrum, under the disguise of a minstrel, and being admitted as a professor of the mimic art, to the banqueting room, there was no object of secrecy which he did not minutely attend to both with eyes and ears. Remaining there several days till he had satisfied his mind on every matter which he wished to know, he returned to Ethelingai; and assembling his companions, pointed out the indolence of the enemy and the easiness of their defeat. All were eager for the enterprise, and himself collecting all the forces from every side, and learning exactly the situation of the barbarians from scouts he had sent out for that purpose, he suddenly attacked and routed them with incredible slaughter. The remainder, with their king Gudrum, whom our people call Gourmund, with thirty nobles and almost all the commonalty, was baptized, Alfred standing for him; and the provinces of the East Angles and Northumbrians were given him, in order that he might, under fealty to the king, foster with hereditary right what before he had overrun with predatory incursion. However, as the Ethiopian cannot change his skin, domineering over these tributary provinces with the haughtiness of a tyrant, during eleven years, he died in the twelfth. Such Danes as had refused to become Christians, together with Hasting, went over sea, where the inhabitants are best able to tell what cruelties they perpetrated."

No. 90, to the right of Alfred is another figure, clad in a hauberk, his head covered, and his face concealed by his helmet, with the kite-shaped shield. This is probably Ethelred, the ealdorman of Mercia, who formed the great bulwark of the west, against the incursions of the treacherous East Angles, and the northmen. " He granted London," says Malmesbury, " the chief city of the Mercian kingdom, to a nobleman named Ethelred, to hold in fealty ; and gave him his daughter Ethelfleda in marriage. Ethelred conducted himself with equal valour and fidelity ; defended his trust with activity, and kept the East Angles and Northumbrians, who were hatching rebellion against the king, within due bounds, compelling them to give hostages. Of what infinite service this was, the following emergency proved [1]," &c. &c.

No. 91, is a remarkable statue representing a saint in episcopal costume carrying in his upraised hands, the crown, or upper portion of his own head, surrounded with a chaplet or circle of stars. The face of the saint himself is perfect, but all above the eyebrows has a corresponding deficiency. Such a mode of representation is quite original, and though quaint, is far superior to the ordinary continental mode, which places the entire head in the hands of a headless trunk. St. Denys and St. Firmin appear thus at Amiens and elsewhere.

This can be no other than St. Neot, the uncle, and some say the brother of Alfred, of whom he was the spiritual guide, and earliest teacher on heavenly things. The model of sanctity, he visited Rome seven times as a monk of Glastonbury ; whence he retired to a wild solitude in Cornwall, which he afterwards quitted to build a monastery ; and died 878, seven years after Alfred had ascended the throne. The principal feature of his moral character, is the resolution which he formed of copying the predominant virtue of every person in his cloister. The continence of one, the pleasantness of another, the suavity of a third, the seriousness, humanity, good nature, and love of singing, and of study, in others.

The faults of Alfred, which give us an additional sympathy in his life, have been produced by Sharon Turner, from the life of Neot [m]. He says that " Neot chided him with many words, and spoke to him prophetically. ' O king, much shalt thou suffer in this life ; hereafter so much distress thou shalt abide,

[1] Malmesbury, b. ii. c. 5.
[m] Vol. i. p. 49. of his Anglo-Saxons.

that no man's tongue may say it all. Now, loved child, hear me if thou wilt, and turn thy heart to my counsel; depart entirely from thy unrighteousness, and thy sins with alms redeem, and with tears abolish.' Again. 'Why do you glory in your misconduct? why are you powerful but in iniquity? you have been exalted, but you shall not continue; you shall be bruised like the ears of wheat. Where then will be your pride? if that is not yet excluded from you, it soon shall be. You shall be deprived of that sovereignty of whose vain splendour you are so extravagantly arrogant.'" Even his admirer Asser, speaking of his misfortunes says, "we believe that this adversity occurred to the king not undeservedly."

No. 92, a queen crowned and veiled, and in a remarkable attitude, as if withdrawing with her right the ring from her left. Such an extraordinary action in connection with the surrounding statues, leaves no doubt that Ethelfleda, the daughter of Alfred, and wife of Ethelred, ealdorman of Mercia, is here intended; whose renunciation of the marriage-tie, after the birth of her first child[n], is thus ingeniously expressed by the sculptor. She exerted extraordinary powers of sagacity and fortitude, and was emphatically called "the Ladye," in connection with her brother Edward, in the defence and fortification of the country.

No. 93. A graceful prince, without any remarkable symbols, may be Ethelweard, the second son of Edward the Elder. "Deeply versed in literature," says Malmesbury, "much resembling his grandfather Alfred in features and disposition." His position here may infer some important services, not cited by history, besides his resemblance to the beloved Alfred in person and in character. He may have been active in the wars and fortifications of Edward and Ethelfleda, or he may have assisted in her pious foundation of St. Petrus, at Gloucester. He died in 924, twelve years after his aunt Ethelfleda, and in the same year with his father, Edward the Elder.

---

[n] Hurlington on Ethelfleda says, "Habuit etiam bellicosissimam filiam Esfledam, dominam Merciorum, quæ multa prælia gessit, multas urbes, et castella, partim extruxit, partim munivit et in qua nihil fortissimi viri præter sexum desiderares: ita ut quibusdam non solum domina vel regina, sed etiam rex vocaretur, ad laudem et excellentiam mirificationis sui, et ut æstimatum et dictum est nisi fati velocitate præcepta fuisset, viros virtute transissit universos." Malmesbury adds, "Tantæ etiam castitatis ut experta primi partus difficultate, perpetuo viri horruit complexus protestans non convenire regis filiæ, ut illi se voluptate innecteret, quam tale incommodum post tempus urgeret."—Wise's Asser, p. 119.

No. 94, a dignified priest, without any symbols in his hands, may be the learned Grimbald, provost of St. Omer, invited from Rheims by Alfred; or John Scotus Erigina, the greatest dialectician of his day. The monk of Malmesbury, or Ethelstan, or Werwulf his chaplain, or Werfrith, his bishop of Worcester, who at the king's command translated the Decalogues of St. Gregory, and of his disciple Peter; or John of Corvey, from old Saxony, whom Alfred placed at the head of his new foundation at Ethelingai, (Asser is accounted for elsewhere.) At all events, this statue refers to the literary glories of Alfred, together with No. 98, in a scholar's dress, and No. 99, of the same character which existed in Carter's time. See his engravings.

No. 95, an episcopal figure of great dignity, and placed to the left of St. Dunstan, may either refer to Alfred, or to St. Dunstan. In the first case it might represent Werfrith, bishop of Worcester, or even St. Swithun, the early preceptor of Alfred. In the second case, it might well refer to St. Elphegus, abbot of Bath, bishop of Winchester through Dunstan's influence, and his firm coadjutor in the reformation of the married clergy; and lastly archbishop of Canterbury, martyred by the Danes in 1013. The choice must be left to the deliberation of the reader.

No. 96, an archbishop in full pontificals, in the act of benediction, his feet bare, and his head unfortunately degraded, (the only spiritual personage presiding and enthroned on a buttress in this the temporal side,) is undoubtedly St. Dunstan, whose prodigious influence for unquestionable good, both temporal and spiritual, during more than forty years, and extending through the reigns of six monarchs from Athelstan to Ethelred II., cannot be too highly estimated. "This extraordinary man was formed by nature to act a distinguished part in the varied theatre of life. The great battle of which, the establishment of celibacy amongst the clergy, has subjected his memory to be disfigured by much extravagant tradition by the enthusiasm of the monkish writers. Happily he accomplished this first desire of his heart and understanding; for a married priesthood in the then state of society, possessing at the death of Edward the Confessor one third of the lands of the country, would soon have degenerated into a caste of sacerdotal nobility, holding their lands as a patrimonial inheritance, by the nominal condition of serving at the altar, but neglecting, in fact, every duty they were charged to perform °." His second object, the political integrity of the empire, was abundantly obtained, as the annals of his time declare, during the reigns of the impetuous Edmond, the feeble Edred, the vicious Edwy and Edgar, Edward the Martyr, and the beginning of that of Ethelred. Shortly after his death, all fell into confusion and ruin, and indeed a more striking instance of the loss to a country of a master-mind, can hardly be cited. His title by one of his biographers, "Rex et Regis Imperator," could not have been better selected.

No. 97, a remarkable figure, raised upon an ornamental corbel, having (apparently) a cap of maintenance on his head, a spear in his right, his left raised to his breast as a confessor, with a robe peculiarly pointed at the bottom, and an aged royal foe crushed under his feet. These symbols agree admirably with the chancellor Turketul, grandson of Alfred, who as a legal administrator, a warrior, a loyal subject, and eminent churchman, is one of the most venerable and amiable characters of antiquity. His useful life was passed in the service of the state. "In the great battle of Brunanbury," says Malmesbury, "fell Constantine, king of the Scots, a man of treacherous energy, and vigorous old age;" (the crowned king, exhibited under the feet of this statue;) " five other kings, twelve earls, and almost the whole assemblage of barbarians. The few who escaped being preserved to embrace the faith of Christ."

Other authorities state that it was a son of Constantine who fell by the hands of Turketul. The brothers of the valiant chancellor, Elfwine and Ethelwine, fell also in this battle. "No greater carnage," says the poet, "had ever taken place in the island since those proud ' war-smiths,' the Angles and the Saxons from the east, first came over the broad sea to Britain." Turketul's attack with the men of London, upon that memorable occasion, turned the fortune of the day in favour of his cousin Athelstan. He it was, with Dunstan, who infused vigour into Edred's feeble reign. In the continental marriages of his nieces, we find him the chief and most active agent. On the reduction of Northumbria, Turketul renounced the world. He announced in the streets of London by a crier, that he was ready to pay every debt, and if he had wronged any one, to make him three-fold compensation. His habits of sanctity, and love of celibacy, had pointed him out to his uncle (Edward the Elder) as a fitting person to hold the highest dignities;

° Palgrave's Ang.-Sax., p. 242.

but these when offered, he constantly declined, regarding them as snares of Satan for the subversion of souls. Sent by Edred on a mission to the rebellious Archbishop Wulfstan, his way lay by the ruined abbey of Croyland, here he was induced to partake of the hospitality of the three only surviving monks, who still found shelter amidst the ruins of the monastery. Touched with this sight, on his return, he procured the means of restoring the venerable foundation, resolving to enter it as one of the brotherhood. Many learned men accompanied him, and at his death, (975,) forty-seven monks, and four lay brothers, belonged to the society. In the actual front of the abbey of Croyland, the statue of Turketul is still conspicuous, though the deplorable state of neglect in which these interesting remains are now left, does not promise its preservation to future ages, which, however, a small timely expense might secure.

The following figures, 98 and 99, have been already described, and we now proceed to the historical series of the north front.

o

FIFTH TIER OF THE NORTH AND EAST SIDES.

No. 100, a statue in full pontificals, with an archbishop's mitre, so diminished as scarcely to be recognizable, and not as usual enthroned, but *standing*, in the niche immediately above the Confessor, is undoubtedly Robert of Jumièges; one of the Norman adventurers and favourites, whom Edward appointed the keeper of his conscience, and raised to the archiepiscopal throne of Canterbury.

"On the first rumour of this reconciliation," (of Godwin and his party with the Confessor,) "the courtiers of Normandy and France mounted their horses in great haste, and fled in different directions. Some reached a fortress in the west, commanded by Osbert, surnamed Pentecost; others made all speed to a castle in the north, also commanded by a Norman. The Normans, Robert, archbishop of Canterbury, and William, bishop of London, went out at the eastern gate, followed by armed men of their own nation, who massacred some of the English in their flight. They repaired to the coast and embarked in small fishing boats. The archbishop, in his trouble and haste, left in England his most precious effects, and, among other things, the *pallium* which he had received from the Roman Church, as the ensign of his dignity[a]."

Robert's memory could not but be odious to the Saxon feelings, not only as a foreign adventurer, but as an "hireling," who "fleeth because he is an hireling, and careth not for the sheep." The cruelty also with which that flight was accompanied, well deserved the ignominy with which his statue is here represented to us. "The English of our times," says Malmesbury[b], "vilify this person together with the rest, as being the impeacher of Godwin and his sons; the sower of discord, and the purchaser of the archbishopric." "On account of these feuds, as I

[a] Thierry's Norman Conquest, vol. i. p. 224.
[b] B. ii. c. 12.

CATHEDRAL AT WELLS

INDEX, NO. II.

EAST SIDE.   **NORTH SIDE.**

Sixth Tier. The Resurrection.

Fifth Tier.

- St. Nicholas.
- ROGER OF SALISBURY.
- Robert, Duke of Normandy.
- Falk, Earl of Anjou.
- Robert the Saxon.
- Edgar Etheling.
- ALDRED OF YORK.
- Wulstan, Bishop of Worcester.
- Christina, Abbess of Romsey.
- Edburga.
- Edgitha.
- Elgiva.
- ROBERT, Archbishop of Canterbury.

118 | 117 | 116 | 115 | 114 | 113 | 112 | 111 | 110 | 109 | 108 | 107 | 106 | 105 | 104 | 103 | 102 | 101 | 100

Fourth Tier.

- King Henry III.
- King John.
- KING HENRY I.
- Adelais.
- Maude the Good.
- Prince Geoffry.
- Prince Henry.
- WILLIAM, CONQUEROR.
- Henry II.
- Stephen.
- Henry, Emperor.
- Matilda, Empress.
- William Rufus.
- Robert Courthose.
- Prince Richard.
- EDWARD CONFESSOR.

79 | 78 | 77 | 76 | 75 | 74 | 73 | 72 | 71 | 70 | 69 | 68 | 67 | 66 | 65 | 64 | 63 | 62 | 61

Third Tier.

- Gift of Tongues.
- Resurrection.
- Deposition.
- Elevation of Cross.
- Bearing the Cross.
- Before Pilate.
- Last Supper.
- Consultation with high-Priest.
- Entry to Jerusalem.
- Calling of Nicodemus.
- Mount of Olives.

31 | 30 | 29 | 28 | 27 | 26 | 25 | 24 | 23 | 22 | 21 | 20 | 19

Second Tier.

First Tier.

- Theodore.
- St. Berennius.
- St. Bertha.
- St. Augustine.
- Liudhard.

59 60 | 57 | 56 | 55 | 54 53 | 52 | 51 | 50 | 49 | 48 | 47 | 46 45

have observed, my narrative labours under difficulties; for I cannot precisely ascertain the truth, by reason either of the national dislike of these nations for each other, or because the English disdainfully bear with a superior, and the Normans cannot endure an equal."

Next to the archbishop, are three female figures, clad in religious dresses, Nos. 101, 102, and 103.

The two following niches, (104 and 105,) are empty, and may possibly have contained others of the same sex.

No. 106 represents a female in a religious dress, holding a book. "My commendations," says Malmesbury[c], "shall also glance at the names of some maidens of the royal race, (though I must claim indulgence for being brief upon the subject, not through fastidiousness, but because I am unacquainted with their miracles.)" —"Whose sanctity," continues he, "which is abundantly resplendent, may suffice to irradiate both the poles. Holy St. Edgitha, the daughter of King Edgar, ennobles, with her relics, the monastery of Wilton, where she was buried, and cherishes that place with her regard; where, trained from her infancy in the school of the Lord, she gained His favour by unsullied virginity, and constant watchings, repressing the pride of her high birth by her humility. I have heard one circumstance of her, from persons of elder days, which greatly staggered the opinions of men; for she led them into false conclusions from the splendour of her costly dress; being always habited in a richer garb than the sanctity of her profession seemed to require. On this conduct, being openly rebuked by St. Ethelwold, she is reputed to have answered with equal point and wit, 'that the judgment of God was true, and irrefragable, while that of man alone was fallible; for pride might even exist under the garb of wretchedness; wherefore, I think,' said she, 'that a mind may be as pure beneath these vestments as under your tattered furs.' The bishop was deeply struck by this speech; admitting its truth by silence; and reddening with joy that he had been branded by the sparkling repartee of the lady, he held his peace. St. Dunstan had observed her at the consecration of the church of St. Denys, which she had built out of affection to that martyr, frequently stretching out her right thumb, and making the sign of the cross upon her forehead; being extremely delighted at it, 'May this finger,' he exclaimed, 'never see corruption,'

[c] B. ii. c. 13.

and immediately, while celebrating mass, he burst into such a flood of tears, that he alarmed with his faltering voice an assistant standing near him; who enquiring the reason of it, 'Soon,' said he, 'shall this blooming rose wither, soon shall this beloved bird take its flight to God after the expiration of six weeks from this time.' The truth of the prelate's prophecy was very shortly fulfilled; for on the appointed day, this noble, firmly-minded lady, expired in her prime, at the age of twenty-three. Miracles multiplying, at her tomb, it was ordered that her virgin body should be taken up and exalted in a shrine, when the whole of it was found resolved into dust, except the thumb, with the abdomen and parts adjacent."

The first of these, No. 100, from the adorned elegance of the costume, may well have been designed for St. Edgitha, a conjecture favoured by the vicinity of St. Dunstan. Not only the Saxon princesses, but the Norman, may lay claim to the distinction of these memorials, for William had three daughters devoted to the Church; Cæcilia became abbess of Caen, and Adela, who took the veil at Marcegny; another "obtained from God a virgin death; a hard substance was found upon her knees after her death," proving the frequency of her prayers.

"In short," says Malmesbury, "as I have remarked of the nuns of Shaftesbury, all virtues have long since quitted the earth, and retired to heaven, or, if any where, (but this I must say, with the permission of holy men,) are to be found only in the hearts of nuns; and surely those women are highly to be praised, who regardless of the weakness of their sex, vie with each other in the preservation of their continence, and by such means ascend triumphant to heaven."

No. 107, a bishop in the act of benediction, from his vicinity to Archbishop Aldred, can be no other than St. Wulfstan, bishop of Worcester, the champion of the Saxon ecclesiastics against the Norman invaders. "Whose pious simplicity," says Malmesbury, "and holy confidence in God, demand praise and approbation."

"In the year 1076, Wulfstan was cited before a council of the Norman bishops assembled in the church of the western convent at Westminster, near London, at which King William and Archbishop Lanfranc presided. The assembly declared the Saxon prelate wholly incapable of exercising the episcopal functions in England, seeing, says the sentence, that he could not speak French. By virtue of this solemn decree, the condemned was ordered to surrender his ring and pastoral staff. That moment the soul of the peaceful Wulfstan was seized with the same indignation, which formerly had inflamed that of the peaceful Alfred, when he, in his turn, fell under the lash of the Conquest. Wulfstan rose, and holding his staff in his hand, walked straight to the tomb of King Edward, who was interred in the church at Westminster; there he stopped, and addressing the deceased in the English tongue, 'Edward,' said he, 'from thee I received this staff; to thee I return and confide it.' Then turning to the Normans, 'I will not surrender to you what you did not give me; I give it to one who is better than you ; take it from me if you dare.' As he uttered these last words, the Saxon struck the tombstone forcibly with the point of the staff. This energetic action astonished the assembly ; and yielding to an impression of surprise, or to some superstitious dread, they did not repeat their demand, but left the last English bishop in possession of his staff and his office. The popular imagination transformed this event into a prodigy ; and the news was spread that Wulfstan's pastoral staff, when it struck the stone, had entered it deeply, as if it had been soft earth, and that no one could draw it out but the Saxon himself, when the foreign judges had reversed their own sentence. When Wulfstan was dead, and a canon of Bayeux named Samson, had succeeded him in the episcopacy of Worcester, the native English bestowed on him the titles of '*holy and blessed.*' This was the lot of almost all men of any eminence who had suffered for their resistance to the power founded upon the Conquest[4]."

No. 108, an archbishop in full pontificals, his right in benediction, and his left on his knee, and presiding over the Conqueror, is undoubtedly Aldred, archbishop of York, who crowned the Conqueror at Christmas, 1066. "The archbishop of Canterbury, Stigand, who had taken the oath of peace to the Conqueror, in his camp at Berkhamstead, was invited to come and lay his hands upon him, and place the crown on his head, according to the ancient custom of the church of the Western Monastery, (in Saxon, *Westmynster,*) near London. Stigand refused to go and give his benediction to a man who was stained with human blood, and an invader of the rights of others. But Aldred, archbishop of York, being (say the old historians) more circumspect and better advised, and comprehending that it was necessary to conform to the times, and not to go against the order of God, who raises up powers, consented to perform this office for the menacing foreigner."

[4] Thierry's Norman Conquest, vol. ii. p. 93.

Three years after, in 1069, at the siege of York, the Saxon archbishop experienced the ingratitude and contempt of the Conqueror.   The provisions which he had sent for from his own lands were seized at the gate by the Norman men-at-arms, and deposited in the royal magazines.   "When the pontiff, who had been friendly to the Conquest, found himself injured by the Conquest, there arose in his inmost soul an indignation which his calm, and above all prudent spirit, had never felt before.   Aldred immediately departed for the Conqueror's quarters, and presented himself before him in pontifical habits, with his pastoral staff in his hand.   William rose to offer him, according to the custom of the time, the kiss of peace; but the Saxon prelate kept aloof, and said, 'Hear me, King William.   Thou wert a foreigner, nevertheless it being the will of God to chastise our nation, thou obtainedst at the cost of much blood the kingdom of England.   I then anointed thee king; I crowned thee; I blessed thee with my own hand; but now I curse thee and thy race; because thou hast deserved it, because thou art the persecutor of God's Church, and the oppressor of its ministers.'   A year afterwards, when the Saxons, having rallied once more, were advancing to attack the town of York, Aldred's languor and chagrin were redoubled; and as if he feared death less than the presence of the men who had remained faithful to their country, he prayed God, (say the chroniclers,) to withdraw him from this world, that he might not behold the total ruin of his native land, and the destruction of His Church*."

East of Archbishop Aldred, No. 109, is a youthful palmer, in his left is his pilgrim's hat and staff.   This can be no other than Edgar, the nephew of Edward the Confessor, the last remaining scion of the Saxon stock, in whom the affection of the nations was fondly fixed: "He was young and handsome," say the Saxon annals, "and was descended from the true race, the best race of the country."

"Their beste kund that Engelande hadde to be kynge[f]."

He was regarded as the hope of England, and more than once espoused by the people in their insurrections as king; popular songs were sung, in which he

---

* Thierry's Norman Conquest, vol. i. p. 374.
[f] Robert of Gloucester's Chronicle, p. 377.

was styled

Edgar Ethelinge,
Engelande's dareling.

The policy of William induced him to pardon his offences; which he might
well do, for he was a man of no talent; he made him a liberal allowance, and
retained him in his court many years. "He silently sunk," says Malmesbury,
"into contempt, through his indolence, or, more mildly speaking, through his simplicity." In succeeding times he went to Jerusalem with Robert, the son of Godwin, a most valiant knight (who stands next him, No. 110, in a hauberk, and with
a kite-shaped shield); "this was the time the Turks besieged King Baldwin at
Rama;" who, unable to endure the difficulties of a siege, rushed through the
midst of the enemy, by the assistance of Robert alone, who preceded him, and
hewed down the Turks on either hand with his drawn sword. At length over-
powered, and cast into chains, taken thence to Babylon, as they report, where he
refused to deny Christ, he was placed as a mark in the middle of the market-place,
and, being transfixed with darts, died a martyr.

"Edgar having lost his companion, returned to England, where, as I have
before observed, he now grows old (A.D. 1145) in the country, in privacy and
quiet[e]."

No. 111, a warlike figure, in a very singular costume, a hauberk covers the
body and legs, which are spurred. In front is a kite-shaped shield, on the head is
a kind of turban, and round the waist is a frock or coat terminating in straps.

The oriental character of this dress, and the position immediately above the
Plantagenet family, lead to the conclusion that this is no other than Fulco, earl of
Anjou, the progenitor of that illustrious family, who married the daughter of Baldwin II., by which alliance he became king of Jerusalem in 1131, where he reigned
till 1144. "His panegyrist, the archbishop of Tyre, has dignified him with
the different virtues of a hero and a saint, and then mixing a description of
his mental with his personal qualities, he says, the king had red hair, but
that, contrary to the usual case of such persons, he was kind, affable, and com-
passionate[h]."

[e] Malmesbury, p. 326.
[h] Mill's Crusades, vol. i. p. 277.

No. 112, a warlike figure, clad in the hauberk, a square-topped helmet entirely covering the face, his legs clothed with high boots, and having a kite-shaped shield before him, in the centre of which is a round boss. This may be Robert of Normandy, the father of the Conqueror, the progenitor of the Norman line, and is presented beside the progenitor of the Plantagenet.

"Robert, second son of Richard the Second, after he had with great glory, held the dutchy of Normandy for seven years, resolved on a pilgrimage to Jerusalem. He had at that time (1031) a son seven years old, born of a concubine, whose beauty he had accidentally beheld as she was dancing; and had become so smitten with it, as to form a connexion with her; after which he loved her exclusively, and for some time regarded her as his wife. He had by her this boy, named after his great great grandfather William, whose future glory was portended to his mother by a dream; wherein she imagined her intestines were drawn out, and extended over the whole of Normandy and England; and at the very moment also, when the infant burst into life and touched the ground, he filled both hands with rushes strewed upon the floor, firmly grasping what he had taken up. This prodigy was joyfully witnessed by the gossiping women; and the midwife hailed the propitious omen, declaring that the boy would be a king. Every provision being made for the expedition to Jerusalem, the chiefs were summoned to a council at Fecamp, where, at his father's command, all swore fealty to William. This fidelity continued till the report of Robert's death[1]."

No. 113, an ecclesiastic enthroned in the eastern buttress, immediately above the statue of Henry Beauclerc. It has no mitre; in his left is a large purse, in his right a rescript or charter. This can be no other than the famous Roger of Salisbury, the favourite of Henry, the keeper of his conscience and his chancellor.

"Roger had a church at Caen, at the time that Henry was serving under his brother William; passing that way, he entered in and requested the priest to say mass. Roger began immediately, and got through his task so quickly, that the prince's attendants unanimously declared, no man so fit for chaplain to men of their profession. And when the royal youth said, ' Follow me,' he adhered as

---

[1] Malmesbury, b. iii. c. 1.

closely to him as Peter did to his heavenly Lord uttering a similar command; for Peter, leaving his vessel, followed the King of kings; he, leaving his church, followed the prince: and, appointed chaplain to himself and his troops, became a 'blind guide to the blind[k].'"

"King Henry had among his councillors," says Malmesbury, "Roger of Salisbury, on whose advice he principally relied. For before his accession, he had made him regulator of his household; and, on becoming king, having had proof of his abilities, appointed him first, chancellor, and then a bishop. He committed to his care the administration of the whole kingdom, whether he might be himself resident in England, or absent in Normandy. The bishop refused to embroil himself in cares of such magnitude, until the three archbishops, Anselm, Ralph, William, and lastly, the pope, enjoined him the duty of obedience. He conducted himself with so much integrity and diligence, that not a spark of envy was kindled against him. He was a prelate of a great mind, and spared no expense in completing his designs, especially in buildings; which may be seen in other places, but more particularly at Salisbury and at Malmsbury; for there he erected extensive edifices, at vast cost, and with surpassing beauty; the courses of stone being so correctly laid, that the joint deceives the eye, and leads it to imagine that the whole wall is composed of a single block. He built anew the church of Salisbury, and beautified it in such a manner, that it yields to none in England, but surpasses many; so that he had just cause to say, 'Lord, I have loved the glory of Thy house[l].'"

The niches 114 and 115 are empty.

No. 116, a graceful female habited as a nun, I have not ventured to name.

No. 117. Empty.

No. 118. A small figure, holding two babes in his arms, and his legs immersed in water, this may possibly indicate St. Nicholas, patron of baptism; his position opposite the north porch, in which that ceremony is said to have been performed, has suggested this interpretation.

[k] G. Neubrig. i. 6.
[l] Malmesbury, b. v. p. 203.

P

No. 119, a female in a religious habit, veiled and carrying a book in her left hand. This statue must also be a subject of conjecture, and I have not ventured to name it.

Thus have we terminated the series of the fourth and fifth tiers of the north and east sides of the western front of the Cathedral.

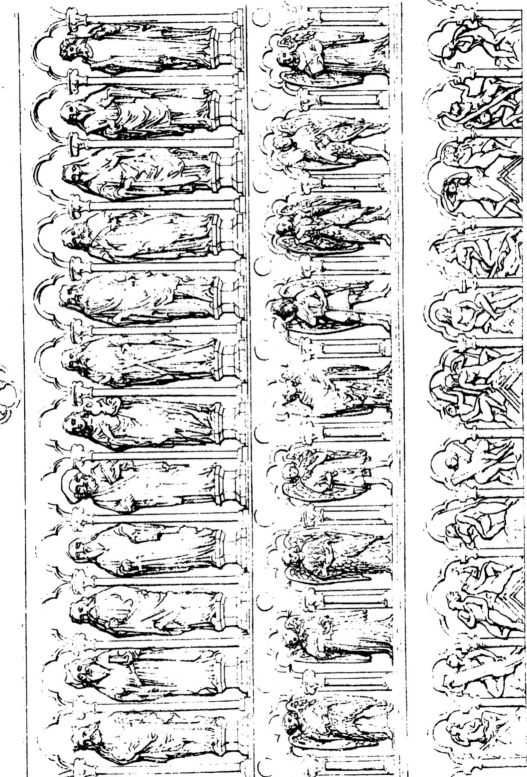

SIXTH TIER.

THE great doctrine of the Resurrection is expressed in this tier in the most awful and affecting manner; ninety-two niches of various dimensions, and containing from one to four figures in each, form the crowning feature or cornice, and surround the north and south towers, and the west front. Immediately above the fourth and fifth tiers, illustrating the most conspicuous of mankind in the lords spiritual and temporal of these realms, these are aptly placed; as signifying the consummation of all things, and that judgment-day, for which all that are on earth must be prepared. And as the climax to the histories explained in the five preceding tiers, no position can be more appropriate or happily chosen.

The composition is thus complete, and the spiritual history of mankind is traced from the reception of the Gospel in the first, the joy that it promises in the second, the history of its revelation in the third; the lords spiritual and temporal, under whom it has been administered to these countries in the fourth and fifth; and finally, the retribution on the judgment-day in the sixth. At the sound of the trump they emerge from their tombs in every variety[a] of expression of joy or despair; some hail the sound full of hope and expectation, some tear their hair, and seem to call upon the rocks to cover them. All are naked and in the common category of mankind, but their rank and sex and professions, and their more serious responsibilities, are often signified by some single symbol; thus kings and bishops, though deprived of all other paraphernalia, have still their crowns and mitres on their heads: and the sculptor appears sometimes to anticipate in these groups, the sentence deserved by the princes below them. Thus over the Conqueror,

---

[a] Carter in his description of the sculptures of Wells (p. 115) has hastily overlooked the merits of these compositions, and this peculiarity more particularly. "On a fourth story," says he, "is a continued range of niches, filled with statues, rising out of the tombs and graves, supposed to represent the Resurrection. But as they are only a repetition of the same attitude, being naked, and of very indifferent workmanship, they are not judged necessary to be given."

a king, naked, but recognised by his crown, and a queen, burst from the earth in terror[b]. Above Alfred, a royal pair seem to hail the glad sound with joy[c].

Over the spiritual side we have a bishop, recognised by his mitre, and hiding his face with his two hands, in shame and despair. And on this side also more particularly, we distinguish some of the fair sex, in lovely proportions, and in those modest and natural attitudes, which such a moment would suggest; placed over the professors of celibacy, they seem to point sarcastically at those affections which their vows have reprobated as sins.

In the figures (not less than one hundred and fifty) composing these groups,

[b] It is extremely interesting to trace from the immortal Alfred's works, the very images which seem to have inspired the sculptor of Wells.

"Hear now" (says he, in his translations of Boetius,) " a discourse on proud and unrighteous kings. We see them sitting on the highest high seats; they shine in garments of many kinds, and are with a great company of thegns standing about them; who are adorned with belts and golden-hilted swords, and manifold warlike appendages. They threaten all mankind with their majesty; and of those they govern, they care neither for friend or foe, no more than a maddened hound. They are very incomprehensively puffed up in their minds from their immoderate power. But if *men should divest them of their clothes*, and withdraw from them their retinue and power, then might you see that they are very like some of their thegns that serve them, except that they be worse."—Turner's Anglo-Saxons, vol. xi. p. 53. "Again, if you saw among mice, one claiming a right to himself, and power over the rest, to what a horse-laugh would you be moved? But if you look at the body, what can you find weaker than man, whom a bite of his flesh or of something within, secretly creeping, destroys?"—Turner's Anglo-Saxons, vol. xi. p. 34.

[c] We may reasonably attribute these figures to Alfred and his beloved Ethelsuitha, to whom he is supposed to refer, especially in his translations of Boetius. The philosopher is called upon to remember that in the midst of his misfortunes, he had comfort yet left him,—a celebrated father-in-law, his wife, and children, which Alfred expands, according to the italics, in the following passage, dwelling with manifest delight on the "vivit tibi" of Boetius, and dilating upon the thought as if with fond recollections of the conduct of his own wife, who shared his adversity with him. "Liveth not thy wife also! she is exceedingly prudent, and very modest. She has excelled all other women in purity. I may, in a few words, express all her merit: this is that in all her manners she is like her father, she lives now for thee, *thee alone; hence she loves nought else but thee. She has enough of every good in this present life, but she has despised all for thee alone; she has shunned it all because only she has not thee also; this one thing is now wanting to her*; thine absence makes her think that all which she possesses is nothing. Hence for thy love, she is wasting, and full nigh dead with tears and sorrow." Turner's Anglo-Saxons, vol. xi. p. 25. For the history of sculpture, it is worthy of remark, that the practice, peculiarly Christian, and exhibited in succeeding periods, of representing the husband and wife prostrate and in prayer, in monumental sculpture, may find its earliest traces in these resurrections of Wells.

we discover a continual variety, often of admirable expressions, as the selection in the annexed lithograph will explain[d].

The eye invited to trace them in succession, as seen against the moving sky, and raised in the building so far above sublunary things, imparts by degrees to the contemplation all the awfulness of the scene. And the solemnity of the doctrine is impressed on the sensitive spectator by the repetition of so many expressions of terror, hope, and despair, in such copiousness and variety.

This effect is greatly enhanced by the justness and propriety of the sentiments and actions throughout, nor do we discover here any of those disgusting and puerile types, which commonly illustrate the Judgment in similar representations. The agency of devils, pitchforks, serpents, and hell-fire, scales and weighing of souls, with all the trivial accompaniments of the common modes of picturing this awful moment, are nowhere traced in these sculptures. The distinctions given to the sexes and professions, the tombstones which they heave up, and their appropriate attitudes, are the only materials which the sculptor has called into use for the carrying out of his difficult task. And if we compare this Judgment with those at Orviedo[e] by Nicola Pisano, and the cathedrals of France[f], as well as

---

[d] In the lithograph, the most remarkable groups have been placed in the niches, under the angels, and brought together from various parts to illustrate their quality and merit. In the plate of the whole front, they are represented precisely as they are, though on a small scale.

[e] See Histoire de l'Art par les Monuments; in plate xxxii. fig. iv., is a specimen, also at Orviedo, very much resembling the sculptures of Wells.—Vol. iii. pl. xxxiii. fig. 8.

[f] In Mons. Gilbert's description of the cathedral of Amiens, we have the following judgment on the large tympanum occupying the arch over the central door.

"Such pictures generally formed part of the decoration of the porches of churches in the twelfth and thirteenth centuries, in order to render, in a more striking manner, to the eyes of the people, the dogma of the Resurrection, and to guard them against the heresies which arose at that time.

This great bas relief is subdivided into four tiers. In the middle of the first is placed St. Michael, the arbiter of human destinies, weighing, in a figurative sense, the souls of mortals; the balance which he held suspended, being mutilated, as also the arm of the archangel, we can see only one of the basins, that which contains the lamb without spot; the other which contained the condemned has been destroyed. It was a striking allegory addressed to Christians, that we can arrive at the dwelling of the blessed, only by good actions, and these were weighed in the balance of equity. By the right foot of the archangel, the vestments of a small statue are distinguishable, which has unfortunately been broken away. Near the left foot is a little devil, which has been preserved; from

in our own country, we shall readily acknowledge the superior taste of Bishop
Trotman, and his able coadjutors.

The great Christian lesson taught by the scenes of the Resurrection and the
Judgment, the awakening of the conscience, and the conviction of responsibility,
were ever the theme of the early writers and artists.   Alfred's expansion of Boetius
is so beautiful and apt, and so apparently the guide and inspiration of the sculptor
of Wells, that its insertion here may be permitted.

"Thou, O Lord," says the royal translator, "wilt grant the soul a dwelling in the
heavens, and wilt endow it there with worthy gifts, to every one according to their desert.
Thou wilt make it to shine very bright, and yet with brightness very various; some more
splendidly, some less bright, as the stars are, each according to his earning.

each side the dead arise from their tombs.   The sculptor, ignorant of the laws of perspective, and
wishing to present a vast field of the dead, has placed them in two ranks of equal heights.

In the second tier, the separation of the elect and the rejected takes place.   The first, clothed
in robes, direct themselves towards paradise, which is at the extremity of this division.   Three
angels stand at the entrance to receive them.   The most elevated places a crown on the head of the
first of the elect, another holds a censer, another a candlestick.   These last figures being in smaller
proportions than the rest, can only be distinguished by the aid of a glass.

A demon with a monkey's head, drives the naked condemned towards the opposite side; one of
these carries a large purse suspended round his neck, another has a crown upon his head, a third
has a crosier in his hand.   These are seized by a demon in the jaws of an enormous dragon.
The terrace which supports these figures is ornamented with oak and thistle, on the condemned side,
and the vine on that of the elect.   And underneath the terrace which supports the third tier,
angels are represented holding crowns over the elect, and chasing the condemned with flaming
swords.

In the centre of the third tier, the Son of Man appears, enthroned on the judgment-seat, to judge
the quick and dead.   His hands are elevated, and his head is supported on a nimbus ornamented
with a Greek cross.   This figure is extremely well draped: at his sides are two statues kneeling, and
suppliants having their hands joined; the one to the right, interceding with her Son, is the Mother of
the Saviour; behind her are two angels; the first standing and holding the symbol of redemption,
the other is kneeling, with his hands joined.   The figure kneeling, to the left of the Saviour, is
clothed in a hood, but without any other distinctive.   This personage appears to be *St. John the
Evangelist*, (says Monsr. Gilbert, and not St. John the Baptist, as is usual,) behind him an angel
standing, bears the nails of the Passion; lastly, another angel is in the attitude of the one at the
other extremity, namely, kneeling.

In the fourth tier over the Saviour, the eternal Father is represented raising His arms, and the
head surrounded with the mystic Triune; at His feet are two angels; the one to the right presents
to the spectator a sun surrounded with rays, the one to the left holds the moon in crescent."—
Description Historique de l'Eg. Cath. de Notre Dame d'Amiens, par M. Gilbert, 1833.

"Thou, O Lord, gatherest the heaven-like souls, and the earth-like bodies; and Thou minglest them in this world, so that they come hither from Thee, and to Thee again from hence aspire. Thou hast filled the earth with animals of various kinds, and Thou sowed it with different seeds of trees and herbs.

"Grant now, O Lord, to our minds that they may ascend to Thee from the difficulties of this world; that from the occupations here, they may come to Thee. With the opened eyes of our mind may we behold the noble fountain of all good. Thou art this! give us then a healthy sight to our understanding, that we may fasten it upon Thee. Drive away this mist that now hangs before our mental vision, and enlighten our eyes with Thy light. For Thou art the brightness of the true light: Thou art the soft rest of the just. Thou causest them to see it; Thou art the beginning of all things and their end. Thou supportest all things without fatigue. Thou art the path and the leader, and the place to which the path conducts. All men tend to Thee."—Turner's Anglo-Saxons, vol. ii. p. 62.

SEVENTH TIER.

It has already been remarked that while six of the tiers of sculpture relate to the history of the faith, the lives and acts of the believers, and their final resurrection to give account of their works done in the flesh in the last day, the three last refer to the Judgment, when " the Son of Man shall come in the glory of His Father with His angels, and then He shall reward every man according to his works."

Thus we have the angels in the seventh, the Apostles in the eighth, and the Saviour in the ninth tier, completing that awful tribunal before which all mortals will have to appear.

Of the angelic host in the seventh tier, nine, special and peculiar, occupy the central space between the buttresses ; in which buttresses, three others on either side, appear (from one still remaining) to have contained angels of an inferior order, who sound the trump. It is remarkable that these nine divisions have no correspondence with the twelve above them containing the Apostles.

Of this mystical number, or of the mysterious nature of the immaterial beings constituting the hierarchy of heaven, it is not permitted to a layman to speak ; nor is it necessary here to do so ; our observations therefore will be confined to the sculptures themselves, and such notices as obviously apply to the usage in similar works, and according to the received forms of Church history.

The invocation of the nine angels occurs constantly in the dedication of lands to sacred purposes, so early as the seventh century[a]; and it is possible that their

---

[a] Ethelred, king of the Mercians, in dedicating certain lands to Malmesbury abbey in 681, thus invokes the nine angels. Ang. Sax., pars ii. p. 10. " Si quis vero hanc donationem augere et amplificare voluerit ; augeat Dominus partem ejus in libro vitæ. Quod si quis tyrannica potestate fretus demere sategerit ; sciat coram Christo novemque angelorum ordinibus rationem redditurum." In 688, Kentwine, king of the West Saxons, conveys lands to Malmesbury, under the same terms. See Ang. Sax., pars ii. p. 11. " Si quis vero contra hanc munificentiam tyrannica potestate inflatus,

introduction here may, besides their appropriate presence in the Judgment-day, have reference to the possessions of the church of Wells, held under similar titles; the infringement of which the ecclesiastics were always jealous and active in deprecating, under the most solemn penalties and imprecations.

We discern four archangels clothed with four wings, and five having two only: the distinction of their particular characters, attitude, dress, and attributes, will materially assist the learned in the explanation of Bishop Trotman's reasons and authorities; and their ninefold order (according to Bishop Andrewes [b]) may perhaps be distinguished amongst these significant and beautiful figures. The careful consideration of them may be safely recommended as fraught with most interesting ecclesiastical matter [c].

The first, the northernmost figure, is an archangel having four wings, and apparently holding a book in his hands.

The second, an angel, holds two crowns.

The third, an archangel having four wings, holds a bowl or censer in his hands, his wavy garment seeming to convey the idea of the vapour of incense rising from it.

The fourth angel, having a short frock-like garment, exposing his legs, and of young and active appearance, holds in his right a formidable sword.

The fifth, the central figure draped in ample and majestic robes, appears to raise his right in benediction.

The sixth, a striking warlike figure, armed from head to foot, holding a spear, and in the menacing attitude of a warrior.

---

venire temptaverit, sciat se obstaculum iræ Dei incurrere, et in ultimo examine coram Christo et angelis ejus rationem reddere."

In 704 Ina is equally solemn in the terms of his gifts to Malmesbury, and it is highly probable that those conferred upon Wells by this pious and magnificent prince, were confirmed by the same expressions, in deeds which the riots of the seventeenth century may have destroyed. He says,— " Si quis vero contra hujus decreti syngrapham venire temptaverit, Sciat se coram Christo novemque angelorum ordinibus in tremendo examine rationem redditurum."—Ang. Sac., pars ii. p. 22.

[b] Angels,	Thrones,	Authorities,
Archangels,	Dominions,	Cherubim,
Powers,	Principalities,	Seraphim.

[c] The nine angels appear again in the east window of the Lady-Chapel of this Cathedral.

Q

The seventh, an archangel with four wings, in a beautiful expression, raising his two hands in adoration.

The eighth, also an archangel, with four wings, holding a flail or flabellum in his right.

The ninth, an angel draped, and holding a book in his hands.

Time has sadly mutilated these figures, but their characteristic symbols, and the beauty of their design, well deserve the research, the comparison, and the illustration which the learned may bring to bear on these venerable remains [d].

[d] The following note on this subject, given at my request by my late learned and most lamented friend, the Rev. T. S. Hughes, cannot fail to be highly acceptable in this place.

ANGELS.

These were anciently denominated seraphim, or cherubim. The word seraphim is derived from *saraph* שָׂרַף denoting a fiery and shining substance. See Dan. x. 6 ; Ps. civ. 4 ; Isa. vi. 1, 2 ; Matt. xxviii. 3, &c., and especially Heb. i. 7. Buxtorf, in voce שְׂרָפִים observes, " Est seraphim angelorum nomen, qui a claritate et aspectus splendore quasi flammantes et ignei usi sunt." They seem to have been denominated *cherubim*, when they were represented under a human figure, from the Chaldaic word *cherub*, which signifies *a boy*. See Buxtorf, Lex. Talm., in voce. Moses mentions them under this name when they were sent to guard the tree of life, Gen. iii. 24. See also Exod. xxv., where they were placed with extended wings over the mercy-seat. They were called angels from the Greek word ΑΓΓΕΛΟΣ, a messenger or minister, being employed as messengers or ministers of God to men. See the SS. passim. The Bible gives no account of their creation, though St. Peter describes them as of a higher order of beings than man. (2 Pet. ii. 11.) And St. Paul seems to designate certain classes or generations among these celestials themselves in Col. i. 16.

ARCHANGELS.

Some uncertainty exists respecting the number of these. They are generally reckoned four : Michael, who stood at God's throne, on His right hand, towards the south, before the standard of Reuben ; Uriel, who stood at His left, towards the north, before the standard of Dan ; Gabriel, in front, towards the east, before the standard of Juda ; and Raphael, behind the throne, before the standard of Ephraim. (See Buxtorf's Lex. Talmud.) Michael signified a leader, who with his angels is said to have fought against the dragon, Rev. xii. 7 ; see also Jude 9. Gabriel is mentioned by St. Luke as sent to the Virgin, and who announced himself as " Gabriel who stand in the presence of God." Raphael and Uriel are only noticed in the apocryphal books of Tobit and 2 Esdras respectively ; the latter is called an *archangel* in 2 Esdras iv. 36. That our own Church considers Michael the chief of all the angelic hosts, appears from the festival which bears his name, that of " St. Michael and all angels." Yet as if in contradiction to this number of four principal angels, Raphael is introduced in Tobit xii. 15. as saying, " I am Raphael, one of the seven holy

The holes immediately under these figures, and which are conspicuous in the building, deserve notice. They may be supposed (amongst other suggestions) to have been made to receive the scaffolding, (technically termed putlocks,) from which these works may have been carved or finished *in situ*.

angels which present the prayers of the saints, and which go in and out before the glory of the Holy One." And though Arnald, in his Commentary, observes that Munster's Hebrew copy makes no mention of seven angels, and that some interpreters take seven for an *indefinite* number, yet he goes on to say "the Jews had an ancient tradition that there are seven principal angels which minister before God's throne, and are therefore called archangels," quoting Clemens Alex. as saying ἑπτὰ μέν εἰσιν οἱ τὴν μεγίστην δύναμιν ἔχοντες, πρωτόγονοι ἀγγέλων ἄρχοντες : to confirm which he adduces Rev. i. 4, iv. 5, and v. 6 ; especially vii. 2, " I saw the seven angels which stood before God," &c. See also Zachariah iv. 2, 10. May we not say that originally there were more than seven, since Satan or Lucifer, who fell from heaven, was evidently a prince or leader of the highest rank ? That the angelic beings were very numerous appears from the number that fell with him ; also from our Saviour's words, Matt. xxvi. 53. The Jews considered that angels were present with them in their synagogues ; especially *three*, who carried their prayers to the throne of God. These were named *Achtariel, Metatron,* and *Sandalphon.* See Eisenmenger, *Judaismo detecto,* pars ii. cap. vii. p. 393. Buxtorf (Lex. Talm.) gives several other names, as *Duma,* the angel "presiding over the last hour of mortals ;" *Juhach,* " a protector of men in journeys ;" *Lajelah,* " presiding over conception," &c. &c. I omit much more which I have collected on this subject ; but I may as well observe that the Teraphim, as well as the Urim and Thummim, mentioned in Scripture, are referred by learned men to the nature and ministry of the angelic host. See Spencer, de Urim and Thummim, &c.

EIGHTH TIER.

THE twelve Apostles in colossal dimensions appear at the foot of the seat of judgment in the utmost dignity; each stands upon a separate pedestal, or throne, as "judging the twelve tribes of Israel," with a canopy above, supported on columns.

As Nazarenes, their hair and beard are long, the costume full, majestical, and various; the writers are distinguished by books in their hands, and the usual symbols are apparent. The characteristics of these sculptures, individuality and variety of physiognomy, beard and hair, costume and attitude, are not less remarkable here than elsewhere. They are extremely well composed, and appear to be derived from received types, which subsequent times have not improved.

The first is undoubtedly St. Peter, he holds a globe in his right, (apparently) the keys in his left, and he has a crown on his head*,—symbols unusual even to the prince of Apostles, and which exhibit the zeal of the bishop, as partizan of the Romish Church, in a very remarkable manner.

The second, differing in costume and in the form of the beard and head, is apparently Matthew, holding his Gospel in his left.

The third holds in his right something which may be supposed to be a loaf, and may designate St. Philip. This symbol of the bread of life, as well as of the material bread which this Apostle administered more especially, is not unusual in

---

* Durandus asserts that " the diverse histories of the Old and New Testaments may be represented after the fancy of the painter, for

Pictoribus atque poetis
Quodlibet addendi semper fuit æqua potestas.

" A false reading of course," say his worthy translators, Messrs. Neale and Webb, " but not without its appropriate sense, the power of adding any ornamental circumstance to the main subject."

the English monasteries, probably as designating their hospitality as well as their sacred ministration.

The fourth holds a sword in his right, and a book in his left. This may possibly signify St. Jude.

The fifth is undoubtedly St. James; he holds his Epistle in his left, and wears his hat and staff.

The sixth is the beloved Apostle John, youthful, with flowing hair; he holds a vase in his left.

The seventh is St. Andrew, with his cross upon his breast. It is remarkable that this Apostle, to whom the church itself is dedicated, is placed on the south, or spiritual side of the centre, as giving more sanctity to the patron saint of Wells. This position as nearest to our Lord may possibly allude to the fact that the festival of St. Andrew immediately precedes the season of Advent.

The eighth has no symbol by which he may be clearly designated.

The ninth is undoubtedly St. Bartholomew, who holds in his left the instrument of his martyrdom, and in his right his own skin.

The tenth is St. James the Less, holding in his right the Fuller's club, the instrument of his martyrdom.

The eleventh is not recognisable by any symbol, save the book which he holds in his right, and may therefore be intended for St. Paul.

The twelfth having a spear in his left, may be St. Thomas, to whom this symbol, as the instrument of his martyrdom, is commonly attributed.

As a new version of the apostolic figures, this series of the sculptor of Wells, directed as it was by the learned Bishop Trotman, and in the vicinity of Glastonbury, the scene, according to tradition, of the early mission to this country of some of the Apostles themselves, deserves the particular attention of the learned in this department.

NINTH TIER.

In this tier we have three niches, in the central one of which only the knees and feet of the Saviour are preserved in excellent position and drapery.

The niches on either side undoubtedly contained, according to the universal practice of the day, the figures of the Virgin in intercession to the right, and of John the Baptist on the left.

CATALOGUE OF THE FIGURES IN THE FOURTH AND FIFTH TIERS OF THE NORTH TOWER, ON THE NORTH AND ON THE EAST SIDE.

In the north we have two prominent buttresses, and one on the east; upon which, as in the west, the most conspicuous personages of the history of the Norman and Plantagenet dynasties are enthroned in large statues, while the rest are standing and in smaller dimension.

On the first is Edward the Confessor, and above him Robert of Jumièges, the Norman archbishop of Canterbury, (unlike the others and as if in penance,) standing; in mean proportions both of figure and of mitre.

On the second William the Conqueror, and above him enthroned is Aldred, archbishop of York, who crowned him.

On the third towards the east, Henry I., and above him his chancellor and obsequious servant, Roger of Salisbury.

The propriety of this selection of personages for these eminent positions cannot be disapproved.

Proceeding then with our series of kings in the fourth tier,

No. 61 is Edward the Confessor, already described; as also his successor Harold, No. 60, in the west front.

No. 69, enthroned on the second buttress, advancing his arms upon his knees, in most imposing attitude and expression of countenance, remarkably preserved, is the dire conqueror of England; if the sculptor has been successful in pourtraying the impassible and benignant Edward the Confessor, he has been no less so in the effigies of the resolute William, characterizing in the liveliest manner the phrase of Horace,

"Impiger, iracundus, inexorabilis, acer."

However imperfect in academic qualities, this figure may challenge any other for its formidable and effective expression.

The character given in the Saxon Chronicle (189, 191) cannot but be service-able in the appreciation of these sculptures and the spirit of the times.

" If any man wish to know what manner of man he was, or what worship he had, or of how many lands he were the lord, we will describe him as we have known him, for we looked on him and some while lived in his herd. King William was a very wise man and very rich, more worshipful and strong than any of his foregangers. He was mild to good men who loved God, and stark beyond all bounds to those who withsaid his will. On the very stede, where God gave him to win England, he reared a noble monastery and set monks therein and endowed it well. He was very worshipful. Thrice he bore his king-helmet every year, when he was in England: at Easter he bore it at Winchester, at Pentecost at Westminster, and in midwinter at Gloucester. And then were with him all the rich men of England. Archbishops and diocesan bishops, abbots and earls, thanes and knights. Moreover he was a very stark man and very savage, so that no man durst do any thing against his will. He had earls in his bonds, who had done against his will : bishops he set off their bishoprics ; abbots off their abbotaces ; and thanes in prison ; and at last he did not spare his own brother Odo ; him he set in prison. Yet among other things we must not forget the good frith which he made in this land, so that a man that was good for aught, might travel over the kingdom with his bosom full of gold, without molestation ; and no man durst slay another man, though he has suffered never so mickle evil from the other. He ruled over all England, and by his cunning he was so thoroughly acquainted with it, that there is not a hide of land of which he did not know, both who had it and what was its worth : and that he set down in his writings. Wales was under his weald, and therein he wrought castles, and he wielded the Isle of Man withal. Moreover he subdued Scotland by his mickle strength, Normandy was his by kin, and over the Earldom called Mans he ruled, and if he might have lived yet two years, he would have won Ireland by the fame of his power and without an armament. Yet truly in his time men had mickle suffering, and very many hardships. Castles he caused to be wrought and poor men to be oppressed. He was so very stark ; he took from his subjects many marks of gold, and many hundred pounds of silver, and that he took, some by right and some by mickle might, for very little withal. He had fallen into avarice, and greediness he loved withal. He let his lands as dear as he could, then came some other hand and bid more than the first had given, and the king let to him who bade more; then came a third and bid more yet, and the king let it into the hands of him who bade most. Nor did he reck how sinfully his reeves got money of poor men, or how many unlawful things they did, for the more men talked of right law the more they did against the law. He also set many deer-friths; and he made laws therewith, that whosoever should slay hart or hind, him man should blind. As he forbad the slaying of harts, so he did of boars; so much he loved the high deer as if he had been their father: he also decreed about hares that they should go free. His rich men moaned and the poor murmured: but he was so hard that he recked not the hatred of them all; for it was need they should follow the king's will withal, if they wished to live, or to have lands or goods, or his favour. Alas, that any man should be so moody, and should so puff himself up, and think himself above all other men. May Almighty God have mercy on his soul, and grant him forgiveness of his sins."

No. 62, to the right of the Confessor, is a prince in a melancholy expression of countenance, whom I presume to be Richard, the eldest son of the Conqueror.

" Richard afforded his noble father hopes of his future greatness; a fine youth and of aspiring disposition, considering his age; but an untimely death quickly withered the bud of this promising flower. They relate, that while hunting deer in the new forest, he contracted a disorder from a stream of infected air. This is the place which William, his father, desolating the towns and destroying the churches for more than thirty miles, had appropriated for the nurture and refuge of wild beasts; a dreadful spectacle indeed, that where, before, had existed human intercourse and the worship of God, there, deer and goats and other animals of that kind should now range unrestrained; and these not subject to the general service of mankind. Hence it is truly asserted, that in this very forest, William his son, and his grandson Richard, son of Robert, earl of Normandy, by the severe judgment of God, met their deaths; one by a wound in the breast by an arrow, the other by a broken neck; or as some say, from being suspended by the jaws on the branch of a tree, as his horse passed beneath it ª."

No. 63, another prince with a cap on the side of his head, his left raised to

ª See Malmesbury, p. 348.

R

his necklace in the conventional attitude, and with his right lifting his cloak and discovering his leg, booted with a short hose of remarkable form, displaying beyond all equivocation, and with the accustomed clearness of demonstration, the unfortunate prince Robert, *courthose*, the duke of Normandy.

No. 64, a crowned and kingly statue, holding his ample mantle in his left, while his right is raised, in the conventional position, to his neck, is William Rufus. Malmesbury's description of the death and the person of this monarch, are so singularly graphic, so illustrative of the style, both in art and in writing, of that day, that its insertion here may be permitted.

" He was, when abroad, and in public assemblies, of supercilious look, darting his threatening look on the bye-stander ; and with assumed severity and ferocious voice assailing such as conversed with him.   From apprehension of poverty and of the treachery of others, as may be conjectured, he was too much given to lucre and to cruelty ; at home and at table with his intimate companions, he gave loose to levity and to mirth.   He was a most facetious railer at any thing he himself had done amiss, in order that he might thus do away obloquy and make it matter of jest.

" Should any one, however, be desirous to know the make of his person, he is to understand that he was well set ; his complexion florid, his hair yellow ; of open countenance ; different coloured eyes, varying with certain glittering coloured specks ; of astonishing strength though not very tall, and his belly rather project-ing ; of no eloquence, but remarkable for an hesitation of speech, especially when angry.   Many sudden and sorrowful accidents happened in his time, which I shall arrange singly according to the years of his reign ; chiefly vouching for their truth on the credit of the Chronicle."

The description of his death is a masterpiece of recital.

" The sun was now declining, when the king, drawing his bow and letting fly an arrow, slightly wounded a stag which passed before him ; and keenly gazing, followed it, still running, a long time with his eyes, holding up his hand to keep off the power of the sun's rays ; at this instant Walter, conceiving a noble exploit, which was, while the king's attention was otherwise occupied, to transfix another stag which by chance came near him, unknowingly and without power to prevent it, Oh gracious God ! pierced his breast with a fatal arrow.   On receiving the wound, the king uttered not a word; but breaking off the shaft of the weapon where it projected from his body, and then falling upon the ground, he accelerated his death! Walter immediately ran up, but as he found him senseless and speechless, he leaped swiftly upon his horse, and escaped by spurring him to his utmost speed[b]."

The successor of Rufus, Henry I., was entitled, by his meritorious reign during thirty-six years, and his pre-eminent love of literature, to the conspicuous place given to his statue on the eastern buttress, as already noted; the preference given to Henry 'Beauclerc' over the princes of the Plantagenet dynasty, then actually reigning, is to be noticed, as displaying the independence, and the love of justice in awarding honorary and historical record, by which Bishop Trotman was actuated. The king is crowned, in his right was a sceptre, his left imposingly advanced upon his knee, the left leg being raised on a footstool.

The next monarch in succession, though never crowned, was the Empress Matilda, (his daughter by the good Maude, the Saxon princess,) to whom he had been careful, before his death, to secure the throne by every possible precaution, in 1126. She had been married to Henry V., emperor of Germany, and their effigies, Nos. 65 and 66, in true conformity with the pompous spirit of these sculptures, are placed side by side. Both are crowned, in princely attitude, and are very elegant statues.

No. 67, a kingly and crowned figure, his left arm *a kimbo*, and his right raised in the conventional manner to his neck, is exceedingly descriptive of Margaret's rival, the handsome Stephen, the dandy of his day.

No. 68, a crowned and kingly statue, his right having held a sceptre and his left sustaining a very full mantle, is Henry II. A reign of thirty-four years, and so remarkable for power and wealth, and important events; and the first of the Plantagenet dynasty reigning during Trotman's episcopacy, is signalized by no other honours than this inconspicuous place. His long protracted contentions with the Church, and his martyrdom of Becket, are thus visited upon the able and powerful king.

No. 70, a prince crowned with a low diadem, his hand in his necklace, is the king's eldest son, who in Henry's anxiety about the succession was anointed and crowned

[b] Malmesbury, b. vi.

R 2

in his father's life-time at York in 1170, but who conspired against his father, and died of fever at Limoges.   "When his physicians acquainted him that they had no hopes of his recovery, his soul was seized with bitter remorse and anguish for his repeated rebellions against his indulgent parent, to whom he sent a message expressing his repentance and earnestly intreating a visit.   Henry, prevented from complying with his request by the representations of his friends, took a ring from his finger and sent it to his son as a mark of his forgiveness; the dying prince received it with much emotion, and pressing it to his lips, soon after expired on a heap of ashes, where he had commanded himself to be laid, with a halter about his neck, and in fearful agonies of mind[e]."

No. 71, a prince, headless, in the costume of the preceding, may be Geoffry, duke of Brittany, (the father of Prince Arthur, who was murdered by King John,) equally rebellious and hostile to his father, who died at Paris, 1186, in consequence of bruises received in a tournament.

No. 72, a staid queen holding a sceptre now broken in her left, her right apparently on a rosary or cross, and to the left of Henry I., can be no other than "Maude the good," daughter of Malcolm Canmore, king of Scotland, and niece to Edgar Atheling; by whose marriage the politic Norman king conciliated his Saxon subjects, 1101.   Her titles to our respect are cited in so characteristic a manner by Malmesbury, that the passage may be here inserted.

"She was educated at Romsey.   Satisfied with a child of either sex she ceased having issue, and enduring with complacency, when the king was elsewhere employed, the absence of the court, she continued many years at Westminster; yet was no part of royal magnificence wanting to her, but at all times crowds of visitants and talebearers were, in endless multitudes, entering and departing from her superb dwelling: for this the king's liberality commanded, this her own kindness and affability attracted.   She was singularly holy; by no means despicable in point of beauty; a rival of her mother's piety; clad in hair cloth beneath her royal habit, in Lent she trod the thresholds of the churches barefoot; nor was she disgusted at washing the feet of the diseased, handling their ulcers dropping with corruption, and, finally, pressing their hands for a long time together to her lips, and decking their tables.   She had a singular pleasure in hearing the service of

[e] Henry's History of England, vol. v. p. 173.

God, and on this account was thoughtlessly prodigal towards the clerks of melodious voice. Her generosity becoming universally known, crowds of scholars equally famed for verse and for singing, came over; and happy did he account himself who could soothe the ears of the queen by the novelty of his song. Nor on these only did she lavish money, but on all sorts of men, especially foreigners; that through her presents they might proclaim her celebrity abroad: for the desire of fame is so rooted in the human mind, that scarcely is any one contented with the precious fruits of a good conscience, but is fondly anxious, if he does any thing laudable, to have it generally known[d]."

No. 73, between the good Queen Maude and King Henry I., the masterpiece of the sculptor of Wells for youthful grace and dignity, can be no other than Adelicia, the second wife of Henry, the fair maid of Brabant, "the maid withouten vice," the theme of the troubadours, and the admiration of all. She was the daughter of Godfrey of Louvaine, descended through both her parents from the Carlovingian line, and one of the most interesting and amiable persons of that period of history. She endeavoured to assuage the sorrows of her husband by her gentle and amiable compliances. Her son-in-law Robert of Glocester, the patron of Malmesbury and of literature, a truly valiant and loyal prince, was used to say and to write,

> " He knew no woman so fair as she
> Was seen on middle earth."

In 1138, three years after her husband's death, she married the king's cup-bearer, the illustrious Count William di Albini, "of the strong arm." He was a knight of great prowess and renown, and an universal favourite; he won the prize at the Tournois of Bruges 1137, where he might have married the dowager queen of France, but for his engagement to the "Eximia Regina" Adelicia. He became earl of Arundel, and was the founder of the illustrious house of Howard still existing amongst us. In 1149, eleven years only after her marriage, this distinguished princess, by a deep religious sentiment, was tempted in imitation of her brother, a monk in the same establishment, to abandon her lovely family and devoted husband to retire into the nunnery of Affligham, near Alost, in Flanders, where two years after she sighed away her gentle life, 1151.

[d] Malmesbury, b. v. p. 516.

Nos. 75, 76, 77, are empty, one of them probably contained the statue of Richard I.

No. 78, bearing a crown, may be King John, a statue of no more remark than the contemptible original, odious alike to clergy and to laity.

No. 79, in a remarkable attitude, standing on his left, and raising his right in conformity with the inclination of the roof which appears in this part, may be King Henry III., thus in the *ascendant*. The crown is not apparent, and this conjecture is hazardous, and submitted only to the reader.

APPENDIX.

THE study of the sculptures of Wells has naturally led to a general survey of the most remarkable specimens of the plastic art, still remaining in our Cathedral churches as well as in those of cotemporary date on the continent, with a view to a comparison of styles, and of the intellectual and moral ideas conveyed by them, and to the history and progress of Sculpture from the twelfth to the sixteenth centuries in this country.

The results of these surveys are given in this Appendix.

In an age so remarkable for the love and veneration of our national medieval antiquities, and of patriotic and holy reminiscences, as well as for the light daily shed upon them by the pens and pencils of the most accomplished historians, archæologists, and even romancers; it is surprising that the luminous illustrations which *figured* Antiquity so obviously affords, should be not only unappreciated but ignored amongst us, and even by our Roman Catholic countrymen : and that in general the tradition of the meaning of those sculptures which have been permitted (by the bad spirit, warring from time to time against every work of art, addressed to the higher feelings and interests of man) to remain in our churches, should have become a dead letter in England; so that works containing extensive and precious indications of general and local history, doctrine, habits, and poetical idea, displaying so advantageously the manners, the learning, taste, and piety, of our ancestors, should be subjected to the hourly dilapidation of time, ignorance, and neglect, without any published attempt to interpret their meaning, beauty or humour, and title to our respect, by any reasonable and timely pains or descriptions.

It would seem strange that while so little honour is done to the Sculpture of the middle ages, medieval Architecture should have been studied with an enthusiasm which extends to its actual adoption and practice in preference to all other styles in this our day, especially in the most solemn and intellectual of all,—our religious edifices; that attributing such mastery in æsthetics to the architects and patrons of those days, we should refuse to see these faculties, or deny their existence, in the sculptors,—

who, nevertheless, speak a language so much more plain, (to those who will read it), and whose works abound in the evidences of mind, character, and sentiment: thus repudiating the speaking statue, while we invest the dumb edifice with hallowed imaginations.

Sculpture is to architecture what the countenance is to the human frame, or what the voice and gesture are to it; namely, the expressive index of the soul which animates its various members; the exponent, in more familiar language than architecture possesses, of the historical, doctrinal, and sentimental motives of the work. Architecture, like Music, may excite the loftiest, but at the same time the most indefinite emotions, while Sculpture explains and details them in plain and distinct terms.

If the Fine Arts present generally the more accurate physiognomy and picture of the times, to those who know how to read them, than even the written chronicle can often do, Sculpture more especially is calculated to describe to distant future ages,

> "The very age and body of the time,
> His form and pressure."

And we may trace in the productions of this art more especially, all the political and moral phases of the history and character of a country, in plain and legible sentences. Under a demonstrative form of Religion, this art was ever considered as the right hand of the ornamental art of architecture, essentially part and parcel of her substance; and stood therefore second to the *ars regina*, amongst the graphic sisters, demanding almost equal intensity of purpose in means and in materials for the execution of their joint labours.

To the architectural composer indeed sculpture affords the most valuable aid, by the variety it communicates to the symmetrical and uniform disposition of parts, and by the contrast of diagonal lines to the rigour of the essential perpendicular and horizontal lines of the architecture; also by the opposition of the round and softer, with the angular and harsher forms inherent in the latter.

But as respects the impression of magnitude and proportion, (always the aim of the architect,) the sculpture of the human figure is of the utmost importance, for we have no other modulus by which dimension is to be estimated; as, the parts of it, the foot, the palm, the cubit, established by the universal consent of language, plainly shew.

The relative scale therefore of the figure to the architecture, so as not to diminish the dignity of the former, while it should give apparent magnitude to the latter, is an artifice of consummate importance, best attained by the Greeks; but not unknown to the middle ages. The abuse of this artifice in the fifteenth and sixteenth centuries, was carried to extremes; and, as we shall see, statues were gradually made more numerous, crowded, and ridiculously small; as well as the members of the architecture itself: so that magnitude was lost in the triviality of both these arts.

With so much to recommend this class of antiquities to the architect, the historian, and the churchman, it is astonishing that so little has been done to elucidate them; for the labours of Gough, Carter, and Walpole, and even of the illustrious Flaxman, have not yet done justice to this interesting subject.

The truth is, that the holy fear of image-worship and idolatry, which haunted our reformers three hundred years ago, and exploded with increased violence through the puritans, has been inherited by ourselves; and has entailed upon us a settled repugnance to this class of antiquities; we are early taught to distrust them as superstitious, monkish, and gothic. We cast discredit, equally upon the correctly scriptural, historical, and beautiful in this art, with the legendary, apocryphal, and grotesque; and in the true spirit of the *odium theologicum*, pluck up the wheat together with the tares also. Thus by a sweeping and undiscriminating injustice, these curious and interesting evidences of history and of the religious sentiments of prayer and of praise, expressed by our Christian fore-fathers, through one of the most ingenious arts which the Almighty has been pleased to implant in the heart of man, are veiled from our eyes; and we are prevented the enjoy-ment, of which this organ is so capable, of the medieval understanding of some of the most consolatory and edifying truths which the Scriptures have left us. For it is through figured antiquity, together with the revered architectural (hardly less than in the literary) remains of a thousand years, still existing in our country, that we trace man's assurance that "Jesus Christ is the same yesterday, to-day, and for ever." And whether in the poems of Dante, the paintings of Giotto, the architecture of the "Lathomus," or the sculpture of the "imaginator," we recognise religion and its blessed influences as the then great business of the world.

The Roman Catholic spirit of these times will naturally be decried by the puritan, "its vices will be graven in brass, and its virtues writ in water:" but with due allowances for all human fallibility, it can never be doubted that religion was the head and front of these costly and noble undertakings; that faith was their deep foundation; and that these worthy sentiments, impressed so indelibly upon them, may well be the edifying and delightful study of the artist and the man of letters, so as to make their investigation at once a homage to the Deity, and a just acknowledgment of the zeal and merit of the men of those days.

It is unfortunate for the reputation of our country in Fine Arts, and equally so for our delight and instruction, (so much promoted by those elegant and refining means,) that from the days of Henry VIII., to the establishment of the Royal Academy by George III., this country has been deprived of artistic succession, and consequently of artistic history.

a 2

The liberal Stuarts struggled in vain against the envious and degrading spirit of puritanism, by the protection of accomplished foreigners; and by the exhibition of the most inspiring examples of taste; the native talents were never deficient, as shewn by many instances, before and since, to the present day; but the want of patronage in a Church and State, constantly infected with puritanism, rendered them abortive then, and still give a Dutch tendency to our schools.

It is of the utmost importance in the artist's eyes, and must be considered as affecting the honour and character of our country for this branch of refinement and genius by every one, (and it is a strong motive of this essay,) to explode this perversion by every means in our power, and to recommend both the ancient and modern examples of excellence existing amongst us.

That such legitimate ornaments in our actual religious edifices are conformable to the canons of the Anglican Church, is largely propounded by Dr. Wilson in his "Ornaments of Churches considered," already quoted, and we can desire no better authority than his unanswered, and indeed unanswerable advocacy affords, of the utility of this study to the members of the Anglican Church at this day.

The natural consequence of the disuse of arts, is the doubt of capacity for them; and to this absurd and degrading imputation we have been subjected, not only by foreigners but even by our own countrymen. Forgetting that culture, patronage, and exercise in them, no less than in all other arts and sciences, are the only means to excellence; and uncandidly refusing to recognise the long disuse and persecution of these arts, through the puritan infection still lingering in our Church; these persons neglect the evidences which are presented by works still existing in our Cathedrals, and in histories relating to them prior to the Reformation; in vindication of the genius of our countrymen in this, as in every other walk of prowess: while they overlook those which our modern school of Fine Art has triumphantly exhibited ever since the encouragement of royalty and of government has been extended to its efforts[a].

It is important to correct these popular misconceptions of an age, by some called

---

[a] Walpole, who is singularly imbued with the popular prejudice of English incapacity in Fine Arts, attributes painting and sculpture alike to foreigners, in his Anecdotes on Painting, vol. i. p. 32; especially in the instance of Queen Eleanor's crosses, which he presumes were designed by Cavallini, who, be it observed, was a Roman artist, and executed the Roman or Byzantine tomb of Henry III., in a Roman taste, while the crosses were in the finest Gothic taste of their day, a style peculiar and only understood in the west of Europe. It is remarkable that Walpole so far forgets his argument of depreciation of native talent, as to quote seven English names against three foreigners; Peter of Stanford, Edward of Westminster, Luvel, Walter, Godfrey of Woodstreet, John of Coventry, John Sutton, against Cavallini, William of Florence, Odon, who are stated to be, and by their names appear to have been, foreigners. But in furtherance of this defence of English talent, the reader is referred to the Appendix on Lincoln Cathedral.

dark, in our country; and in doing so, to make some small additions to the knowledge we possess concerning the arts and artists of our early history, and particularly to assert for England, against Walpole and others, the claim of having produced by the hand of native artists, works in Sculpture, no less than in Architecture, of a merit, equal at least, if not superior, to any other of their day in the continental countries.

Indeed, the argument of common sense, and of all history, biography, and analogy of Fine Art, support the opinion, that the merit we attribute to our English architecture, could not co-exist with incapacity in the other sisters of the triad, namely, Sculpture and Painting; that it is impossible to excel in the one, without a competent knowledge of the others.

Carter, Gough, Walpole, and some others, have indeed given scattered and uninviting notices, with very insufficient explanations of our ancient sculpture; we owe to the academicians, Flaxman and Stothard, (for the labours of the unfortunate son were directed by the illustrious father,) some more definite and becoming explanations on the subject than had previously been published. But no justice has yet been done to our native works of the medieval periods, and it is a desideratum in our literature.

On the continent, where the antique system of Church government and discipline, has undergone no change; we have, from the time of Vasari, a succession of illustrations of middle art, in Ciampini, Aringhi, d'Agincourt, Cicognara, and others; which however we may confidently challenge in merit and interest, both of religion and of art, in the comparison with our own, though not perhaps in number.

When books were so expensive and rare as to have been the subjects of litigation, and the loan of them granted upon pawn and pledge, in the presence of witnesses with the utmost solemnity; and when the eyes and ears were the chief recipients of knowledge, by oral and visible instruction, by the illuminated MS.; the storied walls and windows, the songs, the romances, and sermons; from the time of Aldhelm to that of Wickliffe; then the sculptured Cathedral became the great vehicle and page in which history, doctrine, and title or rights, were recorded and displayed to the public recognition.

During upwards of three hundred years, sculpture flourished in this country in common with the continental states; and attained amongst us in the thirteenth and fourteenth centuries, a degree of merit which was, perhaps, not surpassed in any other, in conception, and sometimes in execution; though certainly deficient in academical dexterity and knowledge.

Its history in this country may thus be briefly stated. More than a thousand years of the Christian era had passed without any traceable productions of the art of sculpture; whatever may possibly have existed in Saxon or anterior dates, belonged assuredly to that family of ecclesiastical art, which came to us direct from Constantinople and Rome, in common with the rest of northern and western Europe; from the fourth to the thirteenth century. Our churches were more or less reproductions of San Clemente at Rome, and the smaller basilicas. Even in these prototypes it does not appear that, through those early ages of struggle, the Church attempted sculpture; or aimed at much beyond the superficial decorations which painting or mosaics could afford; much less likely is it that in these remote regions, sculpture was employed. The few and partial specimens of early Christian art found in the sarcophagi, the tombs, and the chapels of Rome, were traditions from the classical antique[b], of which perhaps the frieze in the western front of Lincoln is an unique example in this country.

Not only the refinement, the leisure, and the knowledge, but the very tools of the art were wanting. Until the twelfth century we trace no other means of carving than the adze[c], with which the stone was hewed; the chisel did not till then appear.

The barbarous enrichments of the eleventh century doubtless display indifferently the Norman and the Saxon art, and are little better than such as the South Sea Islands discover in their paddles and utensils at the present day. It was not until a strong Norman government had fostered improvement in civil acts, by securing internal peace during nearly a century, that sculpture began to shew any signs of revival or of progress. In the twelfth we have, though with great economy of the art, at least the primitive Christian symbols, the Agnus Dei and the cross, and essays of the sculptor in fantastic and romantic devices, chimeras, with ornamental scrolls and foliage, and sometimes scriptural, legendary, or popular subjects, very rudely treated[d].

In the thirteenth century, the progress and enterprise which exhibited itself in all the arts was especially developed in this, and it was then that historical and religious sculpture in great profusion attempted to rival works of classical antiquity, so much seen by our ancestors during the holy wars, and still existing at Athens and in the Mediterranean.

And now it was that the mysterious and symbolical figures by which the freemasonry, as it were, of Christianity, had been heretofore maintained amongst its members, gave way to the more plain lessons of the Scriptures, and the more elegant and poetic repesentations of the sacred history and the parables, addressing the heart no less than the understanding.

The literary and poetic faculty, which in the twelfth century had been fostered and

---

[b] See Roma Subterranea.
[c] See Willis's Canterbury Cathedral, p. 89.
[d] See Lincoln, west end; Worcester, east end; Canterbury crypt, &c.; Rochester Cathedral, &c.

recommended to the world by Henry Beauclerc and his accomplished and virtuous queens, Henry II. and the age of the Troubadours,—now infused itself into the sister fine arts of painting and of sculpture; and the knowledge of the Scripture (which the studies of the schoolmen was unhappily soon destined to divert) imparted a dignity and authority to the works of those days, which proclaims the source from whence they come, and entitles them to our highest veneration and study; and this spirit may be traced in them till the middle of the fourteenth century, when the warlike tendency of the court, the vices of the clergy, and the perversion of their scriptural studies to the trivium and quadrivium, and lastly, the growing dissent under Wickliffe, produced a decay in fine arts. The thirteenth century, to which all writers on art have attributed the title of the revival, produced simultaneously in every member of the European family an extraordinary development of idea and of skill; in this country, as we have already said, and as we shall hereafter shew, art attained a merit, as well as a priority, which has never been duly appreciated, and which, but for the fatal interruption of these studies, by protestant and puritan persecutions which followed, might speedily have attained its climax; and would have shewn itself at least equal, if not superior, to the continental productions in subsequent times, as it undoubtedly does in this age. In the fourteenth century, building had greatly declined, and sculpture was consequently confined in a smaller field, and was less employed in scriptural illustration; but the art continued under the patronage of the secular and ecclesiastical authorities, either in devotional images or sumptuous monuments: and the statues of the individual kings and the monumental effigies are often strikingly beautiful, as may be seen in Mr. Stothard's admirable engravings. It is certain that it had become a lucrative employment and an honourable one, since we have many instances of the practice of the arts by eminent Churchmen: William of Colchester was sacrist of St. Alban's, Alan of Walsingham filled the same office at Ely, and many similar instances might be quoted. Matthew Paris records the names of many artists, especially of Walter of Colchester, whose works were universally admired, and doubtless well paid: Mr. Hunter in the twenty-ninth volume of the Archæologia has revealed to us through the publications by the commission of the public records, the names of sixteen artists, architects, and sculptors, engaged in those beautiful crosses raised by Edward I. to his beloved consort Eleanora, of whom two only bear foreign names; and this is the more interesting because those crosses are justly regarded as not only amongst the choicest and most beautiful works of that early age, so happily combining the effect of sculpture and architecture, but also of the style in which they were executed.

It was in the reign of Richard II. (1382) that occurs a remarkable evidence of the superiority of English sculpture in the licence to Cosmo Gentiles, the pope's collector, given by the king to export three great images of the blessed Virgin, of St. Peter, St. Paul, and a small image of the Holy Trinity, even to Italy, esteemed so generally the school and fountain of Fine Art. And the six kings at Canterbury, the most admirable specimens of sculpture of that time existing in England, offer abundant testimony to the high degree of skill attained at this period. We may also consult the evidence of our own senses in a picture of that time, still at Wilton, and in great preservation, representing Richard II. praying to the Virgin, and the infant Saviour surrounded with a glorious company of angels, and his patron saints, St. John, St. Edmond, and St. Edward Confessor; of which, though the author is not known, it is not too much to hazard, that the physiognomies throughout are eminently English, and thence that little doubt need be entertained of its being a production of one of our own countrymen.

In an illiterate age especially, sculpture as a hieroglyphic and a calendar for unlearned men, had a very important office to perform; moral and religious order was to be enforced by her means in the effigies of kings* and prelates, "the powers that be," as God's vicegerents upon earth; and sacred history and doctrine, "oculis subjecta fidelibus," were thus rendered intelligible to the ignorant while they were delightful to

---

* The satirical Piers Ploughman, Vision, verse 249, describes the kingly office by the voice of a lunatic, an angel, and the commons, both in serious and in humorous guise.

> Crist kepe thee, sire kyng !
> And thi kyng-ryche,
> And leue thee lede thy lond,
> So be leauté thee lovye,
> And for the rightful ruling
> Be rewarded in Hevene.

The angel speaks Latin, because ignorant men had no right to argue or judge, their business is to serve. The commons, without understanding Latin either, all cried out,

> Præcepta Regis,
> Sunt nobis vincula legis.

He likens the king to the cat amongst the mice and rats, whom no one was able to bell.

Passus, 1. verse 647.

> Kynges and knyghtes
> Sholde kepen it (treuthe) by reson,
> Riden and rappen doun
> In reaumes aboute,
> And taken transgressores,
> And tyen hem faste,
> Til treuthe hadde y-termyned
> Hire trespass to the end.

the learned. Kings, saints, and prelates, reverentially pourtrayed, were exhibited in the front of the temple to the public eye, in all their individual characteristics and peculiarities of feature and attribute, through the ablest masters in the art.

When the ill-fated Edward II. visited the convent in Gloucester in 1319, he observed the effigies of his predecessors, and asked for his own. The abbot, like a ready courtier, and as it turned out, like a true prophet, replied that for him he had reserved a more honourable place. And so it was that eight years after the same abbot received the murdered king from Berckley castle, at his great peril, and raised the splendid monument still existing by the choir.

Allegorical and poetical representations of the cardinal virtues and the mortal sins, the parables, and even the sciences, through the signs of the zodiac the occupations of husbandry and the arts of life, awakened the mind and the imagination of the beholders to better things. See notes on Salisbury, Malmesbury, Canterbury, and the French Cathedrals.

Another and more worldly purpose of the art was suggested by the conservative spirit of the Church, namely, the display of those evidences and titles by which its wealth and possessions were held; such as should convey unquestionably the antiquity of their institution, their public utility and services, their undeniable rights and charters, and the kings and benefactors by whom they were founded and endowed. An array of these is often conspicuously presented in the fronts of their buildings, as if to challenge public enquiry; more especially in the beginning of the fourteenth century, when the usurpations of the Church had reached their height, and the public jealousy (which so summarily confiscated the possessions and the order of the Templars) created alarm in vested interests, and threatened to disregard the validity of title deeds, however authoritative and undeniable.

The investigation of title deeds became fashionable in the thirteenth century, (for many forgeries to this effect had been perpetrated, and examples of them are still existing,) and it was a device adopted by Edward I. to fill his coffers, to lay claim to all estates of which the titles were defective. In 1278 he appointed commissioners for these investigations, and history records the shrewd and significant hint given to them

---

' The effigies of the kings are still to be seen at York, from the Conqueror to Richard II.; at Exeter down to Henry VI., with four of the Saxon kings; at Lincoln to Edward III.; at Lichfield to Richard II., together with the Mercian and the Saxon kings of Wessex; at Wells from Ina to Henry III. And as confirmatory of the historical practice we always find the kings from the Conquest chiefly recorded in sculpture, and the Saxon kings only recorded where a strong party spirit against the foreigners prevailed. The effigies of the kings of France cease with Charles VI.

' See descriptions of Gloucester and Croyland in the Appendix.

(and which was not lost) in the case of the earl of Warrene, who, when called upon for his title deeds, produced an old rusty sword, which he declared, while he lived, would be found sufficient to establish his rights and titles.

The king himself, Edward I., in laying claim to the crown of Scotland, did not fail to produce title deeds, by which he shewed his descent and inheritance from " *Brute the Trogan,*" the first conqueror of Scotland; and especially from Athelstan, who in token of supremacy, had, with the assistance of John of Beverley, cut a yard deep with his sword into a rock at Dunbar.

The study of the Scriptures, especially the daily repetition of the Psalms, stored the mind with moral and poetical ideas of the highest order, as well as deeper truths of religion; and these constantly appear with a beauty, ingenuity, and delicacy, which the grossness of modern practicality has entirely overlooked, but which deserve our candid examination, and perhaps our imitation, no less than the architecture they adorned. Here the piety and the ingenuity, and the Christian graces, which many of the ecclesiastics undoubtedly possessed, and which are the legitimate first-fruits of a holy life and sound doctrine and elegant literature, are exhibited with an elevation of idea far above the mechanical skill which was to embody them. The encouragement given to poetry and literature in the twelfth and thirteenth centuries, had greatly enlarged and expanded the public mind, and the kindred fine arts of sculpture and painting naturally exhibited a corresponding enlightenment, and emulated the refinement and the graces now universally demanded. And if Warton has found in the literature of those days much to admire and applaud, we may be assured that sculpture and painting, reflecting no less distinctly the ideas and culture of the times, are equally deserving of our study and regard. In fact the graphic and literary arts are inseparable sisters of the same family, they mutually assist and explain each other, and speak only different dialects of the same language: their fortune is also the same, since they ever flourish and decline together. How far their mutual reflection may be beneficially traced will be seen by some examples in the subsequent descriptions of the Appendix, and may be perhaps better discerned by every learned observer. Winchelman first taught us the relation and the value of the graphic arts of design to the literature of the classical ages, and the importance of the study of fine arts on this single account; the Christian student will equally acknowledge this principle as applied to Christian art.

The sanctity of the faith, its early purity and orthodoxy, its scriptural and classical learning, its decline through the scholastic philosophy, its legendary and apocryphal superstitions, its degeneracy, its corruptions, its alarms and its decay; the sacredness of the kingly office, the abuse and decline of their authority; the value of aristocracy, its degeneracy and abuse, and its comparative eradication under the Tudors; the growth of liberty both of conscience and political position; the virtues and the corruptions of society, are all written in the chisel of the mason or of the sculptor, or by the pencil of the limner in characters too delicate for literary description, but which to the observant eye of the artist are as eloquent as logical, and as evident as the amplest description of history or discourse. Thus regarded the Fine Arts assumed a dignity and an interest which are too often overlooked. We find them thus the companions and the illustrators of history, and amongst the best commentaries on the past, and even the present, that can be consulted. And here we are led to mark the distinction which we must always draw between the ordered sculpturesque symbols, significant for the carrying out of the moral and religious purpose of the edifice, directed always by the high and intellectual authority of the prelates of the Church, and those minor decorations of unimportant meanings which were left to the grosser fancy of the carver; such as corbels, gurgoils, masks, and sedilia, the misereres, the finials, and capitals, &c. &c.

These, especially the wood carvings, while they exhibit the trite and uninformed state of the lower classes of society, are not without their value, as displaying the facetiæ of the builder's school, the tales, traditions, the costumes, and the ideas of those more vulgar annals of our history.

Generally we may safely promise as a reward to the careful and the candid observer of the best of medieval sculpture as well as architecture in this country, (in the midst of technical imperfections, and often apocryphal and superstitious corruptions, which he must know how to discriminate,) a spiritual conception and a religious language of art entirely original and apart from any previous example of classical stamp; a piety, naiveté, and sentiment of truth and simplicity, as of little children, (that "foolishness" of the Greeks,) which impart the indescribable freshness and purity of thought so conspicuous in the Gospel; and in the ideas and the spirit of their inventions he will invariably find the Holy Scriptures first, and then he will trace the homilies of a Gregory, a Bede, and a Thomas à Kempis, with the sentiments and the aspirations of a Boethius or an Alfred, and in a manner often beautiful, as well as highly edifying.

It is obvious that the discredit into which these works have fallen, and often technical imperfection of their execution, require both candour and ingenuity in the interpretation of them; the gross and tasteless observer will bring all things to his own level; there is nothing too doggerel or gross for the apprehension of the vulgar; and such persons will esteem as fanciful and visionary any higher conceptions.

Where there is no written commentary to guide interpretation, this, the natural liability, must be endured. We may say of the imagination in art as in morals, "If thine eye be clear, thy whole body will be full of light; if the light that is in thee be darkness, how great is that darkness!" The sense of the beautiful, as well as of the correct, is one of the great ends of education. *Tò καλὸν*, as well as *τὸ ὀρθὸν*, are of equal and synonymous significance : and that our ancestors had made amidst many errors very great progress in these essentials of the human accomplishment, there can be no doubt.

In fact iconography not only explained the use and purpose of the edifice, but formed the essential element of the ornamental art of architecture in the middle ages, and constantly prescribed the form and order of its most elegant features, which were not only expressly contrived for the figured illustrations of sculpture, but grew out of that requirement.

So general and indeed universal was the use of statues in the thirteenth and four-teenth centuries, that they were the chief motive of the sister art ; the niche and the canopy constituting in fact the most fertile materials of architectural composition, and indispensable to the style, even when applied to purposes and to creeds which protest against the use of images, and demonstrative forms of religion ; and nothing can more ridiculously display the real ignorance of the spirit which animated the architecture from which they are taken, and the incongruity of modern practice, than the employ-ment of these empty niches. The niche void of its statue is the setting without the jewel, the frame without the picture, the stall in the choir or the chapter-house without its tenant.

It was in the fourteenth century that a general decline of the spiritual sentiment of the arts, both of architecture and sculpture, became apparent. The elevation and in-tensity of thought which the Scriptures had hitherto inspired, were now impaired by the scholastic studies of the clergy ; subtilty, affected refinement, and curiosity of workman-ship took the place of beauty and religious character. Sculpture became absolutely subordinated to architecture ; and with a view to enhance the scale of the sister arts, small statues, though increased in number, were employed in architectural compositions, and even these gradually gave way to the vice of heraldry, the pomp and pride of which now began to supersede every other consideration, and cover the building to the exclu-sion of nobler symbols with its endless quarterings, badges, and recognisances ; usurping those positions which were formerly reserved for religion or history, and the inspiration of devotion and piety.

In the fifteenth century this fashion of armorial bearings, the vice of an old aristo-cracy, became a nuisance, covering like a leprosy the whole surface of the architecture, as we see at Canterbury and York ; under this infection every allusion to the Deity or the purpose of the edifice disappears in favour of heraldic record : and these edifices seem rather to have been erected to perpetuate the names and quarterings of the archbishops, the Churchmen, and the nobles, and the *subscribers* of that day, than for the culture of religious sentiment.   The perversion, which Piers Ploughman has so pointedly characterised, was evidently the universal practice [h].

[h] In Piers Ploughman's Creed, vers. 339,

> Than I munte me forth
> The mynstre to knowen,
> And awaytede a woon
> Wonderly well y-bild,
> With arches on everich half,
> And bellyche y-corven,
> With crochets on corneres,
> With knottes of gold,
> Wyde wyndowes y-wrought,
> Y-wryten ful thikke,
> *Shynen with shapen sheldes,*
> *To shewen aboute,*
> *With merkes of merchauntes*
> *Y-medeled betwene,*
> *Mo than twenty and two*
> *Twoyse y-noumbered.*
> *Ther is non heraud that hath*
> *Half swich a roll.*

In the absolution of the Lady Mede (the impersonation of the world) by the friar confessor, Piers Ploughman says in his Vision, vers. 1430,

> Theigh lewed men and lered men
> Hadde leyen by thee bothe,
> And falsnesse hadde y-folwed thee
> Alle this fifty wynter,
> I shal assoille thee myself
> For a seem of whete.
>
> Thanne he assoiled hire soone,
> And so then he seide,
> " We have a wyndow in werchynge
> Wole sitten us ful hye,
> Woldestow glaze that gable
> And grave theronne thy name,
> Syker sholde thi soule be
> Hevene to have."
>
> " Have mercy," quod Mede,
> " Of men that it (lecherie) haunteth,
> And I shal covere youre kirk,
> Youre cloistre do maken,"
> Wowes do whiten,
> And wyndowes glazen,

By this device funds were never wanting for the prosecution of the work : relief from the pains of purgatory, indulgences, and the favour of heaven, were the promised reward to the pious contributors of alms. The eternal interest and personal vanity were alike interested in affixing for all time the badge of a family upon an enduring monument, and the device of armorial record was thus rendered no less fruitful in those times, than the " printing of subscribers' names" is found to be in the present.

By the sixteenth century the art had long lost its religious unction, its grace and sanctity. The wars of the Roses had exhibited the social evils, and had discovered their remedy. The vices of the Church were incurable, and it still maintained its ground, though it had lost all its merit. The patronage of Henry VII. gave a passing encouragement to the manufacture, rather than the art of sculpture. Statues had now become still smaller and more numerous. An arbitrary arrangement and an unscriptural selection, deprive the works of that day of all respect or admiration. The prophets and apostles, saints and martyrs, are confusedly and in ostentatious profusion obtruded upon the spectator, as if to impose upon his credulity. The whole company of saints, and the army of martyrs, as all of equal merit and importance, a polytheism is forced upon the spectator equally deficient in sound religion and taste; proclaiming the crying want of reformation no less in religion and politics than in fine arts. The chapel of Henry VII., and of Prince Arthur at Worcester, are remarkable examples of these errors.

In the latter end of the sixteenth, or the beginning of the seventeenth century, the discredit into which the medieval arts had fallen, and the universality of the revival, soon effaced the traditions of that school which during three hundred and fifty years had done so much for the glory of our country, and the illustration of our history. It was then that the reformers of the Church and of the Fine Arts affixed a stigma to the style, and to figured antiquity in particular, from which it has never since recovered; and Gothic, the term of reproach by which they signalized it, has ever since been appended to that period of taste in architecture and sculpture.

Do peynten and pourtraye,
And paye for the makynge,
That *every segge shall seye*
I am suster of your house.

For—the I leve you, Lordes,
Leveth swiche werkes ;
To writen in wyndowes
Of youre wel dedes, &c. &c.

Of these phases in the art developed by the successive centuries of our own history, that chiefly has occupied the present survey which belongs to the thirteenth and fourteenth centuries, when it was dignified by a deep religious sentiment and scriptural correctness, and all that elevated and interesting taste which ever springs from so noble a source; whatever is apocryphal and legendary, belonging to Christian mythology, as it has been aptly termed, the histories of the virgin or of the local or foreign saints or martyrs, has not been touched on in the following pages, since it can never be considered to belong to the profounder interest of art or of religious history.

To the lover of Holy Writ, as the mistress no less of taste than of truth, and to the artist who sees in its pages the noblest subjects as addressed to the heart and to the eyes, and who believes that far from being exhausted they have never yet been truly reached, because like the subject itself it has never yet been sufficiently felt and understood, no occupation can be more delightful or more informing. Whenever he finds art employed to aggrandise the creature by pompous monuments, flattering human vanity by heraldry and genealogies, or to aid and abet the fallacies of superstition, by apocryphal and legendary impostures, it loses all its dignity and charm, and becomes an idle toy unworthy the occupation of the rational and sentient mind.

Large allowances are relied upon, and will doubtless be accorded by the candid reader towards these essays upon hitherto untried ground; whenever he doubts the interpretation offered as fanciful and unfounded, he will put to himself these questions, Is it possible that works implying so much pecuniary, intellectual cost, and artistic skill, so questionable, and challenging so much attention in the beholder, and directed as we know from history, by minds the merit of which is so well established both in the sister art of architecture and in their literary and historical remains, could have designed these splendid and elaborate works as mere idle and unmeaning decorations, or could have left this portion of their offering to the Deity, so significant and so parlant as it is, to the mere caprice of vulgar and uninstructed carvers?

And if by this reasoning the probability is established of their authoritative and responsible execution, are we not bound, as informed and sentient beings, to read and to interpret their eloquent language, at least as diligently in all that refers to our holy religion and beloved country as Egyptian hieroglyphics or Babylonian arrow-headed inscriptions?

Are we not to look in them for the noblest and most significant scriptural and historical illustration of which the art is capable, especially under the consideration of the then illiterate state of society, and the necessity and duty in ecclesiastics of thus setting before the people those truths which they could not appreciate by reading, consistent as this practice is with the symbolical instruction common in that day?

Another indispensable condition to a conclusive criticism of these essays is that he should also visit the monuments themselves with all that candour, good faith, and leisure, which is undoubtedly due to these monuments of our forefathers, and perhaps to these attempts at interpretation, and the pains which they have cost. By such a proceeding they will be corrected and advanced, and possibly adopted in the graphic spirit of our age. Our religious buildings may thus smile again with these delightful arts, and the hearts and imagination of the faithful will be addressed no less than their *graver* and more intellectual faculties.

APPENDIX A.

THIS spirited and learned work, "The Ornaments of Churches considered," was written by Dr. Wilson, many years senior prebendary of Westminster Abbey, and minister of St. Margaret's church, Westminster, which church has for some centuries been appropriated to the use of the honourable the House of Commons, when in parliament assembled.

During the repairs of the church, (to the amount of £4000,) voted by the House in 1757, on the proposal to introduce the magnificent painted window, now over the communion, great objections to it were raised by a puritan faction as "superstitious," and a prosecution in the ecclesiastical court was instituted accordingly; which gave occasion, with almost universal applause, to the admirable body of arguments, examples, and authorities thus drawn up by Dr. Wilson, in vindication of the use of the Fine Arts in our temples.

This picture was originally designed as a present of the people of Dort to Henry VII., as an ornament to his chapel, but the king's death and other circumstances prevented its arrival at its destination. The adventures of this window during two hundred and fifty years, until its final erection in St. Margaret's church, are curious, and its giving occasion to Dr. Wilson's work will always invest it with a great additional interest in the eyes of artists.

He commences with general observations on the nature of man, and his tendency to be affected by the magnificence which architecture, sculpture and painting supply, in all ages and under all religions. "To confine religion entirely to spirituals," says he, "may perhaps have been the attempt of well-meaning men, but certainly of bad philosophers; they were unacquainted with human nature, and did not foresee that their attempt must end in quietism." "That we do not continue to adorn our churches," says he elsewhere, "is owing to the impious rage of the puritanical faction, and not to the cautious prudence of the reformers." "And if the nation," says Burnet, "should come to be quite out of danger of falling into popery, it would not be necessary to insist upon many of the subjects of the homilies, as it was when they were first prepared." "The necessary Doctrine and Erudition for any Christian Man," published by the authority of Henry VIII., and under the approbation of both Houses of Parliament, explains the second commandment as signifying that we are forbidden to have images to the intent of doing godly honour to them. "But pictures and images may be set in the church, and might not be despised, but to be used reverently." This work was composed by Cranmer, Ridley, Redman, and other learned men. The further injunctions promulgated by Queen Elizabeth and King Edward VI. were chiefly directed against "monuments of feigned miracles."

In the next reign, that of James I., the same spirit still continued to operate, when a great statesman, to whom most parts of human and divine literature were known, Sir Walter Raleigh, thought himself obliged to make the following reflections on it. "The reverend care which Moses, the prophet and chosen servant of God, had in all that belonged even to the outward and least parts of the tabernacle, ark, and sanctuary, witnessed the inward and most humble zeal borne to God Himself: the industry used in the framing thereof, the curious workmanship thereon bestowed; the exceeding charge and expense of the provisions; the dutiful observance in the laying up, and preserving the holy vessels, the solemn removing thereof; the vigilant attendance thereon, and the provident defence of the same, which all ages have in some degree imitated, is now so forgotten and cast away in this superfine age, by those of the Family of Love, by the Anabaptist, Brownist, and other sectaries; as all cost and care bestowed and had of the church, wherein God is to be served and worshipped, is accounted a kind of popery, and as proceeding from an idolatrous disposition; insomuch as time would soon bring to pass (if it were not resisted) that God would be turned out of churches into barns, and from thence again into fields and mountains, and under the hedges; and the office of the ministry (robbed of all dignity and respect) be as contemptible as these places; all order, discipline, and Church government, left to newness of opinion and men's fancies; yea, and soon after as many kinds of religions would spring up as there are parish churches within England. Every contentious and ignorant person clothing his fancy with the spirit of God, and his imagination with the gift of revelation: insomuch as when the truth, which is but one, shall appear to the simple multitude, no less variable than contrary to itself, the faith of men will soon die away by degrees, and all religion be held in scorn and contempt."

Our first reformers were a good deal influenced by the example of Lutheran churches, where pictures were retained, and Luther himself was so far from being averse to them that he reproved Carolostadius for removing them from churches in which they were placed, and observed that they were rather to be removed from men's minds.

Calvin's objections to paintings are founded on the ground only that amongst the pictures hung up in popish churches very few were of an instructive kind, or contained Scripture histories; and the subjects of most of them were either injudiciously chosen, or represented in an unbecoming manner. Vid. Inst. 112.

Erasmus, who expresses entire approbation of such as were adapted to good uses, acknowledges that many pictures in their churches were of a fantastical fabulous nature, nay he adds that "pictor expressurus virginem aut Agatham, nonunquam exemplum sumit a lascivâ meretriculâ; et expressurus Christum aut Paulum proponit sibi temulentum nebulonem."

"Pictures properly conducted," continues he, "besides the honest pleasure they confer, mainly assist the memory and the intelligence of history. Pictures are to the illiterate what books are to the learned, but still the learned may often find in a picture that which a book cannot convey, and by which he may be more deeply affected."

"Painting in fact," says Dr. Wilson, "employed as every art and science ought, in the promotion of virtue, deserves especially the title of *the handmaid of religion*. The temple adorned with historical pictures in which the life and actions of our blessed Saviour should be related, would offer an auxiliary method of conveying part of those truths which it is the intention of the Lessons to make known."

The array of authorities in the English Church cited by our author includes almost all the most illustrious of our divines; among these are archbishops Cranmer, Laud, Wake, and Tennison, the bishops Jewel, Barlow, Burnet, Stillingfleet, Cousing, Butler, More, Hammond, Montague, Hooker; with these Raleigh, Twisden, Clarendon, Chillingworth, Sandys, Mede, Barton, Rogers, Thorndike, and many others.

"What," says the great Chillingworth, "if out of devotion towards God, out of a desire that he should be worshipped as in *spirit* and *truth*, in the first place, so also in the *beauty of holiness?* what if out of fear that too much simplicity and nakedness in the publique service of God, may beget in the ordinary sort of men a dull and stupid irreverence, and out of hope that the outward state and glory of it, being well disposed and wisely moderated, may engender, quicken, increase, and nourish, the inward reverence, respect and devotion, which is due unto God's sovereign majesty and power? I say, what if out of these considerations, the governors of our Church more of late than formerly" (about 1635) "have set themselves to adorn and beautifie the places *where God's honour dwells*, and to make them as heavenlike as they can with earthly ornaments? Is this a sign that they are warping towards popery? Is this devotion in the Church of England, an argument that she is coming over to the Church of *Rome?*"

The evidence of Archbishops Tennison and Wake speak to the sentiments of the Church in the conclusion of the seventeenth and beginning of the eighteenth centuries. The former says, "To say with men that run into extremes, that devotional pictures are no helps to excite memory and passion, is to forget that they are called mute poems, to speak against common sense, and to impute less to a crucifix than to the tomb of our friend, or to a thread on our finger. They may be used as monitors in a Christian commonwealth, where their *worship* is plainly and frequently forbidden, and by all understood to be prohibited. And it is high superstition in those who in our late unhappy revolutions defaced such pictures, and brake down such crosses as authority had suffered to remain entire, whilst it forbad the worship of them; and was in that particular so well obeyed that none of them (it may be) ever knew one man of the communion of the Church of England to have been prostrate before a cross, and in that posture to have spoken to it." "But for the images or pictures of the saints in their former estate here on earth, if they be made with discretion, if they be the representations of such whose saintship no wise man calleth into question, if they be designed as their honourable memorials, they who are wise to sobriety, do make use of them; and they are permitted in Geneva itself, where remain in the quire of the church of St. Peter, the pictures of the twelve Prophets on one side, and on the other those of the twelve Apostles, all in wood; also the pictures of the Virgin and St. Peter in one of the windows. And we give such pictures that negative honour which they are worthy of; we value them beyond any images besides that of Christ, we help our memories by them, we forbear any signs of contempt towards them. But worship them we do not so much as with external positive signs; for if we uncover the head, we do it not to them, but at them, to the honour of God who hath made them so great instruments in the Christian Church, and to the subordinate praise of the saints themselves."

Archbishop Wake, who succeeded Tennison, (1716,) is still more explicit. "When the pictures of God the Father," says he, "and of the Holy Ghost, so directly contrary both to the second commandment and to St. Paul's doctrine, shall be taken away, and those of our Saviour and the blessed saints be by all necessary cautions rendered truly the books, not snares, of the ignorant, then will we respect the images of our Saviour and of the blessed Virgin. And as some of us now bow down towards the altar, and all of us are enjoined to do so at the name of the Lord Jesus; so will we not fail to testify all due respect to His representation." "This passage of Archbishop Wake's," (says Dr. Wilson,) "must undoubtedly surprise those who think they never shew so commendable a zeal for religion, as when their practice or opinions are diametrically opposite to those of Rome. It is the more remarkable as we find it in his Exposition of the Doctrine of the Church of England," page 18.

To those who use the argument of economy, and would withhold such ornaments in temples in favour of the poor, and that we should not be profuse upon stones while we are stones to the poor, the learned Mede (1630) indignantly exclaims, "This battering ram should not be directed against splendid temples only, while splendid palaces both of kings and nobles are suffered to stand! Do the poor suffer? why then do you not sell your palaces, and those of princes and nobles? Do the poor suffer? why then indulge all this apparatus of finery in your drawing rooms, why such splendid carpets in your halls, such delight and splendour in your ceilings, why so many idle and superfluous luxuries? Take away these, I say, and then you will have enough for yourselves and for the poor too."

"I am not ignorant," says Sir Edwin Sandys, (1570,) "that many men, well reputed, have embraced the thrifty opinion of that disciple who thought all to be wasted that was bestowed on Christ in that sort, and that it were much better bestowed upon him or the poor, (yet with an eye perhaps that themselves would be his quarter-almoners); notwithstanding, I must confess, it will never sink into my heart that in proportion of reason the allowance for furnishing out the service of God should be measured by strict necessity, (a proportion so low, that nature to others most bountiful, in matter of necessity hath not failed, no not the most ignoble creatures of the world), and that for ourselves no measure of heaping but the most we can get, no rule of expense but the utmost pomp we list." He adds a little after, "Especially seeing, as in princes' courts, so in the service of God also, this outward state and glory, being well disposed, doth engender, quicken, increase and nourish the inward reverence, respect and devotion, which is due to so sovereign majesty and power."

Finally, in addition to all these written declarations of the most signal divines of our Church, we must not omit those silent but not less eloquent works of the latter end of the seventeenth and beginning of the eighteenth centuries, which bring us closer to our present times, the works of Sir Christopher Wren and his school, under the full authority of some of those, Sancroft and others, whom we have quoted, which works are unquestionably the last in this country of magnificent dedications to the worship of God in which the sister arts have been called in to assist in the beauty of holiness.

NOTE.

To these works, St. Paul's in particular, no additions have been made since their erection, the paintings are suffered to crumble from the walls, and even the gratuitous offers of Sir Joshua Reynolds and others to restore them have been declined ; in the wealthiest city of the world funds only for keeping out wind and weather and white-washing the interior, have been found sufficient during the last century, and were it not for the zeal of our clergy, who have of late spent themselves to uphold this and our other cathedral churches throughout the realm, it would seem that our government would have left them to decay and ruin.

In France, not esteemed remarkable in the last half century for her religious zeal, the most magnificent of the ecclesiastical monuments have been restored with a cost and elegance (especially within the last fifteen years) which will be seen with surprise and admiration. Nothing can exceed the zeal and splendour bestowed on St. Denis, the Sainte Chapelle, St. Germain des Près, St. Germain L'Auxerrois, and others in Paris. Besides these correct, elegant and most expensive restorations, the modern churches of the Madeleine, Notre Dame de Lorette, St. Vincent de Paul, and others, are worthy of all praise, and contrast with the proceedings of our government in this particular with a very unfavourable conclusion. For be it confessed that while this parsimony is so remarkable in respect of the temples of God, the restoration of our houses of parliament, our royal palaces, our arch-episcopal and episcopal palaces, exceeds all former example.

APPENDIX B.

EXETER CATHEDRAL.

THE expressions of the worthy Fuller probably imply no more than that the west front or screen of Exeter Cathedral, ranks second amongst the sculpturesque monuments of England; and that he, at least, in a bigoted age and with a reformer's eye, had sufficient taste to appreciate its deep interest and its intrinsic merit as a work of art. At the same time we may suppose, from the cursory and indefinite nature of his remarks, that he was not much better informed as to its exact import and details, than the men, gentle and simple, and the books in folio, quarto and octavo, of our own and former generations, since the date of its accomplishment. It is indeed surprising that here as at Wells we should look in vain amongst the numerous learned and artistic authorities employed upon the antiquities of this venerable Cathedral for any rational interpretation of the design and impersonation of these remarkable sculptures, (which are however obvious enough to the attentive observer,) replete as they are not only with the merits of art, and vying with the best works of the Italian masters of their day*, but importing to us a religious and historical interest worthy of our most careful study, raising both the authors and the learned patrons who directed them in our estimation to a very high standard of conception and taste, and throwing a light upon the symbolism, the mind and character of that period, which it is no less important than interesting to perceive and appreciate.

Dean Littleton in his tract on the Cathedral, 1754, makes no mention of them whatever, and we look in vain in Oliver's History of Exeter, Kendall's Remarks on its Architec-

---

* Executed as they may be presumed to have been about 1450, the sculptor might have emulated and possibly have acquired the rudiments of his art from Ghiberti, who was now terminating his glorious gates of the Baptistery at Florence, (the gates of paradise, as M. Angelo called them,) or from Donatello, whose works these may challenge.

ture, or Chappell's Collections, for such descriptions as they demand in the mind of every visitor, from the magnificent folio work of the Royal Society of Antiquaries, in which amongst other fine plates from the drawings of the Roman Catholic Carter, is one on a very costly scale, delineating this screen and its sculptures. Edited by Sir Harry Englefield, also a Roman Catholic and a professed antiquary, we were certainly entitled to expect the desired interpretation, and our disappointment is proportionably great in finding none that can be said to throw any light whatever on the subject, except such as is sufficient to shew the outer darkness in which Sir Harry and his age, no less than the present, are involved in respect of this interesting class of antiquities. The only attempt hitherto published is that given by Mr. Britton in his Cathedral Antiquities from Mr. Davey's MS., but which is erroneous in most of its conclusions.

It is to the old superstition of the reformers, the holy fear of images as idolatrous, that we are to look for that deficiency of intelligence of historical and plastic art which is now so remarkable in all classes of the Anglican society, and even as we see amongst the Roman Catholics.

The English gentleman who justly prides himself upon his graphic taste as far as landscape is concerned, has from his childhood been taught the holy fear of image worship, and a repugnance to all that may be taxed as superstitious, monkish, and legendary art. Haunted with these misapprehensions, even the archæologist and the historian shut their eyes to the large field of religious, historical, and tasteful instructions which these remains so abundantly display, and which seem destined to perish before we have been awakened to the delight and knowledge which they are so well calculated to afford.

Meanwhile our archæological societies are zealous in their investigation of the minutest architectural fragment, our architects reproduce their antique forms with reverence in all that belongs to the mechanical and masonic proportions, even to the niche and canopy and the pinnacles which surmount it, but the statue within is ignored as an idle ornament, and thus we are deprived of all the light and grace, and all the most parlant and elegant conceptions of antiquity. And yet it is certain that until sculpture is better understood, we are but half informed of the merit and the value of our architectural monuments, and we throw away the fairest portion of our inheritance in them.

The science of architecture may express energy, power, order, the sublime; but the magnificent and the beautiful must be added by the sister art of sculpture. Sculpture is the voice of architecture, the lively and expressive vehicle of the purpose and leading conception of the edifice, and it is only by her aid that the record of history, of doctrine, and of sentiment, can be intelligibly expressed. Our present purpose is to shew that the study of the sculptures of the middle ages opens a new page in the archæological and historical no less than the doctrinal and sentimental or poetical records of our country, and that it is worthy to engage the attention of our ablest artists and antiquaries, so long supine in this department.

Rarely indeed have we seen some scion of the academic school of England, (and thus acquainted with the human form divine,) as Stothard in his Monumental Effigies, vindicating the character of our country in this respect, or the dilettante society in classical archæology, who have employed the most accomplished pencils, and cultivated this proscribed walk of art; while the Royal Society of Antiquaries, without regard to beauty and significance, publish at an enormous expense and in grand folio, this magnificent monument of the taste and skill of our ancestors, without an intelligible hint of the religious and historical records involved in them; treating this extensive series of nearly one hundred statues and high reliefs of the utmost significance as unimportant, and the mere effervescence of the sculptor's chisel, as a kind of toy only (erroneously attributed to Bishop Grandison, and appended by him to the seven arches of his new nave), as an idle adornment left to the mason and the handicraftsman, containing indifferently "royal and religious personages, some in robes, some in splendid armour, Evangelists, griffons, virtues and vices, angels," &c.; as if the learned and pious founders of these noble works would have subjected their memories to such inept conclusions, and could have employed so much expense of cost and thought in an array of sculptures to no serious purpose, without any other sense or meaning than that of empty decoration.

In the description of plate VII., representing the grand screen or façade at the west front of the Cathedral of Exeter, Sir Harry Englefield says, " It is divided into three parts, separated in some degree by two projecting parts or buttresses; but which both make part of the regular design. In the centre part is the principal entrance into the church, and on the right of it are the small windows of *Bishop Grandison's chapel*; in the two other divisions are the smaller entrances, which differ in their form. The angles on each extremity of the screen are different; the principal parts of it are a plinth with mouldings, on which rises a regular number of divisions, separated by small angular buttresses, enriched. Each division contains two tier of niches; the lower one has a pedestal of three sides with panels, and embattled at top; from which issue angels, either placed against or embracing small clusters of columns; they display an elegant variety of attitudes, &c. On the pedestals of the small windows there is but one column, though there are three capitals, corresponding with the rest of the several capitals. They support *an assemblage of royal personages, who are seated, some in their robes, and others in very splendid armour*. Those statues on the buttresses which *are standing, are religious; the one* that is perfect, to the right, a bishop. Over

d

the entrance of the left part of the screen are three of the cardinal virtues; the fourth destroyed. The first, from the scales, Justice; the second, from the lance and shield, Fortitude; the third, from the religious dress, and the heart in her hands, Discipline: they each have crowns on their heads, and are trampling under their feet prostrate figures emblematic of their opposite vices. In the spandrels of the arch of the principal entrance are *four angels reposing;* and in four small niches on the side of the architrave are small statues *of royal personages* seated. Over the entrance of the third part issue from small ornamented brackets *two royal personages,* and between them *a griffon.* On the returns or sides of the buttresses are four more royal persons. The canopies to the *niches differ on the* buttresses, and to the four first divisions on the third part. In the second tier, all the statues are standing, except in the niche joining the centre small angular buttress, in which is a *royal figure seated;* in his right hand the remains of a sceptre, and in the other a book; his foot on a globe which is divided into three parts: below is a shield with the arms of the see, quartered with the old Saxon kings, supported by two kneeling angels. The corresponding statue is gone, though the shield with the arms of England, and Edward the Confessor, supported like-wise with angels, remains. The five statues on each side comprehend ten of the Apostles with their attributes. *On the buttresses are the four Evangelists with their symbols at their feet:* the rest of the statues which fill the remaining niches, *have no particular badge to distinguish them.* There are likewise four more statues in this line, on the returns of the buttresses; but they have no distinguishing marks. The statue on the angle at the extremity to the right in this tier, *is St. Michael triumphing over Lucifer.* The heads of the niches differ again in the buttresses; but those in the third part alter their design entirely. The line of the entablature continues to the right hand buttress, and then loses part of its width. The battlements on the first and third part are of a most un-common fancy; angels appear between the openings: some playing on musical instru-ments, and others in attitudes of devotion: the battlements of the centre part and but-tresses are open, and are much enriched."

So writes Sir Harry Englefield upon this work of the dark ages, without throwing any other light, it must be confessed, than such as to make darkness of the present visible. The following essay towards a better understanding of it, without pretension to that conclusion which only the union of the Churchman, the archæologist, and the artist can effectually arrive at, may therefore be the more readily accepted. It is but just that we should give credit to our forefathers for the same skill and understanding in their sculpture which we attribute to their architecture so unreservedly, and the fruit of such reliance will abundantly repay our pains.

The screen is about 82 ft. long, and 28 ft. high, and projects about 7 ft. before the western wall of the Cathedral itself. And it is apparent, both from the style of its workmanship, and the internal evidence of the statues themselves, that it is posterior to the work of Bishop Grandisson by at least three quarters of a century. The bishop during his episcopacy of forty-three years, had accomplished a great work, namely the addition of seven arches at the west end of the Cathedral, and with the piety of those days, he had prepared for his own last home a chapel dedicated to St. Radegundus, attached to the western termination of his glorious work, and thus forming a kind of portal to it. St. Radegundus was one of the earliest Saxon saints and harbingers of Christianity, and was thus associated with the bishop possibly in the spirit of those times as symbolising the vestibule and the door-keeper to the Church of Christ, embodying the conception of the eighty-fourth Psalm, " How amiable are Thy tabernacles, O Lord of hosts. Yea, the sparrow hath found an house, and the swallow a nest for herself, where she may lay her young: even Thine altars, O Lord of hosts, my King and my God. For a day in Thy courts is better than a thousand. I had rather be *a door-keeper* in the house of my God, than to dwell in the tents of wickedness."

This chapel, on the south side of the central door, projecting unsymmetrically, and perhaps very inconveniently for the traffic of the narrow street, in front was apparently reduced in size at a subsequent period, the beginning of the fifteenth century, and limited to the projection of the great western buttresses of the Cathedral Church.

The chapel of St. Swithun at Winchester Cathedral had been taken down and reduced about sixty years before for the same reason. The new front was admirably designed to adapt itself to the doors and windows required by the original building, without derangement to the proposed series of illustrative sculpture, and extended over the entire width of the west end; and it is a masterpiece of freedom and ingenuity of design, and of artistic magnificence; presenting a splendid iconographic picture of the great founders of the Faith, the Prophets, Apostles, and doctors of the Church, and the semblances of those vicegerents of Providence, the kings of this country, under whose protection the Church had flourished, more especially during the preceding six hundred years, for the glory of the temple and the edification of the people.

This screen is divided into three parts by the projecting buttresses of the west front, sustaining the thrust of the nave arches; these material buttresses and supports of the temple receive upon their fronts, with admirable symbolical propriety, the four Evangelists and the four doctors of the Church, the *spiritual* supports and buttresses of Christianity itself.

In the upper tier of the northernmost buttress are the Evangelists St. Matthew and St. John holding scrolls, and with their symbols the angel and the eagle; these are under canopies highly elaborated, and standing on five pillars battlemented as representing Christendom. And under these are the two doctors of the Church, now headless; they may probably be intended for St. Jerome and St. Gregory. These stand on pedestals supported by a single column, which reposes on a battlemented octangular pedestal, from which rise half-length angels playing on instruments of music.

On the southernmost buttress are in the upper tier St. Luke and St. Mark, holding long scrolls, and designated by their usual symbols, the calf and the lion. They are sustained in the same manner as the preceding. In the second tier are two episcopal figures, also headless, probably intended for St. Ambrose and St. Augustine, sustained on single pillars and pedestals as before, accompanied by angels holding their hands to their hearts in the attitude of confession.

The same divisions into three compartments by these buttresses, admit in the uppermost of the two tiers of sculpture, the four greater and the twelve lesser Prophets, the Apostles, the Saviour and the Virgin, and St. George the patron saint of England; and in the lowest tier five Saxon kings and special benefactors of Exeter, and the Norman and Plantagenet kings from the Conqueror down to Henry VI.

The central great entrance doorway, 7 ft. 3 in. by 11 ft. 9 in., is in one entire opening, (and unlike the earlier doorways, divided into two by a central pillar.) It is adorned in the sprandrels of the arches with four symbolical figures of angels, grouped in two on either side, having extended wings; far from reposing, they are looking towards the door in extatic attitudes, but holding their hands to their eyes, and in gestures of admiration, as if dazzled by the splendour of the object they encounter; no doubt intended to embody the idea of the twenty-fourth Psalm, in their phonal and antiphonal exclamations, in which David apostrophises the citizens of his spiritual kingdom, and exhorts them to receive their king, through the gates of righteousness, into his tabernacle[b].

The same idea seems to have been carried out in the battlemented parapet which crowns the screen, in which a choir of angels sounding the trump, the cymbal, and all manner of music, in prayer, and in rejoicing, seem to hail the coming of the Saviour or of the arc of God from the walls of a new Jerusalem. These are preserved in the north and south extremities of the screen, but the central portion appears to have been

---

[b] " This is the generation of them that seek him, that seek thy face, O Jacob!

Lift up your heads, O ye *gates*, and be ye lift up, ye *everlasting doors*, and the King of glory shall come in.

Who is the King of glory?

The Lord strong and mighty, the Lord mighty in battle.

Lift up your heads, O ye *gates;* even lift them up, ye *everlasting doors*, and the King of glory shall come in.

Who is the King of glory?

The Lord of hosts, He is the King of glory. Selah."

WEST FRONT OF EXETER CATHEDRAL.

Left section — Development of the return of Screen:

Angels.

1	Alfred.
2	Athelstan.
3	Edgar.
	Justice.
	Fortitude.
	Temperance.
	Chastity.
4	Canute.
5	Edward the Confessor.
6	ST. JEROME.
7	ST. GREGORY.
8	William the Conqueror.
9	William Rufus.
10	Henry I.
11	Stephen.
12	Henry II.

Angels.

Angels.

Angels.

13.14	Richard I.
	John.
	Window.
	Window.
15	Henry III.
16	ST. AMBROSE.
17	ST. AUGUSTINE.
18	Edward I.
19	Edward II.
20 21	} Edward III. Richard II.
22 23 24	Henry IV. Henry V. Henry VI.

Angels.

Development of the return of Screen to the Cathedral.

Right section:

Angels.

1	Isaiah.
2	Jeremiah.
3	Ezekiel.
4	Daniel.
5	Hosea.
6	Joel.
7	Amos.
8	ST. MATTHEW.
9	ST. JOHN.
10	St. Philip.
11	St. Bartholomew.
12	St. Matthew.
13	St. Thomas.
14	St. Andrew.
15	St. Peter.
16	Virgin.
17	The Christ.
18	St. Paul.
19	St. John.
20	St. James major.
21	St. Simon.
22	St. James the Less.
23	St. Jude.
24 25	ST. LUKE. ST. MARK.
26	Obadiah.
27	Jonah.
28	Micah.
29	Nahum.
30	Habakkuk.
31	Zephaniah.
32	Haggai.
33	St. George.
34	Zechariah.
35	Malachi.

North aisle window.

Great west window.

Angels.

South aisle window.

repaired with a more modern parapet, in which this poetical and very beautiful thought has been entirely overlooked and obscured[c].

In the range of statues of the Apostles above the door, St. Peter and St. Paul, to whom the church is especially dedicated, are conspicuous; and the Saviour (now converted into James I., with a sceptre in one hand and a book in the other) and the Virgin, whom He was in the act of crowning, divided the centre, now wanting; and who by the same rule ought to have been replaced by the jolly Queen Anne of Denmark. Over the north door, in small statues, are the four cardinal virtues, Justice, Fortitude, Temperance, and Chastity, the last wanting; this was probably the door chiefly used by the laity; over the south door, which differs materially in its architecture, are the *busts only* of Edward III. and Richard II., having their symbol, the swan with two necks, (*and not a griffon,*) between them.

The south angle, conspicuous from the narrow street, (which originally took its course along and opposite the west front in a very confined area,) is ornamented richly, and the figures of the upper tier continued to the western walls of the Cathedral. In the second or lowest tier the niches never appear to have been occupied, Henry VI. being the last king, and evidently by another and very inferior hand to that which elaborated the other portions of this elegant work. Proceeding to the particulars of these tiers, it is to be remarked that the Saxon kings, and the Prophets and Apostles, are conventional, and by an inferior hand, the costume of the second resembling such as are seen in Henry the Seventh's chapel at Westminster, of the last resembling those conventional symbols and dresses attributed to the Apostles at all times without much variation; while in the kings from the Conquest downward the sculptor has evidently dwelt upon the historical records of them, and has rendered his conception of their individual characters often in a most racy and dramatic manner, displaying at once the great interest which he himself, no less than his spectators, would feel in rulers comparatively so recent and so influential on the history and happiness of the country.

In the upper tier are thirty-five niches; the first, Isaiah, is clothed in long robes with a kind of veil on his head; 2, Jeremiah, 3, Ezekiel, and 4, Daniel, wear a kind of hat; they are in long robes, and most of them carried scrolls, on which originally were inscribed, perhaps in letters of gold, now obliterated, their proper names. The following, the minor Prophets, on the north side, are, 5, Hosea, 6, Joel, in a singular and female costume, which has led Mr. Davey to entitle it Deborah, and for no other reason that can be imagined; 7, Amos, is in the corner. In the front of the buttress are,

[c] The introduction of angels in similar situations is traced over the gateway of the college of Henry VI. at Cambridge, and in profusion throughout the chapel of Henry VII. at Westminster.

8, St. Matthew, and 9, St. John, as above described. In the returning angle is the figure of an Apostle holding his mantle full of what may be supposed loaves or provisions, and which may be presumed therefore to represent, 10, St. Philip the Deacon; next to him and in usual company and order is 11, Bartholomew, holding his skin in his own hands; 12, Matthew, who appears again as an Apostle with a book in his left; and 13, Thomas, who holds some object in his left not distinguishable.

No. 14 is St. Andrew, recognised by his cross; and next to him is St. Peter, 15, not (as at Wells) crowned.

No. 16, an empty niche which originally contained the Virgin; No. 17, the Saviour, His foot upon a globe, in the act of crowning the Virgin, but now altered in adulation of James I., with a sceptre in his right, and a book in his left.

No. 18, a venerable figure with a long beard, representing St. Paul.

No. 19, a graceful young figure, representing John again, in his character of an Apostle.

No. 20, St. James, with his palmer's hat, and reliquary suspended to his girdle.

No. 21 may be Simon, and No. 22, James the Less, having the fuller's club in his left.

No. 23, now broken, may be St. Jude, in the corner of the buttress.

No. 24 and 25, in front of the buttress, are St. Luke and St. Mark, with their respective symbols as Evangelists.

The following figures, very finely and variously draped, 26, 27, 28, 29, 30, 31, may be Obadiah, Jonah, Micah, Nahum, Habakkuk, Zephaniah; 32 is St. George destroying the dragon; 33, 34, 35, Haggai, Zechariah, Malachi.

In the second tier are twenty-seven niches and twenty-four statues; those on the return being empty. Commencing from the north is, in all probability, Alfred, whose hands, now broken, appear to have held forth something which was most probably a book. Like all the kings, he is seated on a throne under an elaborate canopy in a well-proportioned niche, and supported by a cluster of three columns, round which guardian angels, in a variety of attitudes, significant of their care of their lives and acts, are entwined, some with books and instruments of music, others in expressions of grief or repose; they figuratively uphold the pillars of the state, the pillars being triens; they spread their wings around them in gestures full of expression and variety, and are composed by no mean hand; they issue from an embattled pedestal, springing from a projecting plinth.

No. 2 is probably Athelstan, the 3rd may be Edgar, the 4th Canute, the 5th Edward the Confessor, the founder of the see of Exeter; the dean and chapter were enjoined to pray for the three first, the latter, through acknowledged benefactors, are not cited by Bishop Lyttleton. The bidding prayer, composed in the time of Edward IV., enjoined that "ye shall praye for the soule of Kynge Athelstan, the first founder of this place, for Kynge Edgar, Kynge Alfrede, Kynge William Conqueror," &c. &c.

Nos. 6 and 7, already mentioned.

No. 8 is William the Conqueror, with his legs and his arms crossed, in a sullen attitude, his head, which has suffered much injury, as indeed is the case with most of these statues, somewhat sunk between his shoulders.

No. 9 is unquestionably William Rufus, a well-composed and beautiful statue, full of the abrupt vivacity attributed to his character. The red king, his legs crossed, with his right hand on his left knee, and his left *a kimbo*, seems earnestly to address his brother Henry Beauclerc. His hair in wavy tresses spread upon his shoulders.

No. 10, the accomplished and politic Beauclerc, in gentler guise, and like an older and more sagacious prince, listens to the address of the lively king, his left on his left knee, and his right raised to his breast. This statue is full of meaning. The legs are in all instances crossed, and a certain quaintness of attitude and gesture strike the beholder at first, which afterwards disappears in the intensity of their character, and the appropriateness of their semblance and the delicacy of execution which accompanies them.

King Stephen, No. 11, is less successful, the beauty attributed to him in history is not conspicuous, but Henry II., No. 12, is full of all the dignity and wisdom for which he was distinguished.

No. 13, on the south side of the central door, a very remarkable figure, admirably composed in full and elaborate armour, his legs crossed and spurred, a dog between them, and holding a large sword, now broken, in both his hands, his face mostly concealed in his helmet, but exposing his large mustachios and a fierce and terrific countenance, is undoubtedly the Cœur de Lion, Richard I. The popular idea of the warrior of the Holy Land, and romantic hero, and the pride of the English song, could hardly be conveyed better than by this figure; the splendid armour quoted by Sir H. Englefield is confined to this and Henry the Fifth's statues.

Next to him, No. 14, the detested and abject King John, is caricatured by the sculptor, a mean figure crouching, with one shoulder higher than the other, his head on one side sunk between them, and partly hiding his face with his left hand. There cannot be a moment's doubt of the intention of the artist, though possibly overcharged to gratify the popular aversion.

The two following niches are pierced for windows to the chapel of St. Radegundus, and evidently remained at all times empty. The form of the niche, the canopy, the order of the architecture, and the obvious use made of them for an intelligible purpose, all excused and reconciled the apparent irregularity in the succession of the statues. No. 15 in the corner is Henry III., a statue of no great remark or character.

The two figures standing in the front of the buttress, Nos. 16 and 17, have been already described.

No. 18, Edward I., is not remarkable, but No. 19 is a most engaging statue. The young king, crowned, debonnaire, and splendidly attired, with incipient beard, his wavy tresses spread upon his shoulders, a tight dress, displaying the fine form of his figure, embroidered throughout, his legs crossed, and in a graceful attitude, holding in his right his sceptre, and in his left his usual symbol a flower, the careless and ill-fated Edward II. His follies and extravagance, his Gaveston and his prodigality, all crowd in to aid the spectator to appreciate this remarkable statue.

It is strange that the glorious King Edward III., No. 20, and his reckless grandson, Richard II., No. 21, are represented only in bust over the south entrance. The triumphant king turns his head towards his progenitor as if ashamed of his degenerate successor: between them, as has already been remarked, is the swan with two necks, the symbol of the family.

The statue of Henry IV., No. 21, is not less happy than the rest of the preceding as respects character and expression. The care-worn sleepless countenance of the usurper betrays a conscience all alive and sick with pondering and distressing apprehensions. Shakspeare's description is depicted to the life, and we are convinced that no common mind could so conceive and produce the characteristics of the melancholy wily Bolingbroke. See second part of Henry IV. It is remarkable that these last four kings have canopies different from the others.

No. 22, the statue of Henry V., is equally remarkable for character and expression. The warlike king perfectly composed, encased in mail, the visor of his large helmet up and prominent, casting a shade over his face, and reminding us of the Pensiere of Michel Angelo, without any vaunting action like the statue of Richard, it strikes us as the very model of deliberate valour. His legs are crossed, the left enclosed in steel, the right enveloped in drapery; his hands are also crossed, his right holding his keen sword; his breastplate seems covered with chains and orders. All the "modest stillness and humility," the quiet wit and intensity of the quondam madcap, come before us, and we feel persuaded that Shakspeare himself had stood before this admirable work, and had borrowed inspiration from it when he makes Vernon describe our hero in this very semblance,

> All furnished, all in arms,
> All plumed like estridges, that with the wind
> Bated like eagles having lately bath'd;
> Glittering in golden coats, *like images.*
> I saw young Harry,—with *his beaver* on,
> *His cuisses on his thighs, gallantly armed,*—

Rise from the ground like feather'd Mercury,
And vaulted with such ease into his seat,
As if an angel dropt down from the clouds,
To turn and wind a fiery Pegasus[4].

No. 23 is a deplorable falling off: the hand that executed the preceding statues, had ceased to work; some wretched imitator of that, or possibly long succeeding time, has stuck up the emblem of Henry VI., which is below criticism: the other niches are empty.

From the entire change of style in this statue, and the want of the succeeding ones, the presumption that this work was executed during Henry the Sixth's reign acquires a high probability. In 1452 the king visited Exeter accompanied by a prodigious concourse of country gentlemen and yeomen. The mayor and chamber, with upwards of three hundred persons in the city's livery, went forth to meet him to the high cross, where the king, after receiving the incense and kissing the cross, mounted on horseback. Then alighting at the entry of the Close, he advanced in procession to the Cathedral, attended by the bishop, canons and choristers; and having performed his devotions at the high altar, and made his offerings, he retired into the episcopal palace, where he continued two days, during which time he renewed the charters of the city. See Britton's English Cathedrals, p. 43.

These works, long consigned to neglect and disrepute, their features defaced by wanton mischief and degraded by dirt and soot, require all the faith and all the knowledge of design and of sculpture which the spectator can bring to bear upon them. Fashion and favour, hardly less capricious in taste than in other matters of opinion, may at some future period bring these sculptures into favourable notice again, and the treatment they now receive, will be counted in a future generation amongst the sins of a past age, and as unceremoniously attributed to those now most concerned in their respectful preservation, as is customary with the castigators of the by-gone times.

[4] Henry IV., part I. act 4. sc. 1.

e

APPENDIX C.

NORWICH CATHEDRAL.

THE Cathedral Church of Norwich, so remarkable for its internal decorations of sculpture, exhibits very little use of this elegant art externally. The west front is a simple tetrastyle of Norman architecture, subsequently altered to receive a vast window and doorway; built of a coarse and friable stone, it was ill adapted to sculpture; the few specimens, however, which exist are of great interest; especially the statue of Bishop Herbert de Losinga, the magnificent founder of this noble Cathedral Church in 1096, which affords perhaps the only ascertained example of the art of this date. This figure is affixed to the north transept (see pl. x. Britton's Norwich Cathedral) immediately over the door into the church; and nothing can be more barbarous than its design and execution, nor indeed more remarkably contrasted with the eloquent historical portrait of him given in the Anglia Sacra, pt. i. p. 407. "Erat quippe vir omnium literarum tam sæcularium quam divinarum imbutus, scientia, facundia incomparabili, venustus corpore, jocundus aspectu, ut solo visu plerumque a nescientibus quod esset episcopus deprehenderetur. Mentis quippe gratia radiabat in vultu; et morum tranquillitas corporis officium suo famulatui subigebat."

His magnificent foundations in the Cathedral and other churches, his services to the State in his public character, were no less active and suited to the rapid progress of his day.

"In growing and enlarging times," says Sir Henry Wotton, "arts are commonly drowned in action," and a more apt illustration of this truth can hardly be found than in the barbaric effigies of the animated and illustrious Bishop Herbert.

Of the great period of sculpture of the thirteenth century no specimen exists; the Lady Chapel, built from 1244 to 1257, has been unfortunately removed.

Over the buttresses which sustain the apsidal choir, the twelve Apostles are grandly seated, as at Peterborough, presenting an architectural motive of great propriety, effect, and indeed use, since they give stability by their weight. They are, however, somewhat diminutive, and are probably of the fifteenth century.

The best specimen of the art is presented to us in the prior's doorway at the north-east angle of the cloisters, said to have been erected about 1299; and the style well corresponds with that period. See title-page of Britton's Norwich Cathedral.

Upon the face of the archivolt are seven canopied niches radiating from the centres of the pointed arch, in which are admirable statues, of the Saviour in the centre, pointing to the wound in His side: an angel on either side elegantly disposed holds the lance, and the reed and sponge; an archbishop holds a church on one side, and a king on the other, with his right hand in his necklace or rosary in the conventional attitude of that day: these trample upon hideous figures signifying the Vices. St. John the Baptist in camel's hair, and a prophet, probably Moses, on the other side, complete the number seven. Not far from this gate, south of the choir, was a chapel dedicated to St. John the Baptist.

But the unpromising and unadorned exterior of Norwich Cathedral is amply compensated by the magnificent interior, which employed four hundred years in its accomplishment, (1096 to 1535.)

Its Norman pillars of the eleventh and its admirable vaulted ceiling of the fifteenth century, the most beautiful in its structure, order, tracery, and sculpture in England, its rare apsidal termination, its presbyterium, and the choir, especially when viewed from the western gate of the screen, constitute one of the most interesting specimens of medieval art we possess; beautiful and instructive in all respects. See the elegant plates xii. and xiii. of Britton's Norwich Cathedral.

The vaulted ceiling and its sculptures were justly accounted a peculiar glory to the Cathedral Church of Norwich; and the Anglia Sacra records accordingly the last embellishments which Bishop Nix bestowed on this feature (pt. i. p. 419): "Ecclesiæ Norwicensis laquear pulcherrime decoravit, atque alam ejusdem aquilonarem construxit." This illumination and gilding was still apparent in 1806, when a ruthless and impartial "light colour," says the lenient Britton, in other words a white-wash, obscured its remaining lustre and that perspicuity which can be given to such distant ornaments only by colour and illumination. Not only the beauty but the meaning of this remarkable series appears to have been equally veiled from modern eyes, for I find no notice of their order and meaning in any accounts I have been able to consult, worthy as it is of all respect and observation.

First, in the ceiling of the nave, which extends 237 feet from the central tower to the western front, are fourteen bays, in each of which are twenty-two subjects, making three hundred and eight in all.   Seven of these bays relate to the Old, and seven to the New Testament.

In the first bay, against the tower of the transept, we distinguish a head surrounded with rays, illustrating the sublime passage of Genesis so well approved by Longinus: "Let there be light, and there was light."   The creation of the world, of the angels, of the fallen angels, of man, of woman, of beasts, of fishes, of herbs, of creeping things, of the eagle, of the dove; the temptation; the expulsion; the curse of Cain, &c.

In the second bay, Noah building the ark; the ark with numerous arches shewing divers animals; the dove with the olive branch; the sacrifice on Ararat; the covenant, &c.

In the third bay, a mason at work with his adze, his square hanging on a tree; the tower of Babel; Abraham builds an altar, receives the angels, angels on either side prepare the repast; he casts forth Hagar; the cave of Machpelah; the sacrifice of Isaac; the young men and the ass; the ram caught in the thicket; the angel; the faithful Abraham opens the door of a church as the founder of the faith, &c.

In the fourth bay, the aged Isaac; Esau and Jacob prepare the savoury meat; Jacob's journey to Padan-aram; the vision of the ladder; he feeds the flock of Laban; Rebecca and Leah; he struggles with the angel; the death of Jacob; his prediction of the last days, &c.

Fifth bay, Joseph is put into the pit; sold into bondage; the journey into Egypt; Joseph before Pharaoh; the interpretation of dreams; the sheaves bowing to Joseph's sheaf, &c.

Sixth bay, the finding of Moses; the fire in the bush; the cloud behind the camp; Pharaoh's chariot floating; the Egyptians drowning; Samson and the lion; Samson carries off the gates of Gaza, &c.

Seventh bay, David kills Goliah of Gath; he cuts off the skirt of Saul's garment in the cave Engedi; he carries off the spear and cruse of water; Solomon in all his glory, sitting on the throne of David; his temple, &c.

These are the most conspicuous subjects traced of the Old Testament; the following are of the New.

Eighth bay, the Annunciation; the Visitation; the birth of John; the birth of Christ; the wise men enquiring of Herod, who sits with one leg crossed over the knee of the other, in the conventional attitude of kings in council; Herod slays the children of Bethlehem; the flight into Egypt, &c.

Ninth bay, Christ amongst the doctors; baptism in Jordan; on either side an angel ministers, the one holding a shirt, the other His garment; turning of water into wine; the raising of Lazarus; the sick man takes up his bed, &c.

Tenth bay, the Last Supper, the Apostles radiating round the table, forming a star well adapted to the boss; the twelve baskets of fragments; the lad with five barley loaves; Christ rides into Jerusalem; in the garden of Gethsemane; the Apostles; the betrayal, &c.

Eleventh bay, Christ before Pilate; mocked by the soldiers; crowned with thorns; before Caiaphas; Peter cuts off the ear of Malchus; Christ led to crucifixion, &c.

Twelfth bay, the elevation of the cross; the Crucifixion; the soldiers casting lots for His vesture; Christ laid in the tomb; descends into the jaws of a monster signifying hell; the soldiers parting His garments amongst them; a soldier with the spear, &c.

Thirteenth bay, the Resurrection; the Ascension conventionally represented, the soles of the feet only of the Saviour being seen, the Apostles radiating round in the form of a star; angels adoring in the conventional attitude of raising the hands; Christ in the garden; Mary kneeling with a book before her; the day of Pentecost; on either side two prophets cast down monsters which they hold by the tail or the hind legs, &c.

Fourteenth bay, the Resurrection; all rise from the tomb; kings and bishops naked, but recognised by the crown and mitre; angels on either side sound the trump; the elect are invited; the cursed are seized by devils, and cast into the enormous jaws of hell; Christ, the Virgin and St. John, in judgment.

Thus terminates the central nave. In the transepts are four bays similarly disposed, with sixty-eight subjects in each transept, by no means easy of interpretation. That to the north relates to the prophets, especially the book of Daniel; we distinguish Shadrach, Meshach, and Abed-nego; they walk unhurt in the midst of the fire; the dream of Nebuchadnezzar; the king is in bed, and a monster stands before him.

The second bay appears to relate to the adoration of the Magi.

The third bay to the death of the Virgin, her ascension, her transfiguration, &c.; a ladder, to signify possibly that through the Virgin we ascend to Heaven; a door closed; a person standing at it as if knocking for admission through the intercession of the Virgin.

In the south transept we discover the marriage of the Virgin. A boat appears; general councils are held, &c. &c. In these, both the subjects are obscure and the art inferior to that of the west nave.

It is very remarkable that the nave of the east end is deficient in historical and sacred subjects, rebus and armorial badges taking their place. From a well which appears to have been gilt, we may suppose that Bishop Goldwell (1472) erected the vaulting of this portion, and from the hart lying, in several parts of the western nave, we may safely conclude that Bishop Lyhart (1449 to 1472) was the munificent and learned prelate under whom these significant and admirable sculptures were executed.

The taste for this interesting and instructive decoration appears long to have prevailed at Norwich; as we may judge from the cloisters, which are of unexampled magnificence and extent, being about 176 feet on either side, in thirteen bays on one side, and fourteen on the other, admirably groined and carved with series of scriptural subjects. They appear to have been begun in 1297, and finished in 1430; a remarkable example of the confidence with which the works of those days were begun, continued, and ended, during, in this instance, 133 years.

Proceeding southward from the prior's door to the chapter-house, we have, in the first bay, the jaws of hell and the damned therein; and in the following four, the flagellation; the bearing the cross; the crucifixion; the resurrection; and on the corbels against the wall are the four Evangelists. The aptness of these subjects to the brotherhood in this important and much used passage is striking. From the entrances to the infirmary and chapter-house, southward, we have only foliage and architectural ornaments in the bays.

In the north cloister proceeding from the prior's gate westward, we have from the Acts, the Apostles in mount Olivet; the Ascension, expressed by the impress of Christ's feet upon a stone; against the wall, on a corbel, is the crucifixion of Peter, his head downward; Thomas puts his finger into the wound; Christ in the garden; Peter taken up into the boat; the death of the Virgin, &c. &c.

The south and west cloisters are wholly devoted to the Revelations, and some are sufficiently obvious. Commencing on the west we have the illustration of chap. i. 16, "One like unto the Son of Man, out of His mouth went a sharp sword;" four only of the seven Churches appear, the "faulty" Ephesus, Sardis, and Laodicea are omitted*.

"The great dragon, that old serpent," ch. vii. 9, is represented in the usual conventional form of hell.

The beast, "who is like unto the beast," ch. xiii. 4, a woman riding on a beast, "mystery, Babylon the great, the mother of harlots and abominations of the earth," are singular representations; two wells appear, possibly the bottomless pit; the pouring out of the vials of wrath, ch. xvi. 17; the angels singing "the song of Moses," "the song of the Lamb," ch. xv. 3; the elders assembled, "a great voice of much people," ch. xvii. 12; the Lamb triumphant, ch. xvii. 14; the dragon vomiting, "and I saw three unclean spirits like frogs, come out of the mouth of the dragon;" the angel conversing with John.

On the south side are plainly the Saviour on His throne, "one like the Son of Man," enclosed in the usual figure of the mandorla or vesica piscis; the Lamb triumphant, in

* When I visited these places in 1812, they were a desolation, while Thyatira, Pergamos, Smyrna and Philadelphia still flourish. It would be interesting to discover, if possible, whether such was the state of these seven cities in 1400.

the same figure; the Lamb and the book; John writing his Revelations; the four beasts round about the throne; five stars and five candlesticks, possibly alluding to the seven stars and seven candlesticks. One more of the seven Churches is admitted than in the west cloister, possibly alluding to Ephesus, "I will remove thy candlestick out of his place except thou repent;" death on the pale horse; the horse that was red; the angel crying, "Woe, woe, to the inhabitants of the earth."

Such are some of the subjects of the Norwich sculptures, and it is certain that they deserve all that study and illustration from learned hands which their importance both as to history and art bespeak even in these crude notes.

APPENDIX D.

THE SOUTH GATEWAY OF THE CHURCH AT MALMESBURY.

To those who delight in tracing the localities of our early Saxon civilization, and the first scenes of that religion and learning which we have enjoyed, now more than twelve hundred years, Malmesbury possesses a peculiar interest: for while Glastonbury asserted the title of "the mother of saints," in this country, Malmesbury, or Maildulfs-burgh, certainly deserved that of the mother of literature and science, in the west of England. It was here, that Maildulf (one of those learned Scoti who spread the light of religion and of letters to all the surrounding nations from the schools of Ireland, the sacred depositaries of Christianity during the fifth and sixth centuries) succeeded in establishing a branch, which was destined to confer the greatest lustre on the English name; and his barbarous pupils long confessed their obligations to him, by giving his name to their town; for during three centuries Maildulfsburgh was the only designation by which it was known.

Aldhelm, afterwards Saint Aldhelmus, was the first-fruit of this school and master, disputing with the venerable Bede, his cotemporary, the claim of father of Saxon literature. His poem and treatise "de Virginitate" is the most celebrated of his literary works; he successfully applied his talents, as a poet and musician, for the spiritual improvement of his countrymen, and we have the characteristic anecdote of his sacred hymns and recitations on the bridge at Malmesbury to the country people, as they flocked to the market town. He was distinguished in politics as the confidential adviser of the Lycurgus of Wessex, King Ina; he became bishop of Sherborne, and was ultimately canonized, after his death in 708. "In after times," (893) says William of Malmesbury, "allured by the munificence of Alfred, Johannes Scottus, a man of clear understanding and amazing eloquence, came into England, and at our monastery, as report says, being pierced with the iron styles of the boys whom he was instructing, he was even looked upon as a martyr."

In 937 King Athelstan adopted Aldhelm as his patron saint, and in the great battle of Brananburg the king, "invoking the aid of God and St. Aldhelm," recovered the sword he had lost, and finally vanquished the barbarians: "with some of the presents he had received, he enriched succeeding kings; but to Malmesbury he gave part of the cross and crown; by the support of which, I believe, that place now flourishes, though it has suffered so many shipwrecks of its liberty, so many attacks of its enemies!" "After his death at Gloucester his noble remains were conveyed to Malmesbury, and buried under the high altar. Many gifts both of gold and of silver, as well as reliques of Saints, purchased abroad, in Brittany, were carried before his body; for in such things, admonished, as they say, in a dream, he expended the treasures which his father had long since amassed, and had left untouched. His years though few were full of glory."

Lastly, in the twelfth century, 1142, a fresh renown was given to this place by the celebrated William of Malmesbury, the Herodotus of English history, the best and most authentic English historian after the Venerable Bede; a most instructive and delightful writer.

The abbey must have well maintained its merit and importance, as the subsequent remains clearly shew, both of the twelfth and fourteenth centuries, for the church is longer and wider than those of Lichfield, Hereford and others of the second class, and vies even with the cathedral churches of our metropolitan towns.

The gate, which forms the subject of this note, furnishes the most remarkable and unique specimen of English sculpture of that period, and exhibits the character of the Byzantine style according to its northern phase, and long before the English sculptors had dared to think and to design for themselves. It may be suggested as anterior in date to the church; which in its military, but not unadorned style may be supposed to be of the latter end of the twelfth century; but for the silence of William of Malmesbury on this subject, and the injurious terms in which he speaks of Roger of Salisbury, as the usurper, rather than the benefactor of the church, it might well correspond with the style and magnificence of that illustrious prelate.

The arched gateway consists of eight ornamental ribs, in recess, of Caen stone: of which number, five are purely ornamental, while three are of sacred history; the Old and New Testament, in thirty-eight subjects upon the voussoirs of the arches; and upon the upright portions forming the piers are thirty-two subjects, apparently relating to astronomical science, and the occupations of the seasons of the year; these are carved in low relief on ovals (or vesica piscis) formed by the intersection of elegant scrolls of foliage. It is to be lamented that the limits of this work do not admit of the engravings desirable for its elevation, but it has been finely engraved by Basire for the Antiquarian Society, and by Britton in his Architectural Antiquities, vol. i. No attempt, however,

f

has yet been made to decypher and describe these seventy very curious subjects of art and science; which ought to reveal to us more especially the state of both, and of the intellectual spirit of those days.

The historical subjects begin on the west side of the smaller or inner rib, which contains on the eleven voussoirs, eleven scenes. 1, the creation of Adam; 2, the creation of Eve; 3, the paradise; 4, the temptation; 5, the fall, Adam and Eve hide in the garden; 6, the Almighty (in the key-stone) discovers them; 7, the condemnation; 8, the expulsion from paradise, the gate of which is seen; 9, Adam delves and Eve spins; 10, the Almighty enthroned and a small figure before Him, possibly the acceptance of Abel's sacrifice; 11, much defaced, may be the murder of Abel or the lamentation over his body. Returning to the west side, and recommencing at the springing of the second arch, we have fourteen subjects; 1, the command to Noah; 2, Noah builds the ark; 3, the family in the ark, which is supported by many pillars; 4, Noah's sacrifice; 5, the sacrifice of Isaac; the ram caught in the thicket, &c.; 6, the promises to Abraham; 7, the Almighty in the burning bush; 8, Moses and Aaron; these two last forming the centre and key-stones of the arch, not without their symbolical meaning; 9, Moses stretches his rod over Egypt; 10, Samson rends "the lion as he would a kid;" 11, he carries off the gates of Gaza; 12, he diverts the Philistines; 13, David slayeth the lion and the bear; 14, David slays the Philistines: thus, five out of the fourteen last subjects are heroical, as if suited to the rude and warlike spirit of the times. Returning again to the west side to describe the third and outer rib, we find thirteen subjects, each comprising two stones, or twenty-six voussoirs, while the preceding occupied but one stone or voussoir. The subjects are consequently larger: they relate to the New Testament.

No. 1, is the Annunciation; 2, the Nativity; 3, the adoration of the magi; 4, the flight into Egypt; 5, the dispute with the doctors; 6, the Saviour betrayed; 7, the Saviour's entry into Jerusalem, in the centre or key-stones; 8, the Last Supper; 9, the crucifixion; 10, the entombment; 11, the resurrection; 12, the ascension; 13, the day of Pentecost.

As it has already been observed, these thirty-eight subjects commence and terminate from the spring of the arches, but there is no impost-moulding to divide the upright or pier ribs from the voussoirs; and the scroll and subjects are continuous to the hearth or ground, but the subjects distinct and different; and it most unfortunately happens that within reach and exposed to injury, these very curious pieces are so obscure as to leave the possibility of surmise only as to their original intention.

Commencing again on the west, and with the inmost and smaller arch, immediately under the first (the creation of Adam) sits a figure which may be supposed to represent the Almighty, and the sculptures below may signify the creations of the previous days.

And I presume the subject to continue in the second pier alternately.   Thus under the command to Noah is an angel, which may possibly signify "the Spirit of God which moved upon the face of the waters."   Under the Almighty are two goats, which may signify Capricornus, the zodiacal sign of January; thus, the creation of time, or the first season is synonymous with "let there be light and there was light."   Opposite to Capricornus stands a male and female figure, the latter draped; on which I offer no other conjecture than the possibility of their meaning "the morning and the evening were the first day."   Under Capricornus the subject is defaced.   To the right is another human figure much defaced also, the action unintelligible; possibly Aquarius, the month of February.   In the remaining ten on this, the west side, we trace two other human figures, birds, fishes, and beasts; but too degraded and imperfect to attempt an illustration.   On the east side, the sixteen are scarcely more intelligible; here are five human figures, and groupes, and we trace Leo, Virgo, Gemini, and Sagittarius (like a centaur), sufficiently to confirm the belief that the corresponding months, and perhaps their labours and productions, were intended.   For two centuries before the probable date of this work, astronomy (at least with a view to astrological predictions) had been studied in the schools.   "Ingulphius" (1091), says Dr. Henry, "laments the loss by fire of an astronomical table, at Croyland, more than anything else; he calls it a Nadir, and thus describes it.   'We then lost a most beautiful and precious table, fabricated of different kinds of metals according to the variety of the stars and heavenly signs.   Saturn was of copper, Jupiter of gold, Mars of iron, the Sun of latten, Mercury of amber, Venus of tin, the Moon of silver.   The eyes were charmed, as well as the mind instructed, by beholding the coloured circles, with the Zodiac and all its signs, formed with wonderful art of metals and precious stones, according to their several natures, forms, figures, and colours.   It was the most admired and celebrated Nadir in all England.'"

Astronomy was considered the highest attainment of learning, and in Guido Colonna's war of Troy (1260), Lancelot, Rowland, Gawain, Oliver, and other Christian heroes were united with Achilles, Jason, and Hercules; and the latter is taught astronomy and the seven liberal sciences[a].

There can be little doubt that such was the general intention of these thirty-two subjects, and we have only to lament that they cannot be traced more satisfactorily, together with the collateral symbols and figures, designed to be exhibited to the rude but devout admirers, by the learned inmates of the monastery, of whom William of Malmesbury may have been one, at the very moment of the execution of this work.

In the description of the north porch of Notre Dame de Paris (building from 1163 to

---

[a] See Warton's English Poetry, vol. i. p. 130.

f 2

1225, nearly a century after the work at Malmesbury), by Mons. Gilbert, we find the signs of the Zodiac, with their seasonable labours, their temperature, and the ages of man, in thirty-six subjects, sculptured upon the jambs or piers of the doorway. Beginning from the bottom on the north side, we have 1, two figures riding upon a fish, partly immersed in water, one carrying a boat: this is reasonably supposed to be Aquarius, or February; 2, at the side of the foregoing, a figure with two faces, a Janus bifrons, sits at a repast, as if enjoying this season of repose in rural labour, and considering the past and the future; 3, a monk warming himself by a fire; 4, Pisces, March; 5, a man dries his feet by the fire; 6, another carries a bundle of faggots; 7, Aries; 8, a husbandman prunes the trees; 9, a man puts on his winter habit; 10, Taurus, a woman gathers the young herbs: 12, a man with a double face, Bifrons, in repose; 13, Gemini, the lovely June; 14, a youth with flowers, and a bird in his hand; 15, another takes off his upper garment; 16, Leo, singularly misplaced, being August instead of July; 17, a man gathering hay; 18, another naked, as oppressed with heat.

On the opposite and corresponding jamb we have, 19, Cancer; 20, a mower sharpening his scythe; 21, which should be Virgo, is represented by a mason at work on a stone; and it is very plausibly supposed that the Blessed Virgin on the central pillar of the doorway is referred to for this sign; thus continuing the series, and at the same time conveying a homage to the patroness of this glorious building: 22, a reaper; 23, Libra, a damsel carrying scales; 24, a vintner treading out the October grapes; 25, Scorpio, November; 26, a sower; 27, Sagittarius, December, in the form of a satyr; 28, a husbandman beats down the acorns for the swine beneath; 29, Capricornus, January, a goat; 30, a butcher killing a hog.

The six remaining figures appear to symbolize the ages of man; 31, a youth, his hands raised to his heart, as pure and innocent; 32, another looking at a bird, as if to express his volatile age; 33, another with a hawk on one hand, and leading a dog with the other, describing the love of the chase; 34, a mature man, at the studious age, sitting in contemplation; 35, a more aged one, presiding as a judge; 36, an old and decrepit person, with a venerable beard, much clothed, a drapery also over his head.

Such is the interesting description by Mons. Gilbert of these curious illustrations, which are of a date not long posterior to that of Malmesbury, and shewing very conclusively the prevailing use of these calendars of seasons in similar positions, accompanied with their scientific, and at the same time their more familiar symbolism. They supply in some sort the uncertainty which seven hundred years of degradation occasioned to the subjects at Malmesbury.

We now proceed to the subjects of the outer rim (of the New Testament) and its corresponding uprights or piers. These contain four angels in each, who are vanquishing vices or demons, in various attitudes; and these eight, together with the Gabriel in the annunciation, of which they form suite, complete the nine angels, the constant accompaniment of ecclesiastical symbolism, and the fitting guardians of every sacred right and locality.

The design of this gateway, in its seventy subjects of sculptured history of religious, moral, and physical philosophy, is thus shewn to be in no way deficient in the sublime and awful appeal to the neophyte worshippers. It describes very finely the Genesis creation of the six days, the history of man before the flood, the promises to the patriarchs Abraham and David; the fulfilment of those promises; accompanied by the angels of judgment, the expressions of every Christian grace; and the mind is filled with all those ideas and associations which are accounted most affecting and interesting to the mind of man.

The porch within exhibits two very fine alto-reliefs of the twelve Apostles on either side, as preparing the way and opening the heavenly gates; they are seated on thrones, embattled, as in the new Jerusalem; over them is an angelic figure suspended in the air, reminding us of the victory in the classical sarcophagi which they so much resemble in style. Although of barbarous execution, there is a very grand and religious expression about them, and their careful delineation is a desideratum to the artist not only for their intrinsic merit, but as conveying the Byzantine character of art, universally adopted in this country and on the continent in the twelfth and previous centuries, as the model of art and refinement.

On the west side we distinguish St. Peter, with his keys; Andrew, his legs crossed, and the only Apostle holding a scroll; James with a book; John, his head reclined, and his hands in an attitude of devotion; Bartholomew holding his knife; and Philip.

On the east side, Matthew is nearest the church, his Gospel in his hand. The five other Disciples are not distinguishable.

Over the smaller church door, "the strait gate," is the Saviour in the oval nimbus, supported by two angels. In all these are still the remains of painting and gilding; so that the whole was doubtless very splendidly illuminated. Mons. Gilbert reports the same of the subjects above described of the north porch of Notre Dame at Paris, in which he traced the decorations in gold, red, blue, and green.

As already suggested, this "beautiful gate of the temple" at Malmesbury may have been added to an anterior and more antique church; which, in its turn, was removed for the actual one, apparently of the end of the twelfth century: the one circular arched, and the other of the earliest pointed, with other indications of style, seem to warrant this conclusion.

Again about the year 1390, when the church was vaulted in stone and other great repairs performed, such was the just estimation of this " beautiful gate" that the exterior was cased anew, the symptoms of its decay were effectually removed, and the exterior was fortified with a new rib and water-table, strong buttresses, and whatever else might perpetuate it for a thousand years.

The chief approach to the abbey church was from south, the west being close to the road; the cloisters and conventual buildings being to the north and east: it was therefore the most frequented entrance to its holy offices. Warmed by the sun's rays, glittering in its glorious imagery and painting as " the gates of praise," venerable in its ample seats, and ampler alms-giving to the pilgrim and the poor, we are reminded of those passages of the Psalms so habitually recited by the brotherhood of the monastery, and which undoubtedly inspired these very noble and appropriate features of the Lord's holy tabernacle. " Open to me the gates of righteousness: I will go into them, and I will praise the Lord," &c.

In three other very signal French examples, these symbols of the providential order of the universe are conspicuously exhibited, viz., at Chartres, Amiens and Rheims. The coincidence of the famous planisphere at Dendera will not be forgotten by the reader; shewing, as it does, the cosmic acknowledgment of this subject in mankind, as one of the most sublime contemplations of which our nature is capable; at the same time that it is an evidence of the existence, and of the superintending care, and constant presence of the Deity,—of which the humblest rustic, no less than the philosopher, was hourly sensible; and of which they might so appropriately be reminded in approaching the tabernacle of the holy One.

In the northernmost portal of the west front of Chartres, Mons. Gilbert traces nine only of the signs of the Zodiac, illustrated with thirteen corresponding rural labours of the year. The former are carelessly disposed by the sculptor; July is the first, then follow February, June, December, September, August, May, November, April, in their nine appropriate signs. The latter (the illustrations) resemble those of Notre Dame at Paris, except that in November, the woman sows instead of the man, shewing the antiquity of the practice existing at this day of female rural labour in France.

Again, in the northernmost portal of the west front at Amiens, the zodiacal signs and the corresponding labours are exhibited, Cancer, or July being again the first month of the year.

At Rheims, in the jambs of the central portal, the history of Adam and Eve, and the labours of the year, with the four seasons, are represented, but not by the signs of the Zodiac.

APPENDIX E.

CANTERBURY CATHEDRAL.

THE pilgrim to the hallowed temple of renovated Christianity established in these islands under our Anglo-Saxon ancestors in the sixth century, will experience some disappointment in discovering no remains of a more ancient date than the beginning and the end of the twelfth century. Nothing of the four Saxon centuries, nor even of the Norman restoration by Lanfranc, much less of Roman era, is to be found, save in the pages of the admirable Professor Willis.

Indeed the greater portion, the actual west end, erected when the art had lost its unction and Gothic architecture was in decline (1378 to 1501), will, by its smart newness, affected refinement and anomalous proportions*, shock those sentiments of veneration, with which he approaches a site of such antique religious interest. Finally, the recent conversion of the Arundel, or rather St. Martin's tower, north-west, with its characteristic evidences of epoch, and interesting peculiarity of style (see Britton's Cathedrals), into regimental uniformity with the south-west tower, built by Archbishops

---

* The *plan* of the choir, restored by William of Sens on Lanfranc's and possibly still older foundations, displays the ancient Basilica model, used before the "pariquadrate" of Cesarianus (the equal squares, discovered at Romney, and described by him, nearly four hundred years after) at Milan Cathedral was employed; while the western portion of the church (about 1420) shews a total disregard of this approved masonic ichnography, as indeed do most of the works of the fifteenth century. No less in the height of the naves of both, the masonic rule which determined the apex of the vault by the equilateral triangle, was equally disregarded; in the latter, the point of the vault is even higher than a square on the diameter of the church, and partakes of the French extravagance in this particular.

Sudbury, Chichele and others, fulfil the bathos the antiquary is thus prepared for. Some effort of his imaginative faculty and of his organs of veneration will indeed be required, duly to people this Zion of our country with all its affecting and important historical recollections; to figure the first ardent and devoted missionaries, even from the Apostles themselves; the martyrs who have nourished it with their blood under the frequent Danish devastations; the long list of holy and enlightened men who have sanctified it with their prayers and their exemplary lives; the learning which has been repeatedly planted there, and so providentially fostered and advanced within its walls; the gradual improvement of the barbaric creature to national civilization which flowed from its schools and its example; and then, the abuse of sacerdotal assumptions, the fashionable changes of opinion, the shortcomings, and the slackness, which by turns have darkened its sacred precincts. All these should be summoned to interest and to quicken the contemplation of this glorious site.

The purpose of these notes, the iconography attached to our medieval architecture, will be not less disappointed in the remains of Canterbury, so far as the rise of the art and the great epoch of sculpture, the thirteenth and beginning of the fourteenth, are concerned, though the fifteenth will be well illustrated in the choir screen. If our limits did not exclude the consideration of monumental sculpture, this Cathedral alone might supply us with ample materials for a history of the art in these islands.

The Christ Church gateway, by which we enter the precincts of the Cathedral, had, in its perfect state, considerable iconographic and sculpturesque pretensions, and exhibits the last stage of the art before the introduction of the revival, under Henry VIII. and his adviser Holbein. It was completed, as we learn by a large inscription graven in relief along its front, in 1517, under Prior Goldstone II., whose initials and shield charged with his rebus, three gold stones, is conspicuous above the wicket gate. It is a pompous and somewhat confused composition of three stages bounded by octangular towers of small relief. The jambs of the larger gateway are in *Corinthian* pilasters, panelled and sculptured in arabesque; in the archivolt, monkeys and reptiles and fantastic carvings take the place of former holy subjects. The oaken carved and panelled doors might be supposed Italian; the vaulted ceiling is very elegant, and reminds us of Wolsey's taste at Hampton Court. Over the gates is a frieze charged with fifteen shields of the royal Tudors. In the centre is a niche, formerly perhaps containing the Saviour, or rather the Virgin and infant Christ, and on each side two smaller niches. Above is a broad frieze containing twelve angels of large dimensions, holding shields in the fashion so much employed during the fifteenth century.

Through this we approach the Cathedral pile, advantageously, on the south-west angle. Whether the south porch which presents itself to our view is the " Suthbupe, so often mentioned by this name in the law books of the ancient kings, for all disputes from the whole kingdom which could not be legally referred to the king's court, or to the hundreds or counties, wherein to receive judgment[b]," or the gateway we have just passed, is not apparent. Its three sides, and the buttresses attached to the west door, are crowded with two rows of niches, 29 above and 17 below; these forty-six (now entirely empty) may have contained the hagiology of Canterbury. They were probably erected about 1453, and are of greatly improved proportions as compared with that of earlier times, having space enough for the free and unconfined development of the statue: over the door are five ample niches, the central one much larger, (binary,) the two canopies being artistically united for a larger composition. Here we are to seek the only authentic account of the imagery of this porch, namely in the Pilgrim of Erasmus (1497), in which Ogysius is made to say: "In the porch of the church which is towards the south are stone statues of the *three* knights who with impious hands murdered the most holy man" (Thomas à Becket): their names are inscribed, Tuscus, Fuscus and Bereus. We know, however, that the assassin knights were *four*, de Tracy, Fitzurse, de Morville and Brito. Yet no doubt Erasmus relates exactly what he saw.

Hasted, in his History of Kent, supposes that the statues mentioned by Erasmus stood in the *four* niches still remaining over the doorway of the south porch of the Cathedral. Gostling repeats this difficult proposition, videlicet, the placing of the *three* named murderers in *four* niches; which, however, the modern pilgrim will discover to be *five* niches. Under these errors and irreconcilable contradictions we are at liberty to suggest the probable occupants of these five ample niches above the door.

The largest may well have contained the martyrdom, in such a composition as we discover in the great seal of the See, in which the knights dispatch the saint, who is on his knees before an altar, and on the tympanum of the niche we very plainly trace the crucifixion in bas-relief at this day.

The two large niches on either side may well have contained the capital saints of Canterbury, St. Augustine, St. Cuthbert, St. Alphege, and St. Dunstan. In the two niches below these on either side the doorway were probably the statues of St. Peter and St. Paul.

Over this porch in the key-stone of the south window of the tower will be observed a remarkable carving, representing the head apparently of the Virgin carried by an angel, the meaning of which is not clear.

The ceiling of the porch, like that of the west end church, rebuilt by Archbishops

[b] See Willis's Canterbury.

Courtney, Arundel, and Chichele (1381 to 1443), is charged with armorial bearings to the exclusion of all religious symbols; and in the adjoining cloisters (which have the exceptional position of the north side) we count 683 badges and reconnoisances; the personal records of a people who may have been paynims for any thing expressed by the architectural sculpture, though we are quite ready to admit with Gostling "that it was certainly an excellent method of inviting contributors to the works, by such lasting memorials of them and their families." He adds "that a curious observer remarks that we see none of the ceilings thus adorned till the time of Prior Chillenden, 1391. So late was the introduction of this vanity accepted at Canterbury, and so rapidly did it grow."

Thus the iconographic and symbolic sculpture attached to religious architecture, the special purpose of this note, offers nothing to remark upon in the west end; that noble taste having in this age (the 15th) been superseded by the leprosy of vain genealogies, and the aristocratic pride of rank, "the fashion of this world which passeth away." But before it had attained its vigour, we trace in "the key-stone or clavis of the ciborium of the choir, where the crosses as it were seem to meet," the Agnus Dei, with four angel, heads and wings, filling up the points; a quaint and interesting specimen of that period, (1178.) This was the last work of the "Master" William of Sens, before his relinquishment of his charge to "William the Englishman," and his departure and death from the lamentable fall, which Gervase relates with so much feeling. In the crypt, are some barbaric sculptures in the capitals of the pillars, possibly erected by Lanfranc (1077): they are engraved by Gostling, and appear to be without meaning.

We proceed to the reredos of the choir, adorned with the very remarkable statues of six kings. This is a very beautiful architectural and sculptural composition, evidently of the middle or early part of the fifteenth century. It has not escaped the acute observation of the accomplished Professor Willis that "the present elaborate western screen is of a much later period" than that of Prior de Estria, "and a little examination of its central archway will detect the junction of the new work" with that of the Prior, performed about 1330. Britton and others had overlooked this fact so important in fixing the date.

The use also of large angels bearing shields in the cornice, so much employed in the fifteenth century, reminds us of the pageant on the return of Henry V. to London after the battle of Agincourt, 1415, in which amongst other devices "the angelic hierarchy with white dresses, four shining wings radiant with gold, their hair resplendent with tinsel and precious stones, were represented on the battlements of towers; these as the king approached, seemed to hail him with organs and other instruments, and with an English chant."

The ball of empire carried by four of these kings now first observed, reminds us also of one of the circumstances cited in the funeral procession of this king, through Rouen to England. " The embalmed body was placed within a car, on which reclined his figure made of boiled leather elegantly painted; a rich crown of gold was on its head; the right hand held a sceptre, the left a *golden ball*;" the sollerets also, still pointed, assure us, according to Meyrick, of the middle of the fifteenth century. These evidences assist our conclusions as to the personages intended by these very remarkable statues, which are of the finest execution, and four of them evidently portraits; they vary from 5 ft. 2 in. to 5 ft. 5 in. high.

The writers on the antiquities of Canterbury differ on the very important historical point, to what particular kings these portraits are to be attributed. Gostling supposes them to represent King John, Henry III., Edwards I. II. III., and Richard II.— Britton suggests Ethelstan as one, and gives us an imperfect plate, as does also Gostling. None have investigated this interesting subject with the attention due to the facts, first, that they are portraits, and second, that they exhibit qualities of art altogether unprecedented at that period, and entitling them to the highest estimation of the modern artist. They shew, that though iconography attached to architecture had declined, that of images, idols, and monumental sculpture had steadily progressed; exhibiting a discernment of mind in the artist which bespeaks an education of a higher order, and a more special and professional devotion to this department of art; they entirely confirm the idea of excellence at that period in our schools, which is conveyed by the extract from Rymer's Fœdera already quoted, of a " licence to Cosmo Gentiles, the pope's collector in England in 1382, to export three great images, one of the Virgin Mary, one of St. Peter, and one of St. Paul, and a small image of the Holy Trinity, without paying any duty or custom for them :" and we can readily credit the further observation of Dr. Henry, "that we have good reason to believe, that sculptors and statuaries were more employed and better rewarded for their works in this than in any former period, which must have contributed to the improvement of the art. The followers of Wickliffe condemned the worship of images in the strongest terms, and several of them submitted to suffer the most painful death rather than to acknowledge the lawfulness of that worship."

This alarmed the clergy, and made them " redouble their efforts to inspire the minds of the people with a superstitious veneration for images," &c. " The taste for adorning sepulchral monuments prevailed in Britain and on the continent. We know that English artists were employed in erecting monuments for some of the great princes on the continent; Thomas Colyn, Thomas Holewell, Thomas Poppehowe, made in London the alabaster tomb of John, duke of Brittany, and carried it over and erected it in the Cathedral of Nants, 1408." "Of the five artists employed in the monument of Richard Beauchamp, earl of Warwick (who died 1439), four were Englishmen; two marblers, one founder, one coppersmith, the other a Dutch goldsmith. This monument cost about £24,800 of present money," &c.

With these historical recollections in mind, we may well be prepared for the high degree of merit presented to us in this remarkable series, in which a striking individuality impresses the beholder with the idea of absolute portraiture of personages whom we seem to have already seen, and should again recognise individually; each having that special character and conformation, those distinctions and differences, so constant in human physiognomy, and yet so rarely conveyed by the painter or the sculptor in works of this nature. "Facies non omnibus una" was a merit of art understood by this sculptor, in common with Titian, and few indeed besides either in ancient or modern times. The same variety is observable in the drapery of the regal vestments, which, though uniform (for there were no antiquaries in those days), is distinct in each composition, the folds and their grouping tastefully and variously disposed, and admirably undercut, relieved, and studiously executed, with breadth and truth and intricacy at the same time.

There is a tranquil nobility of attitude, aspect, and gesture in these princely figures, and that impassibility observable in persons of a high caste which shews how well the sculptor had observed the characteristics of a true gentleman, and that he was himself one. Indeed, we may attribute the utter neglect into which these merits have fallen amongst our critics and amateurs, to the unobtrusive and quiet dignity of these kings, who in their conscious majesty and self-possession seem to contemn all vulgar ostentation and theatrical ambition to impose and be conspicuous: like the Stanze of Raphael, their modest worth has left them unnoticed, even by a Reynolds.

Learned prelates, accomplished canons residentiary, members of the Antiquarian Society, travelled connoisseurs, sketching gentlemen, drawing "very quick and very ill," have passed through this screen during several hundred years, some having written on and engraved the subject, yet no one has yet made the comparisons which seem to establish these works as of the highest order of merit and historical interest. Here more than elsewhere the protestant prudery and absolute ignorance of the beautiful in this noble art are most conspicuous, because these statues present to us, not only high art which a Chantrey might emulate, but the lively and authentic portraiture of kings to whose times and characters we attach great importance; and which identify the chief actors against Wat Tyler on Tower Hill, and the French at Agincourt, the wily Bolingbroke and the melancholy Henry of Windsor, in the most truthful and interesting manner.

The attribution of these statues which I venture to suggest, offers it is true an arrangement altogether peculiar and novel in monuments of this description. Commonly we have an historical series of kings, sometimes in regular succession, of Saxon and Norman and Plantagenet kings, sometimes a selection only of the former, with the unbroken line of the latter. In the present case it is evident that the intention was to illustrate first the original founder and the restorer of the church at Canterbury, and secondly the recent royal benefactors to the church, the then glory of their country. To this end they are arranged in pairs or parallels, as I presume, thus :—

Henry the Vth.	Richard the IInd.	Ethelbert.	Gateway to the choir.	William the Conqueror.	Henry the IVth.	Henry the VIth.

The gateway is extremely elegant, having in its archivolt the fastenings by which the twelve Apostles, said to have been in silver, were attached; the Virgin and infant Christ having been placed against the ornamented tympanum which occurs between the arch of the Prior de Estria and the new one.

On the north side is an ideal representation of the patriarchal founder, Ethelbert, who holds the church of St. Augustine in his hand, the sceptre in his right; his flowing and curly Saxon hair and venerable beard spread over his breast and shoulders, at once elegant, appropriate, and well conceived and executed.

The fourth king, on the south side of the screen doorway, is no less a conventional statue; also with a flowing beard, but not the Saxon locks, holding a sword in his left, and his right in gesture as deprecating the use of it. This was probably intended for the Norman Conqueror, the restorer of the church founded by the Saxon Ethelbert more than four hundred years before.

In the common seal of the Cathedral we find these two kings constantly recorded.

The second king is obviously a portrait of softer complexion and conformation than the first, and less refined, energetic, and striking; he is youthful, and somewhat fat, and corresponds with the idea formed of the weak and unfortunate Richard II. This mask should be compared with the well-known picture at Wilton, in which the same traits are observable, though younger.

The fifth king is the parallel to this, and is undoubtedly Henry IV. A comparison of the effigy of this monarch in the presbyterium close by, will demonstrate the exact same stature, and features, the peculiar beard confined to the chin, the rest, together with the hair on the back of the neck, shaven according to the singular fashion of the day, and the identity will be easily admitted.

The first statue needs only to be compared with the portrait in Kensington Palace, or the fair engraving of it in Mr. Tyler's life of Henry V., to discover plainly the lineaments of the illustrious hero of Agincourt, Harry of Monmouth, the same depressed eyelids, "the Plantagenet eye," the impassible aspect of lofty cast, the countenance square, somewhat long, the hollow or flat cheek. Nothing can be more satisfactory, as true and identical, or more clear, that the artist dwelt on his subject with all the enthusiasm it might inspire in that exulting day; and with all the desire to transmit to posterity, and in a sacred place, a faithful and unadorned effigy of this remarkable personage. As we contemplate it, a suspicion of the careful copy of a cast taken after death may well cross the mind: we stand before the very man, the flower of chivalry, the pride and the ruin no less of this country than of France for more than half a century.

The sixth statue bears in the lineaments of the countenance so striking a resemblance of the first, that one is tempted at first to suppose it a restoration and a copy of after times, and of inferior hands; but when we read in history that the young prince, Henry VI., was considered to be "the very image, lively portraiture and lovely countenance of his noble parent," we recognise the unhappy king, and feel grateful to the sculptor for supporting so carefully by his effigy the character of his physiognomy thus preserved by history.

If these conjectures shall be confirmed by competent opinions, we thus recover from the dust and the neglect of ages four valuable portraits, and we establish the date of a work hitherto questionable.

There is still another monument of an iconographic kind behind the high altar, and of singular scientific interest, as respects the attainments of our ancestors in the eleventh and twelfth centuries, in the fourth article of the Quadrivium, namely, "Astronomia;" it has never been described, and is well worthy the consideration of the learned.

On ascending the stairs to the site of the shrine of Thomas à Becket, we arrive at the parvis, from which its western front would be most advantageously contemplated. This is a pavement about 27 ft. by 17 ft., inlaid with an elegant pattern in "opus Alexandrinum," composed of porphyry and other precious stones; but more especially on the north and south sides with thirty-two circular white marble slabs (about 1 ft. 11 in. in diameter), graven with symbols, slightly sunk, and filled in with composition of a dark hue, presenting at once a smooth surface for the foot, and a clearly defined figure to the eye.

Of these, nine are distinctly signs of the Zodiac; four appear also to be constellations; seven are virtues and vices; six are seasons; four are griffons and combats with lions; one, ornamental; one, defaced. Besides these thirty-two (sixteen on either side, north and south) there are eight more in the pavement of the shrine which are much defaced, but generally appear to be ornamental; making forty in all: and it is very remarkable that the gate of Malmesbury exhibits the same number, and in the same distribution, shewing that a systematic arrangement was determined and followed in the symbolical illustration of the physical and moral order of the universe. Doubtless the "nadir" at Canterbury was no less splendid than that of Croyland, described by Ingulphus; and the "Trivium" and "Quadrivium" are no less the subjects of study and admiration in this famous monastery, so conspicuous for learning amongst the scientific schools of England. I believe that these remains relating to astronomical science at Malmesbury and this place are the only ones found in England. At Notre Dame in Paris, Amiens and elsewhere, representations of this subject are found, but I think less complete than in these two instances.

Beginning at the north-east angle we trace plainly the first month of the year, Januarius, represented by Janus, with a double face, "ancipite imagine[*]," a pointed cap, a star on either side the head, his left hand opening a door, and his right closing one. He takes the place of Capricornus.

2. Defaced.

3. A man sowing; one of the seasons: in the border are the appropriate ornaments, moon and stars.

4. Aquarius emptying a vase, the water of which forms a circle round him, boldly and admirably composed. In the border is an elegant Byzantine ornament.

5. Pisces.

6. Aries.

7. Libra, anticipated, for here we should have had Taurus.

8. Defaced, but from the traces of letters in the border evidently a group of a virtue and vice.

9. Ploughing, well expressed, in the border is the appropriate ornament of moons and stars.

10. Much defaced, but appears to have been purely ornamental.

11. Taurus.

12. A griffon and a lion fighting.

13. A virtue and vice. SOBRIETAS, LUXURIA are plainly legible in the border. A queenly figure on a throne menaces a drunkard lying at her feet.

14. A griffon holding a sword in the right and a book in the left; an elegant ornament in the border.

[*] Ovid. fast. i. 95.

15. A virtue and vice; the inscription not legible, but possibly industry and indolence: a queenly figure on a throne chastises a culprit on his knees; a rose or quatrefoil in front, a moon and a lily behind.

16. Cancer; terminating the north side. This constellation is again out of its place, for here we should have Gemini, which, however, will be found the last on the other side. Whether these signs have been at any time displaced, or were originally in this order, or rather disorder, is a curious question yet to be determined.

Proceeding to the south side, and beginning as before at the north-east angle, we have,

17. A season, evidently the vintage; a man is treading out the grapes.

18. Two figures sitting together, possibly Castor and Pollux.

19. Defaced, but from the evidences in the border, a virtue and vice.

20. Draco or Cetes, with two major and two minor stars; an elegant ornament in the border.

21. Sagittarius.

22. Scorpio.

23. Much defaced, but from the remains of inscription in the border, evidently a virtue and vice.

24. A griffon winged: in the border is an ornament not elsewhere employed.

25. A virtue and vice, but much defaced.

26. A knight on horseback, in a wood; possibly intended to represent winter as the hunting season: stars and moons form the border.

27. Appears to be Lyra.

28. A griffon and a lion fighting; an elegant ornament forms the border.

29. The mowing season; a man holding a scythe, surrounded with flowers and trees in leaf: in the border are moons and stars.

30. The reaping season; a man holding a sickle, the sheaves behind and round him: stars and half moons form the border.

31. A virtue and vice, but much defaced.

32. Gemini.

In these seasons it would have been satisfactory to have traced the months, six on either side, north and south, in their regular succession, with the corresponding labours, in all instances accompanying them, together with their proper virtues; but we could not discover them: they have probably disappeared in repairing the pavement.

Meanwhile we cannot but admire the appropriateness of this decoration in a place so suited to raise the imagination of the pilgrim. From hence he might behold in one view the wonders of the surrounding architecture; the chapels containing the ashes and the altars of saints and martyrs; the tombs of kings and warriors of the cross, ranged round the shrine of the (so esteemed) prince of martyrs, Thomas à Becket; the gold and silver offerings and gems of which would make "Crœsus and Midas," as Erasmus says, "beggars" in the comparison. And we may rank amongst these glories, certainly as by no means the least noble in conception, the presenting to his contemplation, and under his feet the symbols of that sublime order of the universe in its physical and moral appointments, the seasons and their due labours; and, above all, those moral virtues and graces, without which these blessings can neither be appreciated nor enjoyed.

The extent and general plan of the shrine itself is plainly indicated by the abrasion of the pavement from the feet of the devout during more than three hundred years. Traced by these plain indications we measure about 29 ft. by 18, as the entire circuit: from this a space of about 7 ft. by 18 seems to have been separated as a kind of vestibule (entered from the south-east), in the paving of which are six circular slabs, too much worn to pronounce them symbols; while two others of the same description are seen in the west side; making together eight of the forty above cited. As the seven already catalogued were the cardinal virtues and their opposite vices, these eight may have signified the social and the private virtues, as patience, gentleness, concord, and obedience, with prudence, temperance, justice, force. In all events we may safely conclude on a substantive meaning attached no less to these eight than to the thirty-two already described.

This very interesting piece of antiquity calls for engraved illustrations (not in the compass of these notes), which would be no less elegant than instructive. That they should have hitherto been a dead letter, is to be ascribed to the supineness of all authorities concerned here as elsewhere, or let us suppose, their extreme preoccupation in other and more essential duties.

h

APPENDIX F.

ROCHESTER CATHEDRAL.

THE west front of the Cathedral Church of Rochester presents us the most ancient example of iconographic art, of ascertained date, in this country; having been begun by Bishop Gundulphus in 1103, in the third of Henry I.; and containing in its central western doorway the statues of the king, Beauclerc, and Molde the Good, the Saxon queen Matilda, in very curious and well preserved sculpture, in Caen stone.

The whole of the western front is exceedingly precious, as exhibiting the style of that era, adopted from the Byzantine; more especially as it was understood and practised in France, in S. Germain des Prés, and other ancient examples. It is to be lamented that antiquaries have set so little store on its unique character and high archæological interest; giving us, as it does, most completely, the style and taste of the Archbishop Lanfranc, under whose patronage it was expressly built, as we learn from the Anglia Sacra, P. i. p. 56; and conveying to us, therefore, an idea of the church at Canterbury, erected by that illustrious prelate.

The front is terminated by two bell-towers in the Norman fashion; the whole decorated, at a certain height from the ground, with six orders or series of small columns and arches, the lowest of which is carried on corbels, carved as lions and other monsters. Many of these columns are twisted.

Three doorways lead to the nave and aisles, the centre one of which is highly decorated; four columns in recess, with elegant and elaborate caps, carry as many archivolts, each voussoir of which is separately enriched with Byzantine foliage, chimeras and doves, forming a rich frame to a tympanum, within the arched head; where is represented the Saviour in benediction, in the *vesica piscis*, accompanied with angels and the four evangelists. This tympanum is supported upon an architrave or lintel, in the usual style of that day, composed of eight stones, each of which is locked into its neighbour in the Saracenic fashion, and having on their faces as many Apostles.

The king and queen are incorporated in the fourth columns. The former holds a sceptre in his right, and over his head in the capital of the column is a lion; the latter holds a scroll in her right, the significant symbol of her patronage of learning, an angel in the capital above proclaiming her virtues; her hair is braided in long tresses; both are crowned and trample on monsters, the impersonations of vices; their drapery is on a good principle, but dry in the extreme, and in the elongated style, so remarkable in the Byzantine examples.

In 1177 it is recorded that a fire took place, and occasioned the commencement of a new choir and transept; here we have Purbeck marble columns of the thirteenth century, on corbel-heads of some merit, and remarkable for the prominence of the ears, which characterises the heads at Worcester, the Camposanto at Pisa, and some other works of the early English period. They do not appear to have any symbolical significance.

The doorway into the chapter-house, supposed of the fourteenth century, is very remarkable. On one side is a female statue blindfold, the Tables of the Law reversed, having on her left a crown falling from her head, and on her right a broken sceptre: opposite is a bishop holding a church. The first symbolizes the Jewish Church and the prophecy of Jacob, "That the sceptre should depart from Judah when Shiloh come." Gen. xlix. 10. A similar representation in painting adorned one compartment of the ceiling in the chapter-house of York, and seems to have been a favourite English subject. The second is undoubtedly symbolical of the Church militant. Above are the four doctors of the Church; two angels sing on either side, and on the key-stone are the emblems of Purgatory.

APPENDIX G.

YORK MINSTER.

THE enquirer into iconographic art, relating either to the early phases of religion in Deira, or to the antique history of the metropolis of the north, will be no less disappointed at York than he has already been at Canterbury.

The birth-place of St. Helena and Constantine the Great; the second Rome of Septimius Severus, connecting York with classical antiquity more than any other site in England; the stronghold and bulwark of Saxon Christianity against the Danish persecutions during so many centuries; the scene of Alcuin's renown; the fountain of religious knowledge and literature in the northern parts of these islands, and indeed of France under Charlemagne, find no echo but in the pages of history. In the actual building their deeply interesting memory seems to have been even forgotten; no archaic fragment identifies them, nor does any symbolical record in the new work recall those venerable epochs or memories so dear to the native Englishman.

In the crypts we may still discover the broad lineaments of the Norman Conquest, the tenth edition perhaps of the Christian temple on the same site; and Mr. Browne has been enabled to trace even the plan of the previous Saxon church. Of the great period, the thirteenth, we have the south and north transepts only (1227 to 1260), but having little sculpture, indeed scarcely any other symbol is seen save of the five wise virgins in the five lancet windows in the north transept, fifty-three feet high, "strangely called" (as Britton innocently says, for he does not suggest their real symbolism) "the five sisters." In the vaulted ceiling may be traced the Saviour in benediction, the Agnus Dei, St. Michael and the Devil, St. William and St. Oswald. See Browne's history of the metropolitan church of York.

The nave, and indeed the whole scheme of the plan and section of this glorious church (exclusive of the lady-chapel) offers the most complete illustration of the three great masonic rules preserved to us by Cesariano*, at the same time that it is the most extensive and the boldest structure ever attempted in this country; for the nave is forty-five feet wide: St. Paul's is only forty.

Neither the original architect, nor any subsequently, has ever dared the execution of the stone vault; which, like that of Wem, has always been of wood or plaster only.

Began 1291, and finished 1336, it displays in a remarkable manner the progressive spirit of design amongst the architects of those days; and here we see for the first time, with equal surprise and admiration, the true vertical principle of Gothic architecture carried out in its perfection, and with magnificent unity of design. The columns unbroken and continuous to the spreading vault, the clerestory and the triforium united into one feature, undisturbed by horizontalities or stages, inherited till now (like the normal features of an aboriginal race) from classical styles, delight the eye, and satisfy us in this result of a thousand years of experiment in basilica building.

The magnesian limestone from the quarries of St. Peter's and Thevesdale is perhaps the most beautiful the island affords, reminding us of Pentelic marble, and the queen of temples in which it was employed; and of the same happy coincidence of skill and material in both examples, as compared with other monuments of our country.

The exterior, especially the western towers, carried up by the Treasurer Birmingham from 1432 to 1457, in the reign of Henry VI., exhibits a no less remarkable growth and culture of taste. The acute pyramid or spire gives place to the square tower and pinnacles, and the pointed gable to the low pediments. These, with the flamboyant window and its multitudinous ornament, combine into a master-piece of architecture, peculiar, and entirely illustrative of the English school. The exterior flanks of the nave and aisles are no less elaborately designed, presenting to the observant artist a novel order of enrichment, especially in the cornice, in which the common kale surpasses the acanthus, and displays, as in a variety of instances in this building, the happy application of the commonest plants to architectural decoration, appealing to the only source of all beauty, nature, rather than the degenerate repetition of an accepted common place.

Mr. Browne has given a valuable chapter on the symbolical character of ornamental foliage, in which he points out the herba benedicta, the avens, the thorn, the oak, the laurel, the crowfoot, the rose, the hop, the hawthorn. The plants of ternate arrangement, the strawberry and the ivy, and those of five, the vine and the maple, &c., symbolizing the Trinity and the five wounds; and he well marks the stores of floral beauty

---

* The first rule, the correspondence of the general plan with the vesica piscis, or two arcs of 120°, will be found to coincide with the extent to the high altar, but not the lady-chapel to the eastward.

which offer to the studious mind those endless motives of ornament which made the Greeks and the medievals such consummate masters of decoration.

That the Cathedral fabrics were schools of art, is nowhere more apparent than in the history of York Minster, in which, from the days of Alcuin, 767, but especially after the Conquest, we have the records of continual building, with more or less activity; and when we call to mind that the chapter-house was sixty years in building, and the screen thirty-nine, we may easily conceive how from the school of York, like that of Milan, many a humble Bramante may have formed himself in its never-dying workshops.

In the windows of the lady-chapel we have an unique example in this country of that cage-work, or exterior screen, used at Wem, Cologne, and other German examples.

Vast perpendicular windows throw in a flood of light, and the fragments of the painted glass, " Rhenyshe, Normandee, and Borgondie glasse," now but a kaleidoscope, give evidence of exalted subjects, and of the best art; communicating an unexampled lustre to the interior, and making "the Sabbath a delight" to the people of York who assemble in its long and lofty aisles to enjoy the sun-beams transmitted through their glories, especially on the Sunday, between the services; justly exulting in one of the loveliest and most splendid temples that can be seen in this noble and very numerous family of architectural art.

With reference to iconography, a singular novelty, arising perhaps out of the chivalry and growing liberality of the times, is remarked in the triforium of the western nave, in the central opening of which, and immediately over the point of the eight pier-arches on either side, are or rather were eight statues, apparently referring to the eight Langues or nations engaged in the holy land in the great cause of Christianity; of which those of St. George of England and St. Denis of France are the only ones remaining at the present day. The dragon opposite that of St. George is conspicuous; what were the opposites of the six others no trace discovers, and we can but suggest the probable idea connected with the other new and singular decoration. Mr. Browne supposes these figures simply to represent kings and queens, and states in a note (vol. i. p. 138), that some of these are deposited "in the doubtful charge of the masons:" the examination of them might clear the question materially.

In the eight claves of the ceiling bays are corresponding bosses of significant and well executed subjects, originally gilt; beginning at the east end,

1. The Annunciation, Gabriel holding a scroll.
2. The birth in the stable.
3. The adoration of the Magi.
4. The Resurrection; the Saviour holding the cross and flag, surrounded by angels.

YORK MINSTER. 63

5. The Ascension, quaintly expressed. The twelve Apostles radiate from the centre, in which are the soles of the feet and the garment forming an ornament round them.

6. The day of Pentecost; the twelve radiating as before.

7. The ascension of the Virgin in a very elegant radiated oval surrounded by angels: selected and described by Flaxman in his sixth lecture.

8. The coronation of the Virgin, who lifts her hands in adoration; the Saviour holding the orb; a choir of angels around them.

Each of these is surrounded with eight inferior bosses of foliage or chimera heads, together with bracket bosses, and springing bosses also originally gilt, quaintly and not ill devised for their position; the whole of which, more remarkable for fidelity than grace, may be seen in Mr. Browne's precious etchings: which, together with those of Halfpeny, form a valuable collection for the imitators of the medieval taste, while at the same time they will serve to shew to the informed and classical eye, how much of dignity and beauty have yet to be added to Christian art for its successful appeal to our actual education, whenever artists and opportunities for its full development shall present themselves.

It appears that the same significant and various subjects were introduced into the ancient ceiling of the choir, destroyed by fire in 1829; and we have to lament the disregard of these tasteful and characteristic decorations on the part of all concerned in the restoration: a disregard very justly censured by the York guide of 1846, for, says he, "those who, looking up towards the ceiling, recollect the endless variety of ornaments in the knots and groinings, will be offended with the constant repetition of the same foliage that now meets the eye."

Our attention in the interior is next drawn to the rood-loft screen, which is an imposing piece of design, containing fifteen kings, from the Conquest to Henry VI. It is of very inferior art to that of Canterbury, but a valuable specimen of symbolism and workmanship, and affords us, through the diligence of Mr. Browne, the name of another English sculptor; in confirmation of our favourite assertion, the equality at least of our natives, in this as in every other fine art, during the middle ages, with those of the continent[b]. The date of its execution is further shewn by the niche

---

[b] William Hyndeley is the truly Saxon name of the sculptor appointed in 1472 as warden of the lodge of masons at the Cathedral, on a salary of 3s. 4d. per week, to which a gratuity of 13s. 4d. was added in 1474, possibly for the skill and activity displayed by him in finishing the north tower. Hyndeley, as did his coadjutors, Islip and Darton, has affixed his name by a rebus on the pedestal cornice under the kings, of a *hind lying* in the foliage. Again, in the principal bosses of the archway he had displayed his qualifications in various quaint figures: a man surveying; three monkeys, the emblems of imitation, two having boxes partially open; a dog, the emblem of his constancy to his art; a work tool, a packing case, a lewis, a

provided for Henry VI.; which is now occupied by a statue of recent workmanship, and we must not omit to remark the same fact at Exeter, while at Canterbury the original statue by the same hand with the other kings is still in its place. In this coincidence we have to note first, the contemporaneous execution of these three works carried on by the encouragement, or possibly by the direct patronage and expense of the tasteful and unfortunate king; the patron of the masonic order, and the founder of the most elegant buildings of that period; and secondly, the remarkable circumstance of the omission of his own statue in two instances. Mr. Browne asserts that this statue was early removed, and long replaced by one of James I., in its turn displaced in favour of the actual very poor performance. The reasons of this may have been the political troubles of his unhappy times, or the superstitious veneration of Henry VI. as a saint by the common people. Certain it is that Henry VII. was urgent with Pope Julius II. for the canonization of his predecessor, but these honours were denied by the sacred college.

Finally, we have to remark that the fashion of honouring the royal succession by their effigies affixed to sacred buildings, which prevailed from the twelfth century, now, in the fifteenth, ceased for ever, no less in France than in this country.

The learned Milner asserts, but without giving his authority, that this work was designed for St. Mary's abbey. He coincides with the enthusiastic Carter, in the belief that these effigies were executed (as a general principle) more or less from authentic records and portraits, though he gives no existing comparisons either here or at Canterbury; nor does he distinguish the very superior quality of the latter.

But Milner, as a most accomplished antiquary, gives some very valuable notes, interwoven in the following catalogue, on these statues, which greatly add to their interest.

The artists of those days were happily no antiquaries; we are not therefore surprised to find William the Conqueror, as well as his immediate successors, with long beards, the direct opposite to the well-known Norman fashion.

Rufus carries a bag attached round his neck, possibly to display his rapacity; and he shews his hose, says Milner, to remind us of the trite story of his objection to them for their cheapness only.

---

strap, a chain; ropes, nails, a satchel, a pair of compasses, a rule or scale, and lastly, a noble hind. The *eye* and the *slip*, the *dart* and the *tun*, express his coadjutors.

In 1367 Robert¦ de Patryngton was appointed master in place of William Holton, at a salary of £10 per annum, on condition of his diligence and his exclusive devotion to the Cathedral works.

The carver of architectural decoration is called "Intayler," and his wages seem to have been 2s. 6d. per week.

Henry's dress and attitude express the Beauclerc: his fondness for the Church is signified by the Annunciation on his broche.

Stephen has a short robe, and shews his legs, expressing the active restlessness of his reign.

Henry II. wears the short cloak of Anjou, introduced by himself, and which gave him the name of "short mantle." His broche displays the swan on her nest, the emblem of purity. He holds a heart in his hands, to signify the ingratitude of his sons, which shortened his days, or Psalm cxix. 109, "My soul is continually in my hand, yet do I not forget Thy law."

Richard I. bears a reliquary, after the fashion of Philip Augustus, and as a knight of the sepulchre.

John has no remarkable symbol.

Henry III. appears to have held two sceptres: on his broche is the Ascension.

Edward I. has no remarkable traits.

Edward II. raises his left to his necklace in the conventional attitude of idle grace in those days.

Edward III. has the long beard, so conspicuous in his effigy at Westminster.

Richard II. displays those personal pretensions "as the handsomest king since the Conquest," for which he was remarkable: his hair is gilt [c]; the under part shaven, as observed at Canterbury, a fashion, says Milner, introduced by King John of France, so long a prisoner in this country.

Henry IV. has a peculiar beard already remarked at Canterbury. The collar SS appears first in this statue, and again in that of his gallant son.

Henry V. has a pelican on his broche, to signify his attachment to the Church, or, as we should say more correctly, the sacrifice of his country's welfare to his chivalrous expeditions.

Henry VI. is a modern statue, like that of the same monarch at Exeter, amply displaying, with tasteless design, the superiority of this art amongst us in the fifteenth century; the original, as above remarked, having been removed to prevent, according to some, the superstitious adoration of the people who regarded him as a saint.

The chapter-house is in the elegant octangular form usual in the beginning of the fourteenth century, but the omission of the central column, and the unobstructed diameter of fifty-seven feet, is without example; and this merit, together with that of the decorations of sculpture, painting and glass, justified the monkish eulogy.

---

[c] It appears from an entry cited by Mr. Browne, 1509, that these statues were all painted; "Paid to John paynter of York for painting one image of King Henry, according to an agreement made, 20s."

The imagery of the exterior abundantly displays the decline of religious sentiment, and the growth of worldliness and ostentation.

The Apostles are crowded inconspicuously round the buttresses of the western towers. John and Matthew are in the north, Mark and Luke in the south. An archbishop precedes them, and a king terminates them.

Under the great east window nearly the same arrangement is observed in seventeen busts: first again an archbishop; Moses, distinctly marked by the horn, and Aaron, the twelve Apostles, the Saviour, and a king terminating the series. But crowning the pediments of the west door, no less than the east end, are archbishops in full pontificals, and right and left the Percys and Vavasours, the benefactors in stone and timber to the fabric; while John de Birmingham, instead of *Gloria in excelsis*, transmits his own glory in a large and legible inscription as the chief purpose of the fabric.

Four equestrian statues never yet explained appear on the lower part of the western buttresses. From the attitude of that to the north, the statue of St. Martin dividing his cloak to the naked seems to have been designed.

The temptation and expulsion, in small and inferior sculpture, are represented in the exterior archivolts of the doorway.

The interior of this doorway presents a niche for St. Peter on the central column; both sides are surrounded with niches, which were undoubtedly intended for as many statues, as we may judge by the paintings and brasses representing these niches.

At St. Mary's abbey, York, are some fragments of sculpture interesting as shewing a motive of unusual character; the roof of wood appears to have had its principals springing from niches in the clerestory, in which were the prophets, eight of which remain. That of Moses is distinguishable as having the tables in one hand and a serpent with a bird's head in the other.

A similar motive may be seen in the church at Harrow on the Hill, still legible on its walls:

Sicut Rosa *Phlos Phlorum*
Sic est Domus ista Domorum.

The ceiling was of wood, in imitation of stone groining, "with ribs and bosses covered with gold, and relieved with the richest colours," the compartments of which were painted with thirty-two religious and historical subjects. Of these we may judge by four still remaining, namely, the Saviour holding the ball of empire in one hand, and the banner in the other; the departure of the sceptre from Israel in the coming of Shiloh, designed precisely as at Rochester; St. Edmund the king, holding three arrows; and an episcopal figure, possibly St. William. The clavis in the centre has the Agnus Dei.

According to evidences produced by Mr. Browne this elegant building was begun in 1280 and finished 1340, dates the more important since those of Lincoln, Salisbury, Wells, and London, are not ascertained, and the beauty and peculiarity of these buildings render the epoch of their commencement and completion highly interesting to the history of architecture. On the pier dividing the two doors stands the mutilated figure of the Virgin trampling "the young lion and the dragon under her feet."

Over the doorway in the interior were thirteen niches, doubtless of the Saviour and the Apostles.

In the windows Mr. Browne discovers the cognizances of Edward II. and III.

In the capitals of the north aisle of the choir Mr. Browne discovers the portrait of Henry IV., and a kind of caricature of the political events of his period, particularly relating to the execution of Archbishop Scrope, but these are wholly deficient in art and ingenuity, and serve only to prove the date of their erection.

APPENDIX H.

BEVERLEY MINSTER.

ALS FREE MAKE I THE
AS HERT MAY THYNKE OR EYHE MAY SE.

BEVERLEY is no less remarkable for this, the earliest charter of popular liberty conferred by King Athelstan, than for the shrine and sanctuary of St. John, archbishop of York, 687, whose relics during eight hundred years shed a lustre over this district, and obtained for it charters and the immunities which rendered it another Elis amongst the provinces of England, and protected it by universal compact from all hostile invasion.

Leland in his Itinerary tells us that in his time (1533) "he could not perceive that ever it was waulled, though they be gates of stone portcolesed for defence." And in the time of the civil war Beverley had no walls, and is termed "an open place by no means tenable," nor does there exist in the patent rolls a single grant (as was customary) of a toll for building or repairing walls.

By the effectual invocation of St. John of Beverley, Athelstan had severed at Dunbar, with his single falchion, a mighty rock "still to be seen," says Fabyan, "in the time of Edward III." And William the Conqueror, in the midst of his ravages of Yorkshire, recoiled before the powerful saints, and confirmed all preceding rights and charters. Henry V. regarded him as his peculiar protector in his glorious career and made a pilgrimage to Beverley with his young queen of France, in 1421; and Henry VI. bestowed those magnificent western towers which exhibit the style of that day in such favourable light.

Neither the venerable Saxon, nor even Norman remains of this ancient sanctuary can now be traced, nor any thing of earlier date than 1299. These, however, exhibiting the finest style and proportions of the Early English, may be studied with peculiar advantage by the architectural aspirant.

Although a minster only, the plan resembles that of the metropolitan church, especially in the peculiarity of the second transept, a feature which seems generally to accompany the possession of a shrine. This has never been sufficiently discussed at Beverley, and yet the exquisite and elaborate screen at the back of the high altar appears plainly to indicate its position there, precisely as that of St. Thomas at Canterbury. Oliver doubts because Leland gives no description of the shrine, but he gives evidence of its existence in Saxon times.

The galilee to the north, and the little chamber above for the warden or porter, for the ready admission of the unhappy refugee to the sanctuary at all hours of the night and day, are also features of peculiar interest.

The iconography of this church is sparing, but valuable in the hints for composition which it affords. On the south side of the nave we observe upon the centre of the parapets (which are continuous, and not battlemented as at York), in each of the nine bays, a groupe or figure raised in small statues, significant of the creation.

1. A figure of comparatively Herculean proportion holding up a veil; possibly intended to represent "the earth without form and void; and darkness was upon the face of the deep."

2. The Creator.

3. Man alone.

4. Woman rising from his side.

5. The temptation.

6. The angel with the flaming sword.

7. Adam and Eve departing from paradise.

8. Adam and Eve in the sweat of their brow.

9. Hell.

The Church and State—the head of a king and a bishop are conspicuously placed upon the buttresses of the east end.

The north front exhibits a more modern style; and we distinguish the figure of a benefactor, Vavasour, as it is supposed, who here, as at York, contributed the fine Tadcaster stone which gives such lustre to the remains in Yorkshire.

And we remark also six subjects on the parapets (as in the south), which appear to be legendary, possibly alluding to the "city of refuge," the entrance to which was especially on this side of the sanctuary.

In the west front, constituted by the above-mentioned elegant towers, we count no less than a hundred and twenty-nine niches in the five tiers. Of these the twenty niches on the buttresses are of the double canopy kind, remarked in the cotemporary porch of Canterbury. The label of the magnificent western window is supported by corbelled images of Mark and Luke. Unlike the Cathedral west front, one only of the side doors into the aisles appears, and that of a very subordinate kind, possibly designed to visit the shrine of the patron saints, or for some other sacred purpose. Indeed the whole order and arrangement of the plan discover peculiarities as applied to the minster which are not in the department contemplated in these notes, but demand architectural enquiry as of great interest.

Finally, these towers, as furnishing the model of the general form and character given by Sir C. Wren to those of Westminster Abbey, will always have an additional interest to the architect.

As might well be expected from the eminent masters who flourished under the patronage of Edward I., the interior displays specimens of beautiful and curious conception.

In the nave, the corbelled columns supporting the vault from the spandrils of the pier-arches are adorned with angel figures holding instruments of music, associating the idea of celestial harmony with the holy offices performed in the church: a beautiful novelty which might have been farther extended with great advantage, for these images are somewhat small. The happy and natural association of music with sculpturesque as well as pictorial productions of sacred character, became common in the following ages; but there was an especial reason for it at Beverley; namely, that a fraternity of minstrels or gleemen had been established there during the reign of Athelstan, and were supported in their "laudable ordinances" and statutes with great pomp for many ages after the Norman Conquest[*], and no institution could be more becoming to this peaceful region.

The instruments used by this angelic choir are, viols, hautboys, guitars, rebecs, or crowds, and the serpent. Such representations were in great esteem amongst the sculptors of Beverley, and they may be observed again in this church at the west end, and at the east also over the monuments of the Wartons, in the lady-chapel.

The side aisles are enriched with arcades in relief on the north and south walls, the capitals of whose columns exhibit the most ingeniously devised chimeras and whims of the sculptors: doubtless significant of some purpose now lost to us. Possibly the nave of this church, as the sanctuary, the city of refuge to him "which killeth any person unawares," might thus be intended to furnish some solace to the anxieties of the irritated and fearful mind, condemned possibly for months to occupy those sacred and secure asylums. The faldstool, or chair of peace, was placed in a conspicuous situation near the altar, as an emblem of protection to the refugee; and near this also was their dormitory, the steps to which are seen on the north side. And though sanctuary extended one mile in a circle from this centre, it alone was the spot on which the culprit would compel the suffering parties to accept pecuniary compensation. Although the renowned Percy

[*] See Oliver's History, p. 167.

shrine does not belong to our subject of iconography attached to building, it is impossible to pass unnoticed a specimen of our best period of the art (temp. Edward III.), nor without especial recommendation to the artist and the antiquary for their studious consideration of taste, execution, composition, and costume. Indeed there are few that would admit more readily of moulding, and thus transporting to the museum of sculpture and the schools of design.

It has frequently been described and engraved with more or less exactness, but never yet to do it complete justice.

Here may be seen on the outside the king and queen, Edward and Philippa, and the Lady Percy, with seven knights in complete armour, admirably expressed, as in grief; not forgetting the "dish-thane," the house steward, with his appropriate costume, each having a distinct coat and shield, with every detail that can be desired by the artist and antiquary. Within the canopy hover angels and archangels, the effigy of the Lady Idonea having unfortunately been removed.

On the finial is the Saviour crowned with thorns, and on the projecting corbel the soldiers are throwing the dice for "the vesture;" two angels in benediction, of very beautiful composition and expression, stand on either side; on the opposite side the Saviour shews the wound in His side, and two angels bear the cross and the nails.

The beauty of the vine in the crockets, the exquisite elaboration of the whole, and the delicacy of the material, apparently from Huddlestone, must be seen to be appreciated.

The parish church of St. Mary in the town is both an elegant building and highly interesting iconographically, as exhibiting the notions of the period of Edward IV., when it appears that considerable repairs were undertaken.

These figured remains refer chiefly to the individuals by whose expense the pillars of the church were restored, and the memorials they justly claimed for their zeal are examples which may not be unedifying in the present times.

On the three first pillars we read:

In front,

" I TAP and hes Wyfe made these To Pyllors and a Halffe."

Behind :

"JOHIS CROSLAY MERCATORIS ET JOHANNE UXOR EIUS
ORATE PRO ANIMABUS."

The fourth speaks well for the dames :

"THESE TO PYLLORS MADE GUD WYFFYS.
GOD REWARD THAYM."

On the sixth the guild of minstrels appears in five figures bearing instruments of music.

"THYS PYLLOR MADE THE MYNSTRELLS
ORATE PRO ANIMABUS HISTERIORUM."

The instruments are a treble flute, a guittern, a bass flute, a crowth, and a tabor or side drum, which together are understood as sufficient to produce a pleasant harmony.

The central tower fell in 1530, crushing many of the congregation, and the melancholy event is recorded in a long inscription.

The ceilings of the church are in very handsome wood panelling; the east end adorned with painted portraits of forty kings of England, beginning with fabulous Brutus, and ending with Edward the Fourth.

On one of the beams is an inscription very elaborately cut and illuminated, interesting in all times.

" Mayn in thy lyffyng lowfe God a bown all Thyng
And euer Thynke at the begynnyng awhat schall cowme off the endyng."

There is still another memorial at Beverley of great interest to the reader who honours loyalty, and sympathizes in the pride of an honest ancestry and an untarnished escutcheon, the insertion of which, by the author of these notes, will be excused for obvious reasons.

The Rev. G. Oliver, in his History of Beverley, published 1829, page 168, on the authority of the parliamentary rolls, 7 and 8 of Edward IV., states that "in the first year of Edward's reign Richard Cockerell of Beverley, Gentleman, was attainted of high treason for the part he had taken in the unhappy contest which had deformed the conclusion of the late reign, and his possessions were confiscated, and conveyed by letters patent to John Fereby, a yeoman of the crown." In the following page, 171, we are consoled by an instance at once of the justice of the king, and of the reward sometimes attained by honour and fidelity, where the author relates that "during the continuance of these struggles (of the houses of York and Lancaster) Richard Cockerell had rendered himself peculiarly obnoxious to Edward, by his inflexible attachment to the house of Lancaster, and his active exertions in favour of the unfortunate Henry, and had suffered the confiscation of all his goods and possessions. But when Edward, by the death of his rival, found himself securely seated on the throne, he made a voluntary restitution to Cockerell of all his fees and hereditaments in Beverley and elsewhere."

APPENDIX I.

LICHFIELD CATHEDRAL.

TRANSPORTING ourselves into the age in which this elegant Cathedral Church was built (apparently from 1235 to 1420), and entering into the local motives and provincial attachments of the builders, we cannot but feel the deepest interest in contemplating the design of the sculptures which profusely adorn the west end, and in recognising the ancient pretensions of the kingdom of Mercia, thus splendidly set forth, to civil and religious renown; and that supremacy in the Heptarchy, which she so long and successfully contended with the other kingdoms, especially with Wessex, which at length achieved, through the house of Cerdic, the imperial domination of the whole of England.

The glories of Wessex and of that illustrious dynasty had been recently illustrated by Bishop Trotman at Wells in a manner which doubtless excited the interest and admiration of the country generally, and more particularly the ancient rivalry of the Mercians (after a lapse of four hundred years), who could justly boast of a renown, scarcely inferior to that of Wessex. Such a work as was designed, therefore, by the authorities in 1235, would be as popular, as it was important, in order to preserve in the minds of the people the history and the merits of Mercia in earlier times. Lichfield, the ancient seat of episcopacy and occasionally of royalty, had been sanctified by the blood of one thousand martyrs to the faith in the reign of Diocletian, and by the peculiar merits of St. Chad, whose magnificent shrine was an object of pilgrimage and devotion to all the surrounding country.

About the year 656, the faith had triumphed under the sons of the Saxon pagan king Penda, and his descendants. Offa had even transplanted the archiepiscopal throne from Canterbury to Lichfield: and the annals of religious history numbered many holy men, saints, kings, and bishops, in the kingdom of Mercia before its incorporation with that of England under the dynasty of Cerdic.

The west front, like that of Wells, had been designed expressly for the display of sculpture, all features which could impede or interrupt this great purpose being carefully

k

dispensed with. The three small doors were essential, as the access to the nave and aisles, but the windows of the aisles are wholly omitted; and one only window in the centre gives light to the interior of the west end. The west front (about 100 ft.) incorporates the two towers in a continued series of niches, which may be said to extend to the extremities of the east angle of the north and south towers; presenting in all about 160 ft. for the illustration of its sacred and temporal history in five tiers. See Britton's elegant work on Lichfield Cathedral.

In the first tier were eight statues (now removed) on either side of the great central doorway, which is itself adorned with a very elegant porch containing five statues, apparently St. Peter, St. John, the two Maries, and the blessed Virgin, and the infant Saviour on the central column dividing the doorway.

In the second tier we have twenty-five canopied niches in a continued zone round the entire front. In the centre is St. Chad enthroned and in the attitude of benediction. To the right or south (always the most sacred and venerable side of the church) we have twelve Anglo-Saxon kings of Mercia and England. To the left, the north, are twelve Norman and succeeding kings of England, down to Richard II., under whom Bishop Heyworth appears to have put the last hand to this elegant work.

These statues are far superior in their design to their execution, and they appear to have suffered in frequent scrapings and restorations, so that they can hardly be said to convey complete or fair specimens of the art of their day, at least in their workmanship, but we recognise in the conception and variety of their attitude, dress, and demeanour, a certain wild dignity and grandeur, and peculiarity of character, suited to the respective historical personages, which well deserve respect and a candid observation. The kings are certainly of the later period, and exhibit a decline in the art, but the few fragments of the saints and martyrs which are traced in the upper tiers, display that elegance and excellence in art which was so well attained in the end of the thirteenth century; specimens of which occur in the interior and other parts of the church in corbel-heads and carvings of the exterior and interior.

In the third tier are ten niches on either side the great window. In the fourth tier is the same number; and in the fifth were twelve on either side, and five figures at the foot and point of the pediment. The purpose of these can only be conjectured at present, and may possibly have alluded to the saints and martyrs of Mercia.

Fuller in his Church History displays his accustomed taste and high sense of the importance and dignity of art, in his quaint description of this church. "But now," says he, "in the time of the aforesaid Bishop William Heyworth, the Cathedral of Lichfield was in the vertical height thereof, being (though not augmented in the *essentials*) beautified in the ornamentals thereof. Indeed the west front thereof is a stately fabric, adorned with exquisite imagerie, which I suspect our age is so *far from being able to imitate the workmanship, that it understandeth not the historie thereof.* Surely what Charles the Fifth is said to have said of the citie of Florence, that it is a pitie it should be seen, save only on holy-days; as also that it" (the bell-tower no doubt) "was fitt that so fair a citie should have a case and a cover for it to keep it from wind and weather; so, in some sort, this fabrick may seem to deserve a shelter to secure it. But alas, it is now in a pitiful case indeed, almost beaten down to the ground in our civil dissensions. Now lest the church should follow the castle, I mean quite vanish out of view, I have at the cost of my worthy friend here exemplified the portraiture thereof: and am glad to hear it to be the design of ingenious persons to preserve antient churches in the like nature, (whereof many are done in this, and more expected in the next part of the Monasticon), seeing when their substance is gone, their verie shadows will be acceptable to posteritie[a]."

The ingenious Dr. Woodhouse is the next authority we have to consult on the interpretation of the historical personages represented by these sculptures; but no sufficient justice has yet been done to their interest and merit.

Returning to the central figure of St. Chad over the west door, and proceeding southward, we observe a king passionately embracing a cross with both hands, who can be no other than Peda, the first Christian Saxon king of Mercia, the son of Penda, who, says Malmesbury (b. i. c. iv.): "In the year of our Lord's incarnation 626, and in the 139th after the death of Hengist, Penda, the son of Wibba, tenth in descent from Woden, of noble lineage, expert in war, but at the same time an irreligious heathen, assumed the title of king of the Mercians." In 655, "Penda added to the number of infernal spirits." "His son Peda succeeded him in a portion of his kingdom, by the permission of Oswy, advanced to the government of the south Mercians; a young man of talents, and even in his father's lifetime son-in-law to Oswy. For he had received his daughter on condition of renouncing paganism and embracing Christianity, in which faith he would soon have caused the province to participate, the peaceful state of his kingdom and his father-in-law's consent conspiring to such a purpose, had not his death, hastened, they say, by intrigues of his wife, intercepted these joyful prospects."

No. 2 is supposed to be Wulphere, the second son of Penda, who next inherited the throne, from 657 to 675. This king's history is stained by early hostility to the faith; insomuch that he is said to have killed his two sons for listening to the persuasions of St. Chad, who had converted them to Christianity: subsequently, however, he was himself converted, and became one of the strongest supporters of the faith.

No. 3 is supposed to represent Ethelred, the third son of Penda, and cotemporary

[a] Cent. xi. book iv. sect. iii. p. 175.

with Ina, who in the thirtieth year of his reign, renouncing the throne, and taking the cowl, became a monk, and ultimately abbot of Barding: thus terminating his earthly career by entire devotion to religious offices.

Dr. Woodhouse is of opinion that the three subsequent kings of Mercia have no record in this memorial, and he considers the fourth to represent Offa, whose political consequence, and services to the Church in discovering and illustrating the remains of St. Alban, and in aggrandizing Lichfield, by the transfer of the throne of Canterbury to that city, and other benefactions, entitle him to this distinction, notwithstanding his peculiar crimes, especially the treacherous assassination of Ethelbert king of the East Angles, who had accepted his invitation to his court as a suitor to his daughter Ethelburga. Dr. Woodhouse also considers that the ten following kings of the Mercian dynasty have no record here, but give place to that of Cerdic: he limits therefore the records of the kings of Mercia to four statues only; and he considers No. 5, 6, 7, 8, to represent Egbert, Ethelwulf, Ethelbert, and Ethelred. No. 9 is clearly Alfred, being plainly designated by his harp. The same learned authority considers the liberty of the omission of the less distinguished princes, to have been taken in respect of the following kings; a selection only being made of those most illustrious benefactors on the Church; he therefore supposes the following Nos. 10, 11, and 12, to represent Edward the Elder, Canute, and Edward the Confessor. With much more certainty at the north end we may pronounce on the royal personages intended.

No. 1 is the Norman William: the Conqueror is designated by his long sword in his right, and Domesday Book in his left.

No. 2 is equally certain, William Rufus, being characterized by his bow.

No. 3, Henry Beauclerc, is expressed by his book in his left hand and his sceptre in his right.

No. 4, King Stephen.

No. 5, Henry II.

No. 6, Richard I., holding the standard of the cross.

No. 7, the detested John, has neither sword nor sceptre.

No. 8. Henry III., holds his sceptre in his right.

No. 9, Edward I., as the reformer of laws, holds a large book in his left, and his sceptre in his right.

No. 10, Edward II., is characterized by his beardless countenance and a flower held in his right, to shew the imbecile and transient career of this unhappy prince.

No. 11, Edward III., a grave figure, in the conventional attitude of the redoubtable king counsellor, having his right leg raised on the left knee like Edward the Confessor at Wells, Herod at Norwich, and elsewhere.

No. 12, the last, next to St. Chad, is Richard II., a beardless king, having a ball and cross in his left, and a sceptre in his right.

Over the south porch we have to notice five large statues; of our Saviour in the centre, the Blessed Virgin to His right, St. Peter to His left, and again St. John and St. Chad on either side, to whom the Cathedral was dedicated.

The most ancient feature of this church at present visible, is the door of the north transept. See pl. v. of Britton's Lichfield Cathedral. Five columns in recesses carry as many archivolts very highly enriched and carved. On the first, the archivolt consists of twenty-seven stones or voussoirs connected by a wreath of foliage in ovals (vesica piscis), one on each; on the centre or key-stone of these is the Saviour, seated on a throne surrounded by the twenty-four elders (see Revelations, c. iv.). At the bottom of the east end is St. Chad converting a heathen; and a piece of foliage only on that to the west. The second column bears a boutell of foliage only. The third supports an archivolt, disposed like the first in a foliage with twenty-four ovals on the voussoirs, having an angel in each, the last two holding, the one two moons, and the other two suns. The fourth again consists of foliage only. The fifth column supports an archivolt of eighteen voussoirs, on each of which as before, in the oval or vesica piscis, is a saint, and in the centre on a key-stone the Saviour crucified. Over the central column is a small niche which probably contained a figure of the Blessed Virgin. And over the point of the archway is a circle on which appears to have been the head of Christ, and an angel administering incense on either side.

Such is the outline of the sculptures of Lichfield, which deserve a more special and diligent examination, aided by designs, as well as by the descriptions of the learned in this highly interesting matter: here as elsewhere in these sacred remains we discover the religious and temporal history of the locality in distinct and characteristic symbols, the great doctrines of the faith, and the special worship to which the temple was dedicated. These sculptures were never regarded as idle ornaments, but fulfilled the most important purpose of illustrating history and religion, with as rigorous an adherence to doctrine and discipline as the missals and written documents deposited in the tabularium, and administered to the faithful. Everywhere new historical confirmations and lights of the utmost importance to the understanding and the meaning of these interesting remains of our ancestors, would not fail to arise from more careful investigations of their details.

APPENDIX K.

WORCESTER CATHEDRAL.

THE present Cathedral Church of Worcester was built in the happiest period of medieval taste[a]; and from the few fragments of sculpture which the senseless fury of the iconoclasts have spared, and the order and positions in which this art was employed, we may discover some important evidences of its history, dedication, and special worship, which appear to have escaped hitherto the notice of those good Protestants whose holy fears have so carefully eschewed all idolatrous imagery, and who have shut their eyes and understandings to the obvious beauty and meaning of the symbolical and elegant arrangements displayed in this beautiful temple.

The exact correspondence of the history of the See with the records conveyed by the sculpture which adorns the fabric, is conspicuous, and displays the great importance very reasonably attached to this art in illiterate days.

About the year 680 it appears that Ethelred, king of Mercia, founded the See, and dedicated it to St. Peter. In 774, the religious house of St. Mary, by a stipulation of Bishop Mildred with the Abbess Ethelburga, merged into the Cathedral Church, which was thenceforth called St. Mary's. In 964 the famous Bishop Oswald, the great enemy (with St. Dunstan) of the seculars, and the reformer of the ecclesiastical societies, placed a prior and monks therein. In 1082 the sturdy Saxon bishop and saint, Wulstan (whose statue we have noticed in Wells Cathedral) built for them a new and large monastery, adding three monks to the twelve already appointed there. In 1216 the body of King John, a great benefactor to this church, was interred according to his own will, in this Cathedral Church. In 1218 King Henry III., with a great concourse of nobility, assisted Bishop Silvester in laying the first stone of the new lady-chapel.

[a] See Britton's elegant work on Worcester Cathedral.

We find these historical facts distinctly recorded in the exterior of the tower over the transept. Thus in the east front we have the statue of St. Peter, to whom the church was first dedicated, and St. Andrew; the third niche (now empty) probably contained the founder, Ethelred king of Mercia.

In the north front is a royal personage, possibly Offa, who was reigning in 774, and a great friend to the church; in the centre the blessed Virgin, to whom the church was subsequently dedicated; and lastly the Abbess Ethelburga.

In the west front is a bishop, probably Oswald; in the centre a priest, to indicate his monastic institution; and the last niche, now empty, may have contained the pious Bishop Wulstan, who augmented it. In the ceilings of the transepts and also in the cloisters we have again to remark the statues of St. Oswald and St. Wulstan.

On the south side are two kings and a bishop, who may be confidently pronounced to have been intended to represent King John, King Henry III., and the Bishop Silvester.

These statues are in a whiter stone than that of which the Cathedral Church is built: they appear to be fully as large as life, and are of remarkably good sculpture. The tower which they adorn is stated to have been finished about 1374.

Proceeding to the interior of the church by the north porch, the principal entrance from the town, we discover a special worship to which the church was dedicated; and which does not either appear to have been noticed in modern descriptions of these noble antiquities, namely, the worship of Christ and His holy angels. This we may presume from the nine niches over the north porch, which from their number may safely be pronounced to have originally contained the nine angels. These have been all removed, as also the larger statues contained in two niches at the sides, which probably represented St. Peter and St. Andrew.

The arches of the western nave consist of the angelic number nine, and on the north side was the altar of the Saviour in a chapel still existing. In the spandrels of the triforium over this chapel, on the north only, and not on the south side, were eighteen bas-reliefs like those of the angel choir at Lincoln. In the same position on either side the choir, were eight, representing no doubt the sixteen major and minor prophets; and in the lady-chapel six on either side, representing the twelve Apostles. All these have been so effectually hacked away and defaced by the ruthless hands of the iconoclasts, as to make it impossible to recover their design, a loss to our knowledge of the art in those days the more to be deplored, as from the style of the ornamental sculpture and architecture, and indeed from the historical records, it is apparent they were coeval with the learned and elegant angel choir of Lincoln Cathedral, and therefore probably not inferior in design and execution. Thus appropriate and significant appear to have been the ornamental sculptures of the interior of the church; and that of the cloisters built posteriorly (1380) is admirably consistent with the rest; and happily they are untouched.

In the north side of the cloisters next to the church are seven bays, in the centre of which, in the ceiling, appears the Saviour, surrounded by the four Evangelists. In each of the three bays on either side are four angels, making twenty-four in all, of whom four to the east are archangels having four wings; and four appear with double heads and flames issuing from them; all these have shields. In the ceiling of the east cloister we trace the Blessed Virgin, the bishops St. Oswald and St. Wulstan on either side, the other bosses are alternately oak and vine with heads of kings and bishops. Over the chapter-house, most significantly placed, is the archangel Michael.

The western cloister is ornamented only with foliage.

In the south cloister, the infant Saviour, surrounded by four prophets, is in the centre, and the root of Jesse is represented in the three bays on either side; in the west, David with his harp is plainly distinguished.

Nothing can exceed the freedom and grace of the carving in the capitals and other ornaments. The corbel-heads have that lively expression of portraiture which we frequently observe in the early part of the thirteenth century; the countenance somewhat rustic, the eyes prominent, the ears remarkably relieved, and the mouth smiling. This fashion of art may be traced in the works of the Pisani in the Campo Santo at Pisa (1278). See Cicognara's History of Sculpture, lib. ii. c. 3. p. 193.

In the lady-chapel, surmounting the screen-work, are some quaint devices of chimeras and foliage, and sometimes scriptural subjects, as the expulsion, the death of Abel, &c., and which appear to have been inspired by the dramatic performances then in fashion, called mysteries, miracles and moralities, by the jestours, minstrels, mimics, and jugglers, in churchyards and sometimes in the church itself; and which "however rude and ridiculous," says Warton, "had a powerful influence in those days, by softening the manners of the people, and diverting their attention from military games and the bloody contentions of the tournaments, to spectacles in which the mind was concerned, in creating a regard for other arts than those in which bodily strength and savage valour were alone concerned."

APPENDIX L.

LINCOLN CATHEDRAL.

"HIS WORKE GREAT TROYNOVANT, HIS WORKE IS EKE
FAIRE LINCOLNE, BOTH RENOWNED FAR AWAY;
THAT WHO FROM EAST TO WEST WILL ENDLONG SEEKE
CANNOT TWO FAIRER CITIES FIND THIS DAY."

SPENCER, FAIRIE QUEENE, B. III. c. ix. st. tr.

THE sculptures of Lincoln, presenting specimens of the first efforts, the excellence and the decline of the art in medieval times in this country, excel those of any of our Cathedrals in archæological interest. The frieze in the west front (in all probability Saxon) offers the only extensive specimen we have of that age. The sculpture of the angel choir, and of the east end generally, is the best of the best period (the thirteenth century) still preserved to us; while the kings over the west door illustrate that rapid and lamentable decline, which a short perversion of the great encouragements and motives to fine art may effect in less than a century.

The Norman bishop Remigius (from 1067 to 1092) transplanted the diocesan church from Dorchester to a new site at Lincoln, and the west front still presents remains sufficient for a restoration of its original design. It was carried up in that rude and hurried manner for which the arrogant conquerors were so remarkable; and a careful examination of the frieze over the three doors in that front, and of the hasty and irregular insertion of its parts and accompanying mouldings, will clearly prove to the professional observer, its adoption from an elder building. It might either have been transported from Dorchester, the site of the ancient see, or from some previous church in Lincoln itself; which, as a fortified and flourishing town, in the practice of the Christian faith under the Saxon rule during the four hundred and fifty previous years, must have possessed conspicuous churches already. However active Remigius may have been in the prosecution of the work, it was left to his successor, Bloet, to finish and consecrate in 1093. A fire having subsequently occurred, to the injury probably of the masonry of

l

the great western door, Alexander, the successor to Bloet, in 1124, inserted a new and magnificent doorcase (still existing), which occasioned however by its augmented volume and elevation, the removal and violation of the most important portion of this interesting frieze; so little was Alexander actuated by any respect for the works of his Norman predecessor of only thirty years, if indeed they were by Remigius; or, in the case we suppose, with such contempt or ignorance were treated those of the proscribed Saxon race. The Normans indeed of the eleventh century have left scarcely any remains of sculpture. The portrait of Bishop Losinga at Norwich, and the carvings still extant upon their buildings, display the utmost barbarity; and it is well known that their illuminations of manuscripts are greatly inferior to those of their cotemporary Anglo-Saxons. I should for these reasons entirely subscribe to the opinion given by Gough in his edition of Camden, that this frieze is of Saxon workmanship. It appears to symbolize the trial of faith, by various witnesses and ensamples of the Old Testament, and the promises of the New.

As usual in England, the Old Testament is described to the south, and the New to the north of the western door. In the centre, now occupied by the voussoirs of Alexander's work, was, probably, the Saviour in the vesica piscis, and at the four corners the symbols of the Evangelists. A fragment with this design, of corresponding size and workmanship, was found a few years ago buried in the Cathedral close, and is now carefully preserved by the amiable and learned architect, curator of the Cathedral fabric, Mr. Willson; and little doubt of its identity with this frieze can be entertained: it was highly illuminated with colour, as the rest had been.

Commencing from this centre southwards, it appears that some intermediate fragments are deficient, and the first now remaining describes the expulsion. The curse is symbolized in a new and most significant manner in the upper corner, by an outstretched hand issuing from a cloud holding *a purse of money*.

The next, evidently out of its proper place in the series, is the death of Isaac: Jacob, Esau and Rebecca appear. In the following the instruction for the building of the ark; the salvation of the family of Noah, and of the beasts, which are escaping on Ararat: the faithless are seen immersed in the waters on the south side, now enclosed in the more modern tower.

We are pleased, and in a measure confirmed in the opinion of the Saxon origin of this work, by tracing in it a subject peculiarly treated by our venerable Saxon Bede. "The ark," says he, "signifies the Church, which swims through the waves of this world. Here all who are saved (the people with their animals) may be carried together; who however, since their merit is not equal, have each their distinct mansions; for all in the Church live under one faith, and are baptized with the same water; but all have not the same advancement: of whom it was said, 'God remembered Noah and the cattle in his ark.' For a multitude of irrational animals, as also of beasts, is contained in inferior places, while those who live by science and by reason are in the upper seats, and they are few indeed, for many are called but few are chosen."

In the middle of this series of subjects of the deluge, is a relief representing Daniel in the lions' den; another proof of the reckless and irregular insertion of these sculptures in the building by Remigius.

Thus terminates the south frieze.

To the north some lacunæ are obvious: the salvation of the just and the damnation of the evil are alone preserved. The former appears in an original manner: a drapery is held by the hands of Abraham, as we may suppose, containing in its folds the souls of the saved. In one of the windows of the Cathedral the same symbol may be seen. In a window of Bourges Cathedral the same subject is traced; also at Moissac-Vezelay, and at St. Trophime, at Arles, in sculptures of an early date; referring no doubt to "Abraham afar off, and Lazarus in his bosom" (Luke xxvi. 22), and to the assurance of our Lord to the "centurion," that "many shall come from the east and from the west, and shall sit down with Abraham, Isaac and Jacob in the kingdom of heaven." (Matt. viii. 11). The perdition of the wicked is expressed in a number of figures seized by demons, or tormented by serpents, and thrust into the jaws of an enormous monster, a "hell" as Spencer calls it conventionally.

These sculptures are of inferior execution; the design and style of the ornamental mouldings, no less than of the subject itself, exhibit a close affinity to the classical or Byzantine as seen in the early Christian monuments given us by Aringhi in the Roma Subterranea; and we are reminded of the sarcophagi of the debased Roman times. The engraving of this curious and very interesting frieze is a desideratum.

As we have in this frieze a remarkable specimen of the earliest efforts of the art in England, so we have immediately above it one of its debasement in this country, in the eleven kings from the Conqueror to Edward III. put up by the treasurer Welbourne about 1377, than which nothing can be worse: nor is it easy to conceive how eyes and judgments, trained under the admirable masters of the previous century, could so rapidly have declined.

As an evidence of the loyal habit of thus recording kings, continued to Henry VI., and as costume, they have still some interest with the archæologist.

The old Norman front was incorporated with the new, and greatly extended front which was building apparently from S. Hugh de Grenoble (1186) to Robert Greathead (1254). On the point of the central gable two angels, in bas relief, in the bold attitude of descent, hold censers over a niche, in which *was* probably the statue of the Saviour.

Below, is the dove, and a niche on either side plainly discover the Annunciation. The statues of Gabriel and the munificent Bishop are now removed: in the extreme niches two kings remain. Two pyramids terminate the front. On the southern point appears a bishop, probably S. Hugh, in benediction; on the northern a rustic figure playing on a pipe, called "the swineherd of Stowe," relating to one of those wild legends so common to our country.

Six tiers of niches, which however do not appear to have contained statues, adorn the vast and imposing front; the west as well as the transept towers having originally been surmounted with lofty leaden spires; a very glorious and imposing groupe.

In the interior of the church, renovated and planned probably by St. Hugh (who is said to have sometimes carried the stones and mortar on his own shoulders), and prosecuted with so much zeal during the following fifty years, little other sculpture appears than of an architectural character in the caps of the pier columns, and bosses of the ceilings.

The eastern end of the Cathedral, called the presbyterium, or Angels' choir, was subsequently extended by the Dean and Canons for the canonized remains of S. Hugh. In 1256 they petitioned for leave to remove the city walls in order to obtain the necessary space for their "new work;" which was accomplished in 1282; and a memorable ceremonial took place on the occasion of the consecration of a golden shrine for the relics of the new saint, long held in high veneration.

In this portion of the Cathedral, consisting of five bays, a cycle of thirty subjects, illustrative of the gradual unfolding of divine revelation, is displayed with most admired learning and taste, and may not only challenge, in these respects, the works of sculpture or painting of any country in the thirteenth or succeeding century, but will possibly be found to establish a priority of merit in the English school, hitherto little suspected. We have already acknowledged the ignorance of the Plastic art, and of historical religious design, which marks the present and the last century amongst us; owing no doubt to the puritan infatuation still infecting our Church and our art education. And it is to this we must attribute the disregard of the just claims of our schools of art in the thirteenth century, and the utter neglect of the Lincoln sculptures and other precious evidences of merit in art still remaining amongst us.

This presbyterium has obtained the name of the Angel choir, from the elegant representations of the angelic host, so aptly adorning the spandrels of the triforium arches; but no one has ever yet attempted to read their noble purpose and design; and they have hitherto been regarded as mere ornament, and the effervescence only of the carver's chisel. Mr. Wild indeed, in his splendid illustrations of this Cathedral, in Plate XIV., and pages 33 and 34, has conveyed some notions of their merit; but neither he nor any other has ever understood or attempted to describe the subject matter of this appropriate and elegant homily in stone; indeed to approach the subject we must begin by dismissing our puritanism, and by learning to appreciate the theological learning of the twelfth and thirteenth centuries in England (so, alas! perverted by the schoolmen of the subsequent æra), and to respect the labours of a Roger Bacon, a Greathead and others, in familiarizing to the popular mind the great truths of revelation by every means which could attract and inform it.

Amongst the many literary productions of the excellent Bishop Greathead was one entirely of this sort, his "Chateau d'amour," now in the Bodleian, entitled "Ce est la vie de D. Jh'u de sa humanite, fit e ordiné de Saint Robert Grossetete qui fut Eveque de Nicholle," the ancient *French* for Lincoln. This piece professes to treat of the creation, the redemption, the day of judgment, the joys of heaven, and the torments of hell; the whole being a religious allegory, representing, under the agreeable ideas of chivalry, the fundamental articles of the Christian belief: it has the air of a system of divinity written by a troubadour. His "Pricke of Conscience" was written in the same view.

And still later Robert Mannynge translated many works for the same great end into English rhyme; amongst others "Medytaciuns of the Soper of our Lorde Jhesu, and also of hys passyun, and eke of the Peynes of hys sweete modyr mayden Marye, the which made yn Latyn Bonaventure Cardinall [a]."

Thus the purpose of the Pilgrim's Progress, in the seventeenth century, was answered in the thirteenth, by these and similar works; aided also by the religious plays called "Moralities" and "Mysteries," conveying sacred and moral truths. So generally indeed had these last prevailed in the thirteenth century, as to have become an abuse, repressed by Bishop Greathead in an express prohibition against the feast of fools " ne de Domo orationis fiat Domus ludibrii [b]."

The Drama has ever been the inseparable companion to the more permanent fine arts of sculpture and painting, of which, in fact, it is the prompter and rehearsal; and the poetic mind expands itself equally in each of these elegant and imaginative pursuits by her aid; producing the groupes of Phidias in Greece, the sculptures of the presbyterium at Lincoln, and the scenic architecture of Inigo Jones.

We shall admire the taste and the scriptural soundness with which this epitome of Revelation has been expressed in the Angel choir, ordered, if not by Greathead himself, who died 1254, two years only before the commencement of the "new work," by a mind hardly less learned and cultivated.

In the easternmost of the five bays, commencing on the south side, we have,

No. 1. An Angel, seated on clouds, having in his hand a scroll of small extent, com-

[a] See Warton's History of English Poetry, vol. i. p. 81.   [b] Ibid., vol. iii. p. 194.

pared with the succeeding ones, and issuing from the *angle* of the presbyterium; thus symbolizing the comparative obscurity of the early Promises to Abraham and the Patriarchs as to the coming of the Messiah.

No. 2, (the central spandrel) is David crowned, and sitting on his throne, his harp in his hand: the Patriarch has extended wings, as shewing his divine relationship and angelic mission.

No. 3. An Angel holding a more developed scroll, as containing the prophecies of David, and more especially the Promise, "The Lord hath sworn in truth unto David; of the fruit of thy body will I set upon thy throne." Thus terminates the first bay.

No. 4. in the second, an Angel sounds a trumpet energetically, as "proclaiming the name of the Lord;" "the fame of David into all lands," "in His seed should all the nations of the earth be blessed," &c.

No. 5. in the centre, an Angel, finely designed, signifying by his remarkable corpulency and extended scroll, the prosperity and wisdom of Solomon; the "fatness" of Israel; the king who "made silver to be in Israel as stones," &c.

No. 6. An Angel in solemn expression and attitude holds a scroll in his outstretched arms, as containing the sentence of the Almighty by his prophet Abijah, that for the sins of Solomon the kingdom should be "rent."

The third bay opens with No. 7. An Angel blowing two trumpets, proclaiming the verification of the prophecy, the sins of Rehoboam and Jeroboam, the division of the kingdom, the "halting between two opinions," Jerusalem and Samaria.

No. 8. An Angel playing the pipe and tabret; a *monster issues* from under his feet; the previous angels being always on clouds. All the evils threatened to Israel are here typified by the direct allusion to the apostrophe of Isaiah: "Woe unto them that rise up early in the morning that they may follow strong drink, that continue until night, till wine inflame them; and the harp and the viol, *the tabret and pipe* and wine are in their feasts: but they regard not the work of the Lord, nor the operations of His hand," "therefore are my people gone into captivity," &c.

No. 9, the last in the third bay, is the Angel of Daniel holding in his left hand the sealed book, and raising his "right;" as described in the vision on the banks of the Hiddekel, ch. xii. 7: under his feet is again the monster.

No. 10, the first in the fourth bay, is the Angel of Isaiah. With an expression of the deepest concern he reads the letter of Rabshakeh, which the king Hezekiah spread before the Lord: under his feet is an *abortion*. "The *children are come to the birth*, and there is not strength to bring forth." 2 Kings xix. 3.

No. 11, the Angel of Ezekiel, robust and beautiful, with gloves, or gauntlets on his hands, a lure on his left, and a large falcon in his right: he smiles, while he holds the dangerous bird at a respectful distance. He is seated on a throne with a *horn* at either extremity, and a monster issues from his feet. The Lincoln sculptor found no more apt illustration of the prophet Ezekiel, than the " Riddle and the parable put forth unto the house of Israel." See Ezekiel, xvii. The manners of the times must explain this type of feudal nobility. " No gentleman appeared," says Warton, "unless going to battle, without a hawk on his fist. On the walls of the royal palace at Clarendon, the Soldan is represented as meeting Richard with a hawk on his fist, and in the tapestry of the Norman Conquest, Harold is exhibited on horse-back in the same manner^c."

No. 12, the last in the fourth bay, is not less plainly the Angel of Jeremiah. He holds in his lap his " Lamentations," which he has just been reading, while he regards the spectator with a desponding expression of attitude and countenance. Thus are the four major prophets aptly and ingeniously expressed.

In the fifth and last bay, terminating the south side, No. 13, an Angel, in extatic action of joy, points to the passages of the minor prophets proclaiming the advent, when the time of the Promise drew "nigh." " The Lord, whom ye seek, shall suddenly come to His temple, even the messenger of the covenant, whom ye delight in," Mal. iii. 1 ; or the triumphant expressions of Isaiah, ix. 6. This Angel is apparently intended as the epitome of the minor prophets. From under his feet issues a monster of *peculiar deformity ;* the father of lies is cast out for ever; for except in the succeeding subject of the blessed Virgin, " the old dragon," which appears first in No. 8, is thenceforth seen no more.

We have remarked before the coincidence of thought in the artists and poets of our early schools, and we might almost suppose Milton to have warmed himself by this noble work of the Lincoln sculptor, when, in his Ode on the Nativity, he says,

And then at last our bliss
Full and perfect is,
    But now begins ; for, from this happy day,
The old dragon, under ground
In straiter limits bound,
    Not half so far casts his usurped sway,
And wroth to see his kingdom fail,
Swinges the scaly horror of his folding tail.

The oracles are dumb,
No voice or hideous hum
    Runs thro' the arched roof in words deceiving.

* See Warton's History of English Poetry, vol. i. p. 179.

Apollo from his shrine
Can no more divine.
    With hollow shriek the steep of Delphos leaving,
No nightly trance, or breathed spell
Inspires the pale-eyed priest from the prophetic cell.

No. 14. An Angel of the utmost dignity and severity of design, holds the soul in prayer (a small figure with upraised hands) towards the Blessed Virgin and the young Messiah in the following spandrel, a napkin enveloping the sacred emblem. At his feet is a female head, possibly signifying the priesthood, or the Church, the spouse of Christ.

No. 15, the last of the fifth bay, presents a groupe of remarkable purity and beauty of design. The Blessed Virgin embraces the Messiah, who stands upon her lap, with His right on her bosom, as confessing the source of His human existence, while with His left he withdraws her veil, and exhibits to mankind Her whom "all generations shall henceforth call blessed." Above, a young Angel ministers incense, and at her feet, for the last time, appears the monster serpent, according to the prediction that "her seed should bruise his head." Thus terminates the portion of the series on the south side, and we cross to the north for its continuation.

In the opposite side of this bay Nos. 16, 17 and 18 express most epigraphically the one great sacrifice, the passion of our Lord, and the Atonement; its occasion, the fall of our first parents. The first Angel holds the crown of thorns; the second, an indignant cherub with a flaming sword, drives the guilty pair from paradise; the third holds up the spear and the sponge enveloped in a napkin, which may possibly allude to that called the Sudarium.

In the following bay, 19, 20, 21, we have the subjects of Resurrection and Judgment. In the first, the Saviour, crowned with thorns, points to the wound in His side, while a ministering Angel holds up a small figure, symbolical of the soul, the hands of which are raised in prayer, as above in the fifteenth. In the second an Angel holds the balance; the weightier righteous fall into his lap, while the lighter, "found wanting," are scattered from the ascending cup and fall to the ground. In the third the Angel with incense propitiates the Saviour. See Rev. viii. 3.

In the next bay we have the doctrine of rewards, the crowns of life held by the central Angel, No. 23, while No. 22, reading from a scroll, a palm-branch in his right, significant of martyrdom, refers to Rev. xx. 4; and 24 seeks anxiously in the book of life for those whose names are not "found written," according to Rev. xx. 11—15.

The following bay is devoted to praise. Nos. 25, 26, play on the dulcimer and viol; while 29, holding a scroll in his left, and a palm-branch in the right, proclaims "the everlasting Gospel to every nation, kindred and tongue," according to Rev. xiv. 6.

The last bay continues the same subject, together with the supremacy of the Church, and the still unaccomplished revelations.

No 28. An angel playing on the harp; refers to Rev. xiv. 1, "harping with their harps."

No. 29. (Rev. xii. 1) an Angel holds up the sun in his left, the moon in his right, and a scroll descending from it. Between the horns of the moon is a female head: the former seeming to represent Christ, the Sun of righteousness; the latter His reflection, the Church, the sacred depository of doctrine.

The terminating Angel, No. 30, holds in his hand a scroll, part of which only is unfolded, according to Rev. xxii. 10; "I am the Alpha and Omega, the beginning and the end, the first and the last."

This description will encourage the reader to examine the lithographs of these figures published in the Lincoln volume of the Archæological Institute of Great Britain and Ireland, which suffice to convey some idea of their masterly composition, the artistic arrangement of the groupes as suited to the space to which they are adapted, the graceful management of drapery, and the variety of character. The delicate shades of these, however, as the more or less force given to the angelic figures, making the sex unrecognisable, sometimes male, as in the Prophets, and sometimes female, as in the doctrinal Angels; the lively anxiety of the Angel of Isaiah reading the letter; the ire of the Angel of Paradise; the peace and joy of the Angel of rewards; the searching diligence of the Angel looking into the "Book of life" in vain for those who are not written, and many such like details, can only be appreciated by the attentive consideration of the originals themselves.

The high order of the merit of these sculptures, not only in respect of the taste and learning displayed in their design, but as works of art, excite the liveliest interest in the English observer. Fully equal to the best Italian works of the thirteenth and fourteenth centuries, we compare them with the earliest specimens known to us of Cimabue, *born* in 1224; of the school of the Pisani, flourishing during this century, and of the renowned Giotto, *born* about 1276, precisely at the period in which these sculptures were first modelled by the sculptor of Lincoln. With these, and the works even of Orcagna, a century later, they vie most advantageously.

Where then are we to look for a record of the school, and the masters to whom they may be attributed? The medieval artists, especially of these northern countries, were overlaid by the aristocracies of the feudal and ecclesiastical lords, and were unrelieved by the guilds and free societies, which, in commercial Italy, pointed to more liberal views. Their humility too has concealed the authors of these works, who might well deserve a place beside the masters celebrated by Vasari. But if we do not possess direct, we possess circumstantial evidences of their English origin, of such weight as cannot easily be controverted. And these we owe to the researches of the Rev. J. Hunter (Archæologia, vol. xxix.), who from the publications of the Record Commission, has recovered the names of nine sculptors, four architects, and two painters, who were employed, shortly after this epoch, in those crosses to Queen Eleanor, which have always been regarded as amongst the most elegant medieval productions of these Arts. The names Mr. Hunter has given us are, Richard de Stowe, John de Battle, Dymenge de Legeri, Michael de Canturbury, Richard de Crundale, Roger de Crundale, William de Ireland, Alexander de Abyndon, Master William Torrel, sculptors; William de Hoo, William de Suffolk, Roger de Newmarsh, architects; Walter de Durham, John de Bristol, painters. Only two names in this catalogue, the third and the ninth, appear to be foreign, and it is gratifying to vindicate, through such evidences as these discoveries reveal, the genius of our English ancestors, as conspicuous in that century in art and science, as in chivalry and learning; in which they have been pre-eminent in all times.

"To assert for England, against Walpole and others, the claim of having produced by the hands of native artists, most of the beautiful works of sculpture and architecture which are connected with the name and memory of Queen Eleanor, who died 1292," is the worthy object of Mr. Hunter in his interesting paper; and greatly do we rejoice in the conclusive proofs he has recovered for us, and the reference which we may from thence fairly draw, that in the thirteenth century, as well as at most other periods of history, the talents of this country have yielded to none elsewhere, however favoured they may have been by a more accurate record of their merits.

Finally, of this happy period of sculpture three other specimens may be remarked in the east end. First upon the face of the altar of the holy sepulchre are three Knights Templars admirably composed and executed.

The south gateway is an excellent, and in England an unique example of the apsidal porch so frequent in France; it is profusely adorned with sculpture described by Wild, and referred to by Flaxman in his lecture on composition. It represents the last judgment in the tympanum; but it is by another and inferior hand to that employed in the angel choir. In the archivolts the "careless ones" of this world are represented round the judgment; anticipating by one hundred years the idea of Orcagna in the Camposanto of Pisa. Below were the four evangelists, and the Virgin in the centre.

Against the south-east pier of the presbytery, on the exterior, is a groupe of the king and queen, Edward I., and the beloved wife of his youth, Eleanor. The king bears his shield, and tramples on the enemy: and there is a prodigious grandeur, freedom and energy of style in these figures, which belongs to this period beyond any other of the art in this country. In the adjoining pier is a female statue of equal merit of execution, but affecting great delicacy and refinement in the character, and probably intended for Edward's second spouse, the princess Margaret of France.

The neglect of these fine works, most of which are mutilated, the head of the king having been knocked off within a few years, is disgraceful to the authorities concerned in the preservation of the church, and indeed of the honour of Lincoln. A small expense would suffice to secure to future times, and to the admiration of taste, all that which is now subject to the vulgarest spoliation. Casts in plaster should be taken, and these noble antiquities, redounding so much to the glory of our country, should be illustrated and explained by competent hands.

APPENDIX M.

GLOUCESTER CATHEDRAL.

THE Abbey Church of St. Peter contains some admirable illustrations of the varieties and progress of architectural styles from 1088 to 1457, but unhappily much less completely of the sculptural styles. As an abbey only till 1541, when it was erected into a Cathedral Church, it may not have had the pretension or the wealth sufficient for a greater display of art; yet its high Saxon antiquity, its endowments, and the renown of its founders, might lead us to expect more than we actually find. Great however is the merit of the few fragments of sculpture which remain, illustrating the happiest period of the art in England, just as it had reached that acme, from which it was destined to decline so rapidly.

From 1307 to 1329 the Abbot Thokey rebuilt the south and west walls of the nave, adorning the former with nine buttresses, and the latter with four. The principal approach to the church was from the south; the north, west and east, contrary to the ordinary monastic arrangement, having been occupied by the cloisters, and the other conventual buildings. Here were displayed to the public eye (in the true spirit of an age so attached to the evidences, titles and rights established by historical records and authorities) those illustrious founders and benefactors, of whom the abbey, and indeed the city, might be so justly proud, and whose bequests had been so long respected and enjoyed. The abbey was founded by Wulfere, king of Mercia, about 681, and continued by his successor Ethelred. Osric, the viceroy of the latter, founded and endowed a nunnery here, of which Kyneburga, Eadburga, and Eva, of the royal race, had been successively abbesses. But the ravages of the Danes, and the lawless state of the country, no longer admitted of such institutions, and Bernulph king of Mercia converted it into a convent of secular priests in 821.

History records the benefactions of the renowned Ethelfleda*, the daughter of Alfred,

---

* See William of Malmesbury, chap. v. "She was buried in the monastery of S. Peter, at Glocester, which, in conjunction with her husband Ethelred, she had erected with great solicitude. Thither too she had transferred the bones of S. Oswald, the king, from Bardney; but this monastery being destroyed in succeeding time by the Danes, Aldred, archbishop of York, founded another, which is now the chief in that city."

to the abbey of Gloucester; and we learn that in 1022 King Canute, at the instigation of Wulstan, drove out the secular priests in favour of Benedictine monks.

Robert, duke of Gloucester, as a patron of letters and an honour to his country, might well be recorded here. Finally the unfortunate Edward II. might also have been commemorated in the new work. This ill-fated monarch perished two years before Abbot Thokey retired from the government of the abbey; and his shrine, penitentially visited from all parts of England, in the hope of averting the divine vengeance on the nation, had enriched it greatly.

It may be to these illustrious personages that the mutilated statues on some of these buttresses refer. The two easternmost are the most perfect: they are royal personages; they hold churches in their hands, and tread upon *pigs*, thus quaintly signifying the exaltation of Christianity, through the institutions of Wulfere and Ethelred, over idolatry, which kept mankind in a *swinish* degraded state. One of these, remarkable for grandeur of style, was, it is said, lately moulded by the sculptors of the new Parliament houses, and with great reason. The following three are unfortunately too much defaced to distinguish their characters and attributes without the assistance of scaffolding and closer examination; but they appear to be female statues, and may represent the royal abbesses above cited. The sixth is a king in a most imposing attitude, having held apparently a sceptre in either hand; and thence probably intended for the great King Canute, the ruler of two countries simultaneously. The seventh and eighth statues, obscured by the porch built more than a hundred years subsequently (1412 to 1437), have with their buttresses been removed. The ninth statue is also removed, as are the four from the buttresses of the west end. These buttresses are singular in their architecture, the sides of the lower part being splayed, and having been adorned with canopies and niches for smaller statues. The pinnacles over the great statues of the founders are battlemented, and not, as commonly, in a pyramidal form; possibly attributed to temporal, in contradistinction to spiritual personages or saints[b].

The actual state of the existing statues is greatly to be lamented, and unless speedily repaired, some of the most precious examples of this art and period, still preserved to us, will escape from our hands.

The porch has a niche on either side the entrance, probably designed to receive St. Peter and St. Paul: above are six niches now empty. The groined ceiling presents a beautiful and adorned figure. In the middle the Saviour raises His hands, exhibiting the wounds in them and in His side; four angels are ministering round Him.

At the end of the south transept is the pilgrim's entrance to the shrine of the unfor-

---

[b] See Britton's elegant work on Gloucester Cathedral, Pl. iv.

tunate Edward II., having acolytes or angels on either side of a bold and beautiful design, seeming to welcome the penitential visitors. The groined ceiling of the church, executed in 1242, contains no other sculpture than the usual bosses of foliage. Over the high altar at the east end in the magnificent ceiling, apparently by Abbot Seabroke (1450), is the Saviour in benediction surrounded with a choir of twenty angels; ten of whom hold the symbols of the passion, and ten instruments of music. The rest of the ceiling, though architecturally beautiful, is deficient in sculptural art. The lady-chapel, of very elegant architecture (1472), was adorned with a profusion of small statues, now defaced or removed. The cloisters contain no symptom of sculpture, an omission characteristic of their date, about 1381 to 1412, by Abbot Froucester, who however, in the historical spirit still preserved in his day, is said to have meritoriously transcribed the records of the abbey down to the 20th of Edward III.

The monumental effigies of Robert Courthose and Edward II., with some others, are worthy of the attention of the curious visitor[c]. Our purpose in these notes is however confined to architectural sculpture, never yet noted, while the monumental has already been the subject of so many splendid works.

[c] See Britton, Pl. xxii.

APPENDIX N.

SALISBURY CATHEDRAL.

THE sculptures of Salisbury Cathedral are of the highest interest to us, not only as they compare with the contemporary works of Wells (whose rival bishop actually assisted here at the first celebration of divine service in 1225), but as the epoch of their execution can be fixed with the greatest precision from that year to 1258; and more especially are they gratifying and honourable to our school on account of the great beauty of their style and execution; which happily in their preservation to this day may be proved to be fully equal to the works of any other country or school then flourishing, not excepting those of Florence and Pisa; thus fortifying, in a remarkable manner, our constant assertion of perfect equality of merit (to say the least) of our English school with any others of their day. And it is to be lamented that the limits prescribed to these notices prevent our producing those illustrations by engravings, which would give conclusive evidence of this fact, by parallel comparison with the Italian and other works of the medieval times published by D'Agincourt and Cicognara. As it is, we must refer the connoisseur to such ocular inspection and such elaborate drawings as I have myself made to arrive at these conclusions. They also serve to confirm, in a remarkable manner, the position assumed throughout these observations, that sculptors abounded in due proportion in this country together with the architects and limners, since in each locality a distinct and peculiar hand is to be traced, and (here especially) altogether a different chisel from that of the somewhat rigid style at Wells, and the more pure and learned style of Lincoln. These figures have a flowing grace, and elegance of execution, attributed by D'Agincourt, in Plate xxxv. fig. 3, to the younger Pisani, and by Cicognara, Plate x. and xii., to the same author. Beauty rather than character is at Salisbury the object of the artist: the attitudes assume the line of beauty, reposing on one leg generally, the hip protruded, the arms finely balanced: the cast of the drapery also is highly artificial, ample, broad, and at the same time elaborate: casts of some of these would surprise the modern practitioners.

The scope of Bishop Poore and his successors was not of the same scriptural and historical extent with that of Bishop Trotman at Wells: his design appears to have been confined to the usual illustration of the holy Trinity, the heavenly hierarchy, the apostles, and the saints and martyrs, most of which, very happily, we find recorded in Dugdale's Baronage, vol. ii., having these illustrations in our sculptures just as we might expect them. Even these must have presented a very glorious page, for we find a hundred and twenty-three niches with their proper pedestals in the west front, and nineteen in the north, and apparently as many in the south return; making about a hundred and sixty in all; and if we may rely upon Hollar's view, taken so recently as the reign of Charles I., in which the greater part is displayed, we may conceive the magnificence and value of the work in his day, and we may appreciate the ignorant and deplorable activity of the iconoclastic reformers. Referring to Mr. Britton's valuable Elevation, Plate v. of his Salisbury Cathedral, we find a tetrastyle square front bounded by two turrets and their pinnacles.

The architecture, somewhat capricious, appears to have been disposed chiefly with reference to the iconographic scheme and arrangement.

Over the apex of the pediment, in a conventional form, evidently intended as especially sacred and archaic, the Holy Spirit with the nimbus,

"Dove-like, sits brooding."

The sacred oval below it (from the authority of Bishop Nevil's seal, 1450, published in Hoar's collection of seals, and in another of the College of the Trinity in Salisbury), may be pronounced to signify the first Person of the Trinity. On the apices of the two lofty buttresses of the centre are two figures enthroned and much degraded, which may be conjectured as representing the second Person of the Trinity, and His Blessed Mother.

The niches immediately below these, on the great buttresses, are empty; these, together with contiguous niches on either side, and below, are sufficient for the whole company of the Apostles. The seven niches on either side above, and the six on either side below, must be supplied by conjecture, as well as the eleven immediately above the porch, and those on the extreme turrets.

Proceeding with the existing statues on the two principal buttresses, we may confidently pronounce the upper one to the north as St. Paul, in a magnificent design of drapery and attitude, holding in his right the sword, broken, but recognised by the pommel still in his hand.

Opposite to him on the south is the venerable St. Peter, very finely designed and holding (apparently) the keys, now broken, in his two hands. Pope Honorius threatens the opponents of his Bull to translate the church of Old Sarum, with "the indignation of the Almighty God, and of the blessed saints Peter and Paul." Below is a youthful and almost feminine figure in a most elegant proportion, attitude and drapery, which may be safely conjectured as St. John the Evangelist; and immediately opposite in the south buttress is clearly "St. John the Baptist, clothed in a camel's skin," his characteristic symbol, very gracefully disposed, the head and feet of the camel tied in front, and plainly recognisable. In his right was held a disc having on it the Agnus Dei, to which his left seems to point. The practice of placing the two Johns, the Evangelist and the Baptist, in juxta or corresponding position, is of frequent occurrence. The venerable beard alone of this fine statue remains, the head having been, as indeed almost all the others, most barbarously mutilated to the great disgrace of the town, and still more of the cathedral authorities, who plainly neither traced the characters intended, nor understood the merit of art in them, a merit sufficient to illustrate a school. Below these on the great buttresses were two figures, the southern one of which exhibits the feet of a female statue of elaborate workmanship, which may have been intended as St. Anne, or the Magdalene, both of whom had special altars dedicated to them in the church on its final consecration.

The extreme buttresses do not rise to the summit of the building as the central ones. On the summit of the northern is the statue of Bishop Poore looking towards Old Sarum, and in an attitude of moving rapidly, his garments flowing in the wind; thus represented by illustrative sculpture to express (no doubt) the great act of his life, the removal of the church and the monastic clergy from the dominion and interference of the military at Old Sarum. To the south on the opposite side, on the apex of the corresponding buttress, stands a figure in a secular dress, having a cap of estate on his head, and a bag suspended to his girdle; the costume and the position, added to the well-known history of the building, leaves no doubt that this was designed to record the merits and signal services of William Longespee, earl of Salisbury, the natural son of Henry II. and the fair Rosamund Clifford, made sheriff of the county in 1200 by Richard I., the faithful partizan of John, and afterwards of Henry III., an eminent diplomatist and privy counsellor, as well as a warrior, and a signal benefactor to this church, of which he laid the third stone in 1220. He died tragically, by poison as it is supposed, in 1226, and Bishop Kilwarden, in 1270, granted thirty days' indulgence to those who should pray at the earl's tomb; such was the veneration in which this interesting personage was held.

The image of an archbishop on the northern turret may be attributed either to Thomas à Becket, whose arm was preserved amongst the precious relics in the

Cathedral, or Stephen Langton, who presided as archbishop of Canterbury, in 1225, on the first celebration of mass. In the north front a very elegant statue, a palm-branch in his right, and a stone in the left, held reverentially in a napkin, may unmistakingly be pronounced as for St. Stephen, to whom, with the holy martyrs, an altar was raised on the first opening of the Cathedral church in 1225 by Bishop Poore.

But the cloisters, chapter-house, and the monastic buildings attached to the Cathedral were the peculiar glory of the new work. Relieved from the confinement of the former site in the fortress of Old Sarum, and placed in an unoccupied and open meadow, these appendages assumed an extraordinary development, with architectural conveniences and beauties hitherto unattempted. The cloisters were detached from the church by an open court, which removed the risk of fire, permitted the sun's rays to enter the windows of the south aisle, keeping the church dry and wholesome, and affording a very useful space for materials, repairs and workshops, used to this day. The chapter-house, an elegant invention, having a single column in the middle like a palm-tree supporting the stone vault, was adorned with histories of holy writ and with sculptured and carved stalls most elaborate, windows of coloured glass, and a ceiling painted with exquisite taste. The chapter-house (not attached in the usual manner to the cloister walls) communicated then with a very graceful vestibule, which terminated with an archway, subdivided by a central column and two smaller arches, adding greatly to the perspective and architectural effect; a feature entirely novel in monastic arrangements.

The archivolt of this vestibule archway is richly and very appropriately adorned with fourteen groupes standing on pedestals and under canopies, and which convey with great significancy of character and symbolism the poetical and moral ideas of their day, and present us a very precious and rare specimen of those allegories, or moralities, as they were then called, so well calculated to delight and interest the uninitiated spectator, who might be waiting for admission into the courts held in the chapter-house within, and which were the subjects of writing and of art instruction with the most learned authorities of their day. At the very moment of the execution of these elegant works, the illustrious Greathead, bishop of Lincoln, was indicting his dissertation " de septem vitiis et remediis*."

In the great contemporary work of Amiens Cathedral church, twenty-four bas-

---

* In Price's edition of Warton on English Poetry (vol. i. p. 204 and 205,) we find among the tapestry of Charles V., king of France, A.D. 1370, a piece representing " the seven deadly sins ;" and again in the tower of London, amongst the tapestry of Henry VIII., was also a piece " of the seven deadly sins ;" but their amplification to double this number in the Salisbury sculptures is a novelty of which no other example is cited.

reliefs representing twelve virtues and the contrary vices are placed under the statues of the Apostles; and the same subject is frequently found more or less in England, in France, and in Italy. Even Spencer, three centuries later, could not indulge his native impulse to descriptions of chivalry, without framing such a story as conveyed, under the dark conceit of ideal champions, a set of historic transactions, and an exemplification of the nature of the twelve moral virtues.

Already in the twelfth century, as we have seen at Malmesbury, the medieval artists had been directed to illustrate this portion of the Christian catechism, and to symbolize to the eyes of the people, the practical and moral precepts of the Gospel, no less than the great doctrines and history of the faith. The front of the church at Salisbury exhibited, as we have conjectured, the doctrine of the Trinity, and, as we may more surely see by the distinct remains on this front, the disciples of that doctrine, in the twelve Apostles, John the Baptist and St. Paul, together with the saints and martyrs, who have lived and died for the faith; and more particularly of the founders of this church.

In the chapter-house, as we have already observed, is the history of the Old Testament in sixty pieces, and that of the New simply in the Saviour and the symbols of the four Evangelists. Arising out of this picture of the faith we are now very naturally directed to the fourteen pieces of sculpture representing the three theological virtues, Faith, Hope, and Charity, trampling on their opposites, Infidelity, Despair, and Treachery. Under these are the cardinal virtues, Justice, Truth, Purity, Bounty, and Humility, with their opposites, Guilt, Falsehood, Lust, Avarice, and Pride. On the south side underneath are Devotion, Modesty, Diligence, Almsgiving, Temperance, Fortitude, with their opposites, Worldliness, Impudence, Sloth, Want, Excess and Fear.

Unaided by engravings the description of these, and of the apt and often elegant symbols by which they are expressed, would be tedious: suffice it to say that in poetic fancy they are at least equal if not superior to any figures of the kind and of the period known to us, in any country; and in artistic composition and grace of form they might be adopted by a Flaxman or a Stothard. They remind us of the gates of Ghiberti executed two centuries and a half later, and would do credit to any school.

The sixty subjects of the Old Testament, occupying the spandrels of the stalls within the chapter-house, depart to the south from the symbol of the Saviour, and the four Evangelists, placed most elegantly in the spandrel of the two entrances, and return to the same. They are curious, but of inferior hands to those in works already cited.

No 1, is the chaos; 2, the creation of the sun and moon; 3, of the land and water; 4, the separation of waters below the firmament from the waters above the firmament; 5, the creation of fishes; 6, of man and woman, and of beasts; 7, the rest of the seventh day, in the pointed oval; 8, the placing in Eden; 9, the temptation; 10, the fear of Adam and Eve; 11, the expulsion from Paradise; 12, Adam delves, and Eve spins; 13, the sacrifices of Cain and Abel; 15, sentence against Cain, who has the straw hat of the husbandman; 16, building of the ark; 17, the deluge. Noah enters at one end, and from the other end he welcomes the dove; 18, the voice on Ararat; 19, Noah's nakedness; 20, the tower of Babel: a labourer delivers a stone from his shoulders on the top; on the other side the builder uses the plumb line; 21, the Angels appear to Abraham; 22, Sarah mocks the Angels; 23, the destruction of Sodom; 24, Lot and his daughters escape from Sodom: his wife as the pillar of salt is well expressed; 25, Abraham leads Isaac to sacrifice: he is seated on an ass with the wood; 26, the sacrifice of Isaac; 27, the blessing of Isaac's sons; 28, defaced; 29, Rebecca dismisses Jacob with a wallet on his back; 30, Jacob gives water to the cattle; Rachel leads him to her father's house; 31, three figures kneeling and receiving the blessing of Laban; 32, Jacob's dream (seemingly displaced); 33, Jacob wrestling with the angel; 34, the meeting of Jacob and Esau, their flock; 35, Joseph's dream; 36, departure of the brothers; 37, Joseph put into the well; 38, sold to the Egyptians; 39, Joseph's coat of many colours brought to Jacob; 40, defaced; 41, Joseph and Potiphar's wife; the former in a ridiculous attitude, his feet turning inwards, shewing that the monks looked at this incident like the most profane; 42, Joseph before Pharaoh; 43, cast into prison; 44, the baker hanged; 45, Pharaoh's dream; 46, Joseph's interpretation; 47, Joseph released, and interpreting the dream of Pharaoh; 48, thrashing and storing the corn; 49, Joseph's brethren come down for corn; 50, returning to report the silver in the mouth of the sack; 51, go back to Jacob; 52, return with little Benjamin; 53, journey of the Patriarchs into the land of Goshen; 54, defaced; 55, the discovery of Moses; 56, Moses and the burning bush; 57, passing the Red sea; 58, destruction of Pharaoh and his host; 59, Moses ascends the mount; 60, Moses delivering the tables of the Law.

Such are the interesting subjects of these sculptures, which are curious on so many accounts, and, still well preserved, call for careful engravings.

Above the entrance doorways are heads, which should not be overlooked, in the form of corbels in the cornice: they represent a young king and queen, accompanied by two lions to express her royal rank (these may be Edward I. and Eleanor); a bishop (perhaps Poore), and an ecclesiastic of humble degree, or possibly the architect, complete the series.

APPENDIX O.

PETERBOROUGH CATHEDRAL.

The Iconography of the stately front of this church, so far as it goes, is highly favourable to the argument of these notes; namely, to give a voice, sometimes, to the mute evidences furnished by the sister art of sculpture, as to the grave and interesting purposes of these sacred edifices, and earnestly to recommend a more careful study of a language, formerly intelligible equally to the illiterate and the learned; graven as we find it, so abundantly on the broad pages of these masonic volumes, and so descriptive in the most important cases of the religious intention, the special dedication of the altars, and the legal titles of authorities, by which the possessions and antique rights of these institutions were founded; and had been confirmed from time to time, under the most revered powers, spiritual and temporal, of successive ages. And though the quality of the art in this instance may disappoint the artist, and the connoisseur of the sculpturesque merits of the thirteenth century, these effigies are nevertheless to be regarded as full of historical purpose, and as a clear record of the rise and progress of the Benedictine monastery of Medehampstede, and in perfect correspondence with the annals, by tradition or in writing, which have escaped the disasters and the misrule of the eight hundred years anterior to the date of the actual building.

We learn that A.D. 664, Wulfere, king of the Mercians, granted a charter to the monastery, already begun by his elder brother Penda. "The minster was then hallowed in the names of St. Peter, St. Paul, and St. Andrew; and the king willed that all that to Rome cannot go, should seek St. Peter here." Accordingly we find four tiers of niches and statues illustrative of this dedication, and of the authorities confirming it, down to the thirteenth century.

In the upper tier, and in the points of the three pediments, we plainly discern the enthroned statues of the three Apostles with their appropriate symbols. And in the third tier are the other nine, crowned with the sacred nimbus; three in each of the three pediments in regular "trinal triplicity." In the second tier are two kings in each pediment, who may be safely pronounced as Penda, Wulfere, Ethelred, the founders and the restorers after ninety-six years of Danish devastations, Alfred and Edgar, and lastly perhaps the reigning monarch at the period of the new work, Henry III. or Edward the First.

The sacred purpose and the imperial founders thus duly recorded, we find in the fourth tier the effigies of the archbishops, bishops and abbots, who promoted the work, or fulfilled its holy offices.

Under the central pediment are four ecclesiastical personages, in their appropriate vestments, probably the archbishop, Deusdedit, and the first Saxon abbot, Saxulf, who presided at the original foundation in 664; and the archbishops St. Dunstan and Adelphus, under whom it was restored in 966. The remaining eight may not be so plausibly named, but the merits of many of the historical personages attached to the abbey furnish abundant suggestions. Athelwold, bishop of Winchester, was a great promoter of the work, and under the abbot Kenulphus, the abbey took the name of Peterburgh. Thorold, the first Norman abbot, fortified the abbey; John de Seez, in 1117, began the new choir; and in 1146 Martin de Bec raised the lantern tower and transept, and in 1190, Abbot Benedict carried on the work to the west end; and finally the tasteful but unknown abbot, who, shortly after this last date put a finishing hand to the work by the elegant and unexampled porch which now so much excites our surprise and admiration, well deserved a record.

The nine celebrated historical windows of the north and west cloisters, from which we might have hoped to derive some light in these particulars, disappoint us, so far as we may rely on the thirty-six quaint couplets preserved by Gunton. We must therefore refer these effigies to the leisure and the learning of those whose labours may be rewarded with a more plausible appropriation of names and titles than has been here suggested. These windows, together with those on the south and east sides containing the Old and New Testaments, appear to have been executed about 1450, when from other examples, we may believe that all regard to correct history and to sound scriptural knowledge had comparatively ceased, and the very subjects of the sculpture of the thirteenth century had been forgotten as obsolete. Art was then employed on legendary and superstitious "traditions," and true religion was overlaid with apocryphal story. It was under such impressions that Colonel Cromwell and his soldiers in 1643, "brake in pieces the fair windows of the cloisters," and tore out "the apocrypha" only from the great cathedral bible that lay upon the brass eagle. For the same reasons the statues and evidences which might have revealed to us the real use of the little chapel at the entrance porch, whether of St. Thomas à Becket or other unscriptural saint, were unscrupulously demolished; while the Apostles, kings, and holy men promoters of the original work in the pediments above, were religiously respected; a discriminating conduct in those iconoclasts highly creditable, and remarked at Wells and elsewhere already in these pages.

Although these notes are confined chiefly to the neglected subject of iconography, we cannot descend from the pediments over the triple window of this majestic porch without our tribute of admiration, designed as it is in the happiest and most practised taste of medieval architecture. The style of the sculpture would seem to place it either very early in the thirteenth century or very late; a point still to be ascertained.

And though we know that the little chapel in the central opening was placed there but as an apology to fortify the failing and collapsing pillars on either side, we cannot desire its removal, or imagine any contrivance better suited to its essential purpose, or better calculated to augment by its relative proportions, the magnificence of the vast portal in which, like a swallow's nest, it has niched itself so unobjectionably.

The dedication of this latter work, apparently in the fourteenth century, is still a subject reserved for the ingenious investigator of these delightful antiquities; its spiritual purpose, as the vestibule to the Temple, was doubtless esteemed holy and all-sufficient; and truly it reminds us (in the pious and æsthetical spirit of those times, evinced at Exeter also) of the Psalmist's words, lxxxiv.: "How amiable are Thy tabernacles, O Lord of Hosts. My soul longeth, yea even fainteth for the courts of the Lord; my heart and my flesh cry out for the living God," &c.

On entering the church the doors of the nave shut against the usual central column. On the pedestal of this is a very remarkable and tolerably executed representation of angels casting Beelzebub into the fiery pit. This may be interpreted after the trite commonplace, as an appeal simply to the consciences of the worshippers, and to the salvation from these eternal punishments, which cometh of the holy offices of the sanctuary within; or possibly it may be deemed as the appropriate ornament to the triumphal arch, as the doorway (it may be called) through which we pass from a profane world into the Christian glory; and the illustration of the exulting apostrophe of our Saviour on the return of the seventy first evangelists of His mission (see Luke x. 18): "I beheld Satan as lightning fall from heaven." It is interesting to observe the same representation (in smaller scale indeed) over the lavatory of the cloisters at Chester.

There is no sculpture in the interior of the church. The lady-chapel, built 1274, and which doubtless contained such ornaments and of the usual merit of that epoch, was taken down and the materials sold about the year 1658.

East of the apsidal termination of the church, a novel mode of sculpture is presented to the artist in the twelve Apostles seated on the tops of as many buttresses; and though they may be deficient in style and execution, the idea (observed also over the apse of Norwich Cathedral) may be stored in the artist's mind as a valuable hint in architectural composition, applicable to Gothic no less than classical architecture.

The date of this work, about 1520, suggests the probable imitation of the classical model then so popular on the continent. It was built by the Abbot Kirton, or *Kirk-Tun*, by which rebus (the church over the barrel or ton), in the trite fashion of that day, he has recorded his name in the gateway of the deanery. In the same gateway is a statue of a saint, which Flaxman has put beside Grecian example (see his Lectures, Plate xl.) as an illustration of breadth and dignity in the management of drapery. Britton's elegant illustrations in the fifth volume of his Cathedral Antiquities will assist the reader in the perusal of these notes.

APPENDIX P.

CROYLAND ABBEY.

IN the fourth volume of Britton's Architectural Antiquities of Great Britain, some account of the ruins of the celebrated Abbey Church of Croyland, illustrated by three very accurate and elegant plates, will be found, incorporating the remarks of Dr. Stukeley, who was the first (1744) to assign some of the series of statues on the west front to the individual saints and patrons of this monastic institution, and also those of Mr. Gough to the same purpose. But while we acknowledge our obligations to the diligence and acuteness of these learned antiquaries, for preserving the memory of these fleeting remains, many removed since their time, and now in more danger than ever, we may fairly offer some criticisms and corrections on their conclusions, together with some further and very obvious illustrations of the spirit in which these works appear to have been undertaken, under the fashion, the impressions, and the circumstances of that period of English history.

The exact epoch at which these works were executed, has never been accurately determined; but the internal evidences they contain in respect of style and costume, and their comparison with the annals of the abbey, will incline us to conjecture that they were executed under the Abbot Richard Croyland, who from 1281 to 1303 is recorded to have made very considerable improvements and rebuildings in the church. The elegant and imaginative style of the work confirms the persuasion that the masters who executed the crosses of Eleanor (1292), and who had laboured at Lincoln with so signal a success, must have been employed here; indeed we recognise the same hands. It was thus that a poetic character, that last attainment of the imitative arts, was impressed upon sculpture especially, and in this instance we are struck in a lively manner with the contrast of grace and solemnity given to the sacred and historical figures of the

front, with the grim and hideous monsters on which they tread; impersonations as they
are of the opposite vices of gluttony, violence, sloth, sensuality, &c., so effectively pourtrayed, and so entirely in accordance with the fables and superstitions of the ancient
natives of these localities; whose imaginations peopled these dreary marshes, this "cursed
Croyland" and "little hell," as it was proverbially called, with the goblin, the Will-o'-
the-wisp, and the malignant witch, who tormented the terrified wanderer attempting to
penetrate them, and whose terrors made St. Guthlac's constancy superhuman, no less
than that of his successors, till by degrees they had converted these melancholy sloughs
into a garden, smiling with urbanity, learning and hospitality.

Five tiers of sculpture in the centre of the western front corresponding with the
nave of the church, ranged round the great door, and the finely proportioned window
above it in panels, and standing on corbels.

The first of these nearest the ground, and part of the fourth, and the whole of the
fifth, relate to the religious and legendary illustration of the abbey. The second, third,
and part of the fourth, to the founders, benefactors and abbots, who had endowed and
governed it during the five hundred previous years.

The chief western doorway is composed in the new fashion adopted shortly before in
the south doorway of Lincoln, namely, with a column in the middle to receive the two
leaves of the door. This column carries a spandrel, in which is a large quatrefoil, containing five subjects of the legend of St. Guthlac, the hermit founder in 697. These are
marvellously preserved through the visitations of Cromwell in 1643, and the subsequent
two centuries.

No. 1. The saint in a boat, accompanied by his faithful Bedwin and Tatwin, arrive
at the island of Croyland, signified by a tree, at the foot of which, like another Æneas,
he finds a sow with a farrow of young pigs:

> "Cum tibi sollicito secreti ad fluminis undam
> Litoreis ingens inventa sub ilicibus sus, etc.,
> Is locus urbis erit."   Æn., l. iii. v. 390:

a reading of the ancient legend truly characteristic of the cloister pedants of this learned
abbey.

No. 2. The centre represents the temptations which the saint underwent in this
haunted solitude; a monstrous devil attempts in vain to disturb his constancy.

No. 3. The saint, his loaf and cruise by his side, is visited by Hedda, bishop of
Lichfield, who consecrates the oratory of the holy anchorite.

No. 4 represents the saint in his last moments attended by his faithful sister Pega,
the evil one still tempting him.

No. 5 exhibits his apotheosis and triumph, and his ascension to heaven in the arms of an angel.

On the haunch of this archway are two niches now empty. That to the north contained, according to Stukeley, " a defaced figure setting its foot on a beast," and that on the south, " a corresponding figure now much mutilated;" but what they were is not clearly conveyed.

On either side of the doorway were originally two statues, life size, standing on pedestals and corbels of singular and elegant composition. To the north is a grand apostolic figure in a simple robe confined " by a cord, tied in a knot, which, together with the drapery, is exquisitely carved," but it is now headless; a monster under its feet is also mutilated. On the pedestal is the temptation of our first parents, the serpent conspicuous, in elaborate bas-relief. On the south the pedestal only remains: upon it is an elegant angel searching the scriptures and trampling upon the serpent, admirably expressed, as crushed by the incumbent weight: " there is no piece of workmanship in the front better worth looking at," says Stukeley. Upon this doubtless stood the Blessed Virgin, the destruction of which by Cromwell and his iconoclasts in 1643, is the more to be deplored from the assurance of its pre-eminent merit given us by the surrounding sculptures.

The first probably represents the founder St. Guthlac, who first brought the light of revelation into these parts. The fall of man is thus appropriately described on his pedestal, through the wiles of the Evil One, while his redemption by the seed of the woman, which was to " bruise" his head, is aptly figured on the southern pedestal, which sustained the young Saviour and His Blessed Mother.

Pursuing the sacred illustrations of these sculptures, we omit the second and third tiers for the present, and ascend to the fourth and fifth.

Here we have a remarkable order of the twelve Apostles: the certain are printed in italics. In the fifth tier are, *St. Philip*, *St. Andrew*, St. Thomas, St. James, *St. Peter*, *St. Paul*, *St. Matthew* (these last four are seated on the extrados of the arched window, while the others are erect), *St. John*, *St. James the Elder*, and *St. Thaddeus*: in the fourth tier St. Simon and *St. Bartholomew*.

The certainty is established by the well known symbols which accompany them. The first-called disciple of our Lord, St. Philip, is placed first, and is recognised by the five barley loaves which he carries in his arms (John v. 5). He tramples on a monstrous demon with a wide mouth, into which he thrusts his hands, as if to express the vice of gluttony, the opposite to the Apostle's characteristic virtue of frugality. St. Andrew is recognised by his cross; Peter by the keys. Paul, now fallen, with the two following, were seen by Stukeley. St. James by the club, the instrument of his martyrdom, and St. Thaddeus by the partizan. Monsters in various and hideous appearance are under their feet, expressive

of human vices and infirmities, opposite to the peculiar virtue of each Apostle, while ministering angels hover round and hold shields in the spandrels of the great arch.   The last
in the fourth tier, St. Bartholomew, in the habit of a monk, is recognised by his *whip*,
which together with the *thumb* of the saint, given by the emperor Turkityl, were famous
relics in this monastery.   The pilgrim to these remote and sacred precincts could hardly
mistake the significance of this arrangement, or fail to perceive the moral conveyed by it.
While the glorious company of the Apostles assured him of the *bread of life*, the first of
them, Philip, assured him of that material bread of hospitality which our Saviour had
taught him how to use towards the five thousand so effectually; at the same time that
the last Apostle, the mortified St. Bartholomew, holding the instrument of his voluntary
penance, gave evidence of the habitual austerity of the conventual inmates, the brotherhood of the monastery.   It is remarkable that Stukeley and Gough reckon only ten
Apostles, counting the last as St. Guthlac, and giving no name to the opposite, called
here Simon, nor to the statue to the north of the entrance, supposed here to be
St. Guthlac.   It can however hardly be doubted that the whole of the twelve were intended to figure in this front.

The placing St. Philip first, reminds us of the arrangement at Exeter, and gives
evidence of due precedence, according to the letter of holy writ.   St. Peter no longer,
as at Wells, ranks the first of the Apostles: at the same time enthroned in the centre
with St. Paul, a sufficient pre-eminence is secured to each of those Apostles.

We now proceed to the historical series.   In the fourth tier to the north is a stately
king, who can be no other than Ethelbald of Mercia, the friend of Guthlac and original
patron.   In his right he holds a sword, and in his left the orb.   Under him in the third
tier is an ecclesiastic holding a crozier, who may be Kenulph, the first abbot appointed
by the king.   The next, a warlike figure, may be Egbert, or Alfred, or Edgar.   Below
these in the second tier we may with more certainty pronounce the ecclesiastic to be
Turketyl, the meritorious chancellor of Athelstan, and restorer of the abbey in 950.
He wears a mitre, to signify the increase of dignity bestowed on this second foundation,
and right to represent the abbey in great councils of the nation.   The king beside him,
with a conspicuous jewel on his breast, is undoubtedly the great King Athelstan, " the
precious stone," always designated by this ornament.

On the other side a king, beside St. Bartholomew, holds his sceptre in one hand
and a charter conspicuously in his left, to which is a seal pendant.   Immediately
under this king is an ecclesiastic, and this juxta-position induces the supposition
that the Conqueror and his faithful secretary Ingulph, who gave such lustre to the
abbey by his administration, and his historical writings, are here intended.   On the
level with Ingulphus is a female who may possibly be St. Pega, the sister and tender

companion of Guthlac. And the figure below this is undoubtedly Siward, the famous earl of Huntingdon, and father to the unfortunate Waltheof, the last of the Saxons, slain by the jealousy of William. He holds a battle-axe in his hands, and between his legs is the dragon, which his legend declares that he alone vanquished. As a great benefactor and a Saxon prince, he could not be omitted. The mitred ecclesiastic by his side may be, as Stukeley supposes, Goffrid, or any other renowned benefactor and abbot of the monastery.

We have thus endeavoured to account for the personages here intended. Ethelbald, Turketyl, Athelstan (the last not recognised by Stukeley or Gough), and Siward, are not questionable. The others may be subject to various interpretations by those better acquainted with the annals of Croyland. But the importance of this array of benefactors, one of them with his charter so conspicuously displayed, was obviously great at this period; for one of the first acts of King Edward I. on his accession, 1272, was to institute an enquiry into the land revenues of the crown, and the title-deeds by which all lands were held. It became then fashionable to display on the face of the buildings, both sacred and secular, the effigies and armorial bearings of those acknowledged and historical patrons and benefactors of these institutions, by which, together with the muniments and title-deeds and charters, the rights of the possessors were established to the satisfaction of the officious commissioner, and the envious visitor, always ready to suspect the right to so much wealth and such extensive privileges.

St. Guthlac.	Turketyl.	Kenulph.	Ethelbald.	St. Philip.
	Athelstan.	Edgar.	St. Simon.	St. Andrew.
Legend of St. Guthlac.				St. Thomas.
				St. James
				St. Peter.
				St. Paul.
				St. Matthew.
				St. John.
The Virgin and Saviour.	Siward.	St. Pega.	St. Bartholomew.	St. James Elder.
	Goffrid.	Ingulph.	The Conqueror.	St. Thaddeus.

APPENDIX Q.

BATH ABBEY.

THE Abbey Church at Bath, the successor of the temple of Sul-Minerva, or Minerva Medica of the Romans, of the church of Ache-Mann's-Cester (literally the city of aching men) of the Saxon king Edgar, and, lastly, of that built by the Norman bishop Robert, 1165, offers one of the last and most correct specimens of that ancient ecclesiastical architecture, the rules of which had been so dogmatically and diligently observed during more than five hundred years in this country. It is more particularly interesting as having been erected precisely at that moment (the beginning of the sixteenth century) when the long defection of the Lollards, and the growing spirit of the Reformation were rapidly preparing the overthrow of the ancient system, not only of Church government, but of Church architecture and sculpture no less.

Yet in this elegant example, except in its tedious execution, which lasted a hundred and sixteen years, there is no evidence of the decay of those antique masonic rules, nor of that fond imaginative symbolism, and of that pious and poetic taste, which ever marked the works of our Roman Catholic ancestors. On the contrary, the architectural order of the church exhibits the ultimate refinements of the masonic science; some of which have been described by the architect Wood, of Bath, and by Mr. Britton more recently in his beautiful engravings.

The imagery displays quaintly but warmly all that affection towards "the house in which God's honour dwelleth," so characteristic of the spirit of those days, and so agreeable to trace and to understand, remote as it is from the prosaic and commercial conceptions of the present days.

Of the architectural taste of this period of Transition, Spencer has left us some valuable evidences in his "Fairie Queene." The Trine; the numbers seven and nine;

the triangular, were still held sacred in all that referred to ancient and to holy things; while the classical "Doricke" was applied to "great Venus Temple," and all that was most new and fashionable.

Describing the Palace of "Holinesse," B. I. c. xii. st. xxxix., he says:

> "During the which there was an heavenly noise
> Heard sownd through all the Pallace pleasantly,
> Like as it had bene many an angel's voice
> Singing before th' Eternal Majesty,
> In their *trinall triplicities on hye:*
> Yett wist no creature whence that hevenly sweet
> Proceeded, yet each one felt secretly
> Himselfe thereby refte of his senses meet,
> And ravished with rare impression in his sprite."

Of the House of Temperance, B. II. c. ix. st. xxii., he says:

> "The frame thereof seemed partly circulare,
> And part *triangulare;* Oh worke divine!
> Those two the first and last proportions are;
> The one imperfect, mortall, fœminine;
> Th' other *immortal, perfect,* masculine;
> And twixt them both a quadrate was the base,
> Proportioned equally by seven and nine;
> Nine was the circle set in Heaven's place;
> All which compacted made a goodly diapase."

But of "Great Venus' Temple" he says, B. IV. c. x. st. vi.:

> "And it was seated in an Island strong,
> Abounding all with delices most rare,
> And wall'd by nature gainst invaders wrong,
> That none mote have access, nor inward fare,
> But by one way that passage did prepare.
> It was a bridge ybuilt in goodly wize
> With envious corbes and pendants graven faire,
> And arched all with porches did arize
> On stately pillours fram'd after the Doricke guize."

A short but unhappy period (from 1500, the date of this work, to the latter end of the century, during the agonies of the dying creed and the ruthless triumph of the reformers) divides this last effort of the poetic school of art from the poetic age of literature which quickly followed. Thus we may remark that the symbolical language in stone, which under the Roman Catholics had so long and so acceptably nourished the imaginative faculty, now gave way to a new manner of supplying this essential pabulum of the human mind, namely, by the allegories of a Bunyan, the fables of a Spencer, or the dramatic wonders of Shakspeare and his school.

Oliver King, the pious bishop to whose zeal we owe this elaborate work, appears to have been accomplished in fine art no less than in the business of life and of his sacred office. As secretary to the unfortunate Prince Edward, Edward the IV., and V., and especially of Henry VII., who employed him in his subtle diplomacy with the French king, Charles VIII., he must have had a large and various learning, practical, scientific and tasteful. Promoted to the see of Exeter in 1492, he was thence translated to Bath and Wells in 1496, in the former of which he found the church " per incuriam, multorum Priorum non reparatam, aut refectam, imo funditus dirutam." Pained by this state of the church, and meditating the remedy, the pious bishop dreamt the vision, which, conformably to the taste of his day, he exhibited on the face of his new Bethel as its most appropriate decoration. Like another Jacob he saw the heavens open, and the glorious Trinity surrounded by the celestial hierarchy; while Angels, ascending and descending from earth to heaven, proclaimed " how dreadful is this place! this is none other than the house of God, and this is the gate of heaven!"

The zealous bishop issued his injunctions in 1500, and such was his anxiety to witness its prosecution, that, as Sir John Harrington says, " he would wishe he had paid *above* the price of it, so it might have been finisht, for if he ended it not, it would be pulled down ere it were perfected." He died, unfortunately, in 1504, and fully justified were his apprehensions; for after the dissolution of the Abbey in 1539, the commissioners, says Harrington, " in reverence and compassion for the place, did so far strayne their commission, that they offered to sell the church to the towne under 500 marks: but the townesmen fearing they might be thought to cosen the king if they bought it so cheape, or that it might after, as many things were, be found concealed, utterly refused. Whereupon certaine merchants bought all the glass, iron, bells, and lead; of which lead alone was accompted for, as I have crediblie heard, 480 tunne, worth at this day 4800£."

Long was it the jest of the passing railers; and on its sacred walls in those evil days might be read, says Harrington:

> " O church! I waile thy wofull plight,
> Whom king nor card'nall, clerke nor knight
> Have yet restored to auncient right."

But better times arrived at length, and Bishop Montague in 1611 put the finishing hand to the work, according to the prediction:

> " Be blythe, faire Kerk, when *Hempe* is past,
> Thyne olyve, that ill winds did blast,
> Shall flourish green, for ay to last*."
> Sic esto!

* By *Hempe* understand Henry VIII., Edward VI., Mary and King Philip, and Queen Elizabeth.

With respect, however, to the special subject of this memorandum, the iconography with which the west front is adorned, "Here," says Harrington, "I may by no meanes omitt, yet I can scant tell how to relate the pretty tales that are told of this Bishop King, by what visions and predictions he was incouraged and discouraged in the building of this churche, whether some cunning woman had foretold him of the spoyle that followed (as Paulus Jovius wrytes how a witch deceaved his next successor Hadryan Bishope of Bath); or whether his own mynde running of it gave him occasion, sleeping, to dream of that he thought waking; but this goes for current, and is confirmed with pretty probabilities, that lying at Bathe, and musing and meditating one night late after his devotions and prayers for the prosperity of Henry VII. and his children, who were then all or most part lyving, to which King he was principal Secretary and by him prefered to his Bishoprick, he saw, or supposed he saw, a vision of the Holy Trinitye, with Angells ascending and descending by a ladder; neer to the foote of which there was a fayre olive Tree, supporting a crowne, and a voyce that said—'let an Olive establish the crowne and let a King restore the Church.' Of this dreame or vision, he took exceeding great comfort, and told it divers of his friends, applying it to the King his master in part, and some part to himselfe; to his master because the olive Tree being the emblem or hieroglyphick of peace and plentye, seemed to him to allude to the King Henry VIIth who was worthilly counted the wisest and most peaceable King in all Europe of that age; to himself (for the wisest will flatter themselves sometimes) because he was not only a chief counsellor to the King, and had been his ambassador to conclude the most honorable peace with Charles VIIIth, who paid 745,000 ducketts, besides a yearly tribute of 25,000 crowns; but also he carried both the Olive and the King in his own name; and therefore thought he was especially designed for this church-worke, to the advauncement of which he had an extraordinary inclination. Thus though, as S. Thomas Aquin well noteth, all dreames be they never so sensible, will be found to hault in some part of their coherence, and so perhaps may this; yet most certaine it is, he was so transported with this dreame for the tyme, that he presently set in hand with this church (the ruins whereof I rue to behold even in wryting theis lynes); and at the west end thereof he caused a representation to be graved of this vision of the Trinitye, the Angells and the ladder, and on the north side the olive and the crown, with certain French wordes which I could not reade, but in English is this vearse, taken out of the book of Judges, c. 9:

> Trees going to chuse their king
> Said, 'be to us the *Olive* king.'

All which is so curiously cut and carved as in the west part of England is no better worke than in the west end of this poor church. And to make the credit of all this more authentique, he added 'de sursum est, it is from on high.'—Thus much the stones and walls though dumb witnesses, yet credible, doe playnly testify."

Wood says that the west front is described in an equilateral triangle, thus forming a Trinity in its figure, the sides being about ninety-three feet. Cæsarianus would term the orthography a tetrastyle, the two central buttresses having bulk enough to form turrets of nine feet wide by ninety-five high. There are three doors and three windows.

The tutelar saints of the church being St. Peter and St. Paul, we find their statues on either side the central door. Under the first was the inscription (now illegible):

'Claviger Æthereus factus de Simone Petrus;'

and under the second,

'Ecce Furor Sauli factus est Conversio Pauli.'

On their pedestals we have the portcullis of Henry VII.

In the spandrels of the arch, in an enigmatical and well-contrived figure, we have the crown of thorns, in the centre a bleeding heart, and surrounding it the hands and feet with the stigmata. These are involved in an intricate roll very artistically disposed, the end of which is held in one corner by a hand issuing from a cloud, as if alluding to Ezekiel ii. 9, 10, "And when I looked, behold, an hand was sent unto me; and, lo, a roll of a book was therein; and He spread it before me: and it was written within and without: and there was written therein lamentations, and mourning, and woe."

Above this doorway is a niche, with the arms of Henry VII. beneath it. In this probably stood the Blessed Virgin and Child; with much less probability the statue of the king, as some suppose. Above is a magnificent and elegantly ordered seven-light window: two smaller doors lead to the south and north aisles, with inscriptions no longer legible, but reported as formerly legible: on the south 'Domus oronis,' or orationis, and on the north 'Domus mea.' Over these are four-light windows, on the central munten of which are small statues, possibly commemorative of benefactors, as Priors Birde, Hollewye, or Peter Chapman, and others; one holding a large purse. Above in the spandrels are corbels, the purpose of which is not now apparent: on the extreme buttresses are the olive-tree and the crown.

But the most remarkable features are the turrets, commencing in squares and changing into octagons; on the octangular faces of which are the ladders, quaintly expressed, with six angels ascending and descending in the front, and on the sides of the octagon the twelve Apostles in trines, having an elegant canopy over each three; and these are of remarkable sculpture, much superior to the rest of the carving of this front.

At the foot of the ladder on the north is a figure of Jacob, or of the bishop, represented on one side in sleep, and on the other standing with his wallet on his back, and raising an altar. Above these are large scrolls, on which were formerly inscribed "certain French wordes," says Harrington, "which I could not reade;" already quoted. This ladder has *sixty-seven* grades, and is surmounted with the figure of the Saviour.

On the south turret the same ladder appears, but of *sixty-four* grades only, having 'a hell' at its summit, and upon it are six angels also attached; at the foot on one side a person on his knees before an altar, and on the other another building an altar, with the same scrolls above them as in the north. This may refer to the inscription below, 'Domus orationis,' and the necessity of constant and reiterated prayer to preserve us from this fatal ladder. The smaller number of grades, which do not offend the symmetry of the front, and are ascertained by counting only, may signify that hell is reached by fewer steps.

Above the great window are the three Persons of the Trinity, the Father and Son in the conventional form, and the Holy Ghost below in the front of the window. Four shields surround the central niche, and on either side seven angels, with the olive-tree and crown in the corners.

It is a picturesque and touching circumstance, conformable to all ancient practice, classical and others, that a portion of the old church at the south-east angle was incorporated with the new structure, and its venerable forms may easily be distinguished in the midst of an architecture of a posterior style of nearly four centuries.

OXFORD: PRINTED BY I. SHRIMPTON.

CPSIA information can be obtained at www.ICGtesting.com
Printed in the USA
BVOW03s1116260315

393469BV00014B/124/P